OBLIGATIONS AND PRIVILEGES OF RELIGIOUS PROMOTED TO THE EPISCOPAL OR CARDINALITIAL DIGNITIES

THE CATHOLIC UNIVERSITY OF AMERICA
CANON LAW STUDIES
No. 256

OBLIGATIONS AND PRIVILEGES OF RELIGIOUS PROMOTED TO THE EPISCOPAL OR CARDINALITIAL DIGNITIES

A HISTORICAL SYNOPSIS AND A COMMENTARY

BY
JOSEPH J. MAROSITZ, M.S.C., J.C.L.
PRIEST OF THE CONGREGATION OF THE MISSIONARIES OF THE SACRED HEART

A DISSERTATION

SUBMITTED TO THE FACULTY OF THE SCHOOL OF CANON LAW OF THE CATHOLIC UNIVERSITY OF AMERICA IN PARTIAL FULFILLMENT OF THE REQUIREMENTS FOR THE DEGREE OF DOCTOR OF CANON LAW

THE CATHOLIC UNIVERSITY OF AMERICA
WASHINGTON, D. C.
1948

Imprimi Potest:
JOSEPH J. JANSSEN, M.S.C.,
Superior Provincialis.
Geneva, Ill., die 16 maii 1947.

Nihil Obstat:
JOANNES ROGG SCHMIDT, A.B., J.C.D.,
Censor Deputatus.
Washingtonii, D. C., die 1 iunii 1947.

Imprimatur:
✠ JOANNES M. McNAMARA, D.D.,
Vicarius Capitularis Baltimorensis-Washingtonensis.
Baltimorae, Md., die 3 iunii 1947.

MURRAY & HEISTER—WASHINGTON, D. C.
PRINTED IN THE UNITED STATES OF AMERICA

TO HONOR THE SACRED HEART

TABLE OF CONTENTS

PART TWO

CANONICAL COMMENTARY

FOREWORD

The Church is not forgetful of reward to be given for special service. This reward for merit may take the form of ecclesiastical honors or dignities. Religious, too, may be the recipients. History attests to the fact that religious have been advanced to dignities. But since religious by their very profession must strive after evangelical perfection by the observance of the three vows of religion, namely, poverty, chastity, and obedience, and of the particular obligations imposed by an approved rule, there is need to regulate the inter-relations of the dignitary status and the religious state.

The present historical synopsis is not intended to be an exhaustive study of all dignities to which religious could be raised; the work is restricted to the consideration of two dignities: The episcopate and the cardinalate. An effort is made to summarize the salient points of legislation, which effected important developments on the obligations and privileges of religious promoted to the episcopal or cardinalitial dignities. It must be noted that the historical inquiry, in the same manner as the commentary, concerns not the obligations and privileges of religious as bishops or cardinals; these dignitaries religious in this regard are under the same obligations and enjoy the same privileges as are accorded to any others in the same dignities. The investigation is rather centered about the obligations and privileges of bishops or cardinals religious as religious.

The second part of this study consists in a commentary upon the canons of the Code which pertain to the promotion of religious to ecclesiastical dignities, namely, canons 626-629. An understanding of the significance of the term of ecclesiastical dignities is necessary; hence, the first portion of the initial chapter of the canonical commentary is an inquiry into the usage of the word *dignitas* in the Code of Canon Law. Thereupon follows the commentary on the respective canons which deal with the necessary conditions for the promotion of religious to ecclesiastical dignities outside their religious institutes, with the juridic condition of religious in the cardinalitial or episcopal dignities particularly in relation to their religious state, and with the abdication or dismissal of these dignitary religious from the office or dignity. The obligation of cardinals and bishops religious to retain their religious habit in the dignitary status is set forth in a special chapter. Thus this dissertation endeavors to present as clearly as possible the proper interpretation of the present-day legislation of the Code of Canon Law on the special obligations and privileges of cardinals and bishops religious as religious.

The writer at this occasion thanks the Congregation of the Missionaries of the Sacred Heart, the former and first Provincial of the United States Province, the Very Rev. Joseph Averbeck, M.S.C., and the present Provincial, the Very Rev. Joseph J. Janssen, M.S.C. To the staff of the Catholic University Library for their assistance, to the Superiors of the Holy Cross College and of the Dominican House of Studies for the use of their Libraries, and to all others who by their suggestions and encouragement have made this work possible, the writer wishes to express his appreciation. He likewise extends a sincere expression of gratitude to the Faculty of the School of Canon Law of The Catholic University of America for their kindly consideration and help over the past three years.

PART ONE
HISTORICAL SYNOPSIS

CHAPTER I

INTRODUCTORY NOTIONS

In the earlier centuries of the Church's history there is not much that directly touches upon the subject of this dissertation: *The Obligations and Privileges of Religious Promoted to the Episcopal or Cardinalitial Dignities.* That is due, no doubt, to the fact that a religious state of life in the strict sense of the term with the obligations of the three vows did not begin till the middle of the third century.[1] Besides, even after these beginnings there was still a period of development from the primitive form of anchoretic monasticism to the cenobitic form of monasticism.[2] Certainly, then, in these years of formative development one could not expect to find direct references to the obligations and privileges of religious promoted to ecclesiastical dignities; this matter necessarily belongs to a later period when the process of development was more complete. Therefore, the historical material will be considered in the development of law as gleaned especially from the collections of Gratian and the Papal Decretals.

The title of the present study contains various terms that need definition. The word *obligation* does not require any long discus-

[1] Flanagan, *The Canonical Erection of Religious Houses,* The Catholic University of America Canon Law Studies, n. 179 (Washington, D. C.: The Catholic University of America Press, 1943), p. 1; Devoti (1744–1820), *Institutionum Canonicarum Libri IV* (3 vols., ed. prima Romana post quintam, Romae, Vol. I, 1825), Lib. I, tit. IX, §II; Wernz (1842-1914), *Ius Decretalium ad Usum Praelectionum in Scholis Textus Canonici, sive Iuris Decretalium* (Vol. III, ed. altera, ex typographia Polyglotta, Romae-Prati, 1908), nn. 601, 602 (hereafter cited as *Ius Decretalium*); Bouix (1808–1870) insisted that the beginnings of a religious state of life are to be found at the start of the third century; however, his argumentation proves rather that there were individual cases in which the obligation of the three vows existed, but this fact does not point to a religious state of life in the strict sense, which came somewhat later.—*Tractatus de Jure Regularium* (2 vols., Parisiis, 1857), I, 129-171 (cited hereafter as *De Jure Regularium*).

[2] Heimbucher, *Die Orden und Kongregationen der katholischen Kirche* (3. ed., 2 vols., Paderborn: Ferdinand Schoeningh, 1933-1934), I, 61-114.

sion. Etymologically obligation is derived from the Latin *ligare*, to bind; therefore, it is something which binds. More specifically, it is something absolute, something objective, that imposes a necessity on the will;[3] in other words, it is any duty imposed by law, promise, or contract, etc. It is in this sense, viz., as a duty imposed by law, that this term will be understood.

The term privilege has received a variety of definitions.[4] Derived etymologically from *privata lex*, it may be defined as a grant to a definite person, or to a group of persons, moral or physical, of some special favor or right.[5] The very fact that a privilege is a special favor or right accorded to a particular person or to a group of persons at once shows its principal difference from a law, which is meant for the common good. Those in whose favor a privilege is granted can act lawfully contrary to or beyond the provisions of the law.[6] Strictly, then, a privilege cannot be called a law except by analogy in so far as any privilege puts an obligation on others to respect the special objective rights granted. Taken in this sense a privilege more accurately defined is *a private law granting some special benefit or favor contrary to or beyond the law.*[7]

There are many divisions of privileges. In the present work, however, advertence to one division will be sufficient: a privilege contrary to the law (*contra ius*) and a privilege beyond or outside the law (*praeter ius*). Both arise from their relation to the common law, since a privilege constitutes some permanent right for

---

[3] Vermeersch (1858–1936), *Theologia Moralis* (3 vols., Romae: Pontificia Universitas Gregoriana, Vol. I, 3. ed., 1933), I, n. 143.

[4] It is not necessary here to go into a detailed investigation. Cf. Roelker, *Principles of Privilege According to the Code of Canon Law,* The Catholic University of America Canon Law Studies, n. 35 (Washington, D. C.: The Catholic University of America, 1926), pp. 4-8 (hereafter cited *Principles of Privilege*); Matulenas, *Communication—a Source of Privileges,* The Catholic University of America Canon Law Studies, n. 183 (Washington, D. C.: The Catholic University of America Press, 1943), p. 35, note 4.

[5] Shuhler, *Privileges of Regulars to Absolve and Dispense,* The Catholic University of America Canon Law Studies, n. 186 (Washington, D. C.: The Catholic University of America Press, 1943), p. ix.

[6] Matulenas, *op. cit.*, pp. 36, 37.

[7] Michiels, *Normae Generales Juris Canonici* (2 vols., Lublin, Poloniae: Universitas Catholica, 1929), II, 312: *lex privata speciale aliquod beneficium aut favorem contra vel praeter jus concedens.*

the privileged person or persons. Thus, the former exempts from the common law, which prohibits or commands something; the latter grants something beyond or over and above the common law, which otherwise by law itself is reserved to others.[8]

The title of the present work includes also the word *religious,* the subject of the obligations and privileges. The term religious is wide, a general term. In the present work it is restricted to designate men who have taken the three vows of religion in any religious institute, and so embraces those bound by solemn vows as well as those bound by simple vows.[9]

In the historical sources the terms *Monks, Regulars, Mendicants* occur. The word *monachus* was freely used of those consecrated to God, whether they lived as hermits or in communities. It was a name given to anchorites or hermits who lived a solitary life in continence, in poverty, in fasts and in mortification away from the tumult of the world, either in caves or in deserts, striving for perfection and sanctity by the contemplation of divine things. St. Paul the Hermit (234-347) is considered the founder of the anchoretic life, and St. Anthony the Abbot (251-356) its chief propagator. The name also applied to cenobites who lived together in a group of cells under the common rule of an abbot, and had at least some exercises in common, as established by St. Pachomius (292-345).[10] St. Benedict (480-543) constantly described his brethren as monks, and their residence as a monastery. And from that time on the term *monk* was commonly applied to the members of any religious body of men, which reproduced in some measure the conditions of life as contemplated in the old Benedictine rule.[11]

---

[8] Beste, *Introductio in Codicem* (2. ed., Collegeville, Minn.: St. John's Abbey Press, 1944), p. 117.

[9] Canon 488, 7°—*Codex Iuris Canonici Pii X Pontificis Maximi iussu digestus, Benedicti Papae XV auctoritate promulgatus, Praefatione, Fontium Annotatione et Indice Analytico—Alphabetico ab Emo Petro Card. Gasparri Auctus* (Romae: Typis Polyglottis Vaticanis, 1917; reimpressio, 1934).

[10] Ferraris († ca. 1763), *Prompta Bibliotheca Canonica, Juridica, Moralis, Theologica, necnon Ascetica, Polemica, Rubricistica, Historica* (Ed. novissima, mendis expurgata, 8 vols., Parisiis: Aqud J. P. Migne Editorem, 1852-1857), V, s. v. *Monachus,* nn. 2-7 (cited henceforth as *Prompta Bibliotheca*); cf. Heimbucher, *Die Orden und Kongregationen der katholischen Kirche,* I, 61 ff.

[11] Heimbucher, *op. cit.,* I, 159 ff.

Those who make profession of solemn vows in any religious institute of solemn vows are in the present law called *regulars.*[12] Originally, in the early centuries of the Church, the term *regulars* signified men and women who withdrew from the world into deserts to live under a rule of life established by some saintly man.[13] Mendicants are regulars, but not all regulars are at the same time Mendicants; hence the two terms are not synonymous. "Mendicants are those who according to their institute and in virtue of their primitive constitution are radically incapable of possessing property in common. . . . Since they had no means of sustenance other than by begging, they were given the name *Mendicantes,* beggars; whence the name Mendicant." [14] These Mendicants thus obtained the privilege of begging for their sustenance wherever they were. And some years later this same privilege was extended to other religious institutes, even though they were allowed to possess property in common. They likewise were called Mendicants.[15] In the historical sources, then, the terms *Monks, Regulars, Mendicants* are but more particular names for the general term of religious.[16]

The last phrase in the title of the present work is *Episcopal or Cardinalitial Dignities,* which in their character are ecclesiastical dignities. In a very general sense, a dignity signified any preeminence or precedence with jurisdiction.[17] A dignity, therefore, very early implied precedence and jurisdiction; it was distinguished

---

[12] Canon 488, 7º and 2º.

[13] Shuhler, *Privileges of Regulars to Absolve and Dispense,* p. x.

[14] Shuhler, *op. cit.,* pp. x, xi.

[15] Shuhler, *op. cit.,* p. xi.

[16] Ferraris, *Prompta Bibliotheca,* VI, s. v. *Religiones regulares et militares,* n. 6; Bernardus Papiensis (+1216), *Summa Decretalium* (ed. E. A. Th. Laspeyres, Ratisbonae, 1860), Tit. XXVII, *de regularibus et transeuntibus ad religionem,* §1.

[17] Craisson (+1881), *Manuale Totius Juris Canonici* (5. ed., 4 vols., Pictavii, 1877), II, n. 2184: "Juxta primitivam significationem, *Dignitas* erat titulus beneficialis annexam habens praeeminentiam cum jurisdictione." Tuschus (1534–1620), *Practicae Conclusiones Iuris* (3. ed., Vols. I-VIII, Ludguni, 1634; Vol. IX, *Eminentissimi Cardinalis Tuschi Additiones ad caetera octo volumina Practicarum Conclusionum Iuris*: Opus posthumum a Carolo Tuscho et Raynaldo Cardinali Estensi, Ludguni, 1670), II, Conclusio 419, n. 1: "Dignitas est quaedam praeeminentia ex administratione."

from a personate (*personatus*) and from an office as such: a personate had only the right of precedence, whereas an office lacked both precedence and jurisdiction.[18]

In its broad connotation an ecclesiastical dignity was synonymous with any ecclesiastical office attended with the right of precedence and some participation of the jurisdictional power in the church; in consequence of the usual practice, if that participation had lapsed or been taken away, such offices could still be considered dignities, though *de iure* they were not such.[19] However, the restriction of the term *dignities* to only those offices which actually implied jurisdiction in the external forum was more in harmony with the idea of prelacies mentioned in other definitions.[20] Thus one could define a dignity in a more proper sense as an ecclesiastical office that necessarily implied precedence and jurisdiction.

Dignities are divided into major and minor: the major dignities are the Supreme Pontificate, the cardinalate, the patriarchate, the archiepiscopate, the episcopate, and the abbacy; the minor dignities are the archdiaconate, the archpresbyterate, and in general, the dignities which are found in a chapter of canons.[21] The present work,

[18] Craisson, *loc. cit.*: "*Personatus* est titulus beneficialis annexam habens praecedentiam sine jurisdictione. *Officium* vero ab utroque differt, . . . et est titulus beneficialis absque jurisdictione et praecedentia." Meehan, *Compendium Juris Canonici* (Roffae, 1899), p. 299, nota 2.

[19] Ferraris, *Prompta Bibliotheca,* I, s. v. *Beneficium,* Art. I, n. 26: "Dignitas enim est praecedentia cum jurisdictione, ut sunt, v. g., abbatia, archidiaconus, decanatus, et hujusmodi, et licet alicubi de consuetudine istae dignitates non habeant jurisdictionem, adhuc tamen dignitates censeri debent ex praxi, quamvis de jure sine ulla jurisdictione non sint tales." Tuschus, *Practicae Conclusiones Iuris,* II, Conclusio 419, n. 2: "Signa cognoscendi dignitatem sunt tria, primum, quando is, qui habet officium, praeest administrationi cum iurisdictione; secundum, quando nomen officii sonat in dignitatem, prout Archidiaconus, Archipresbyter, et Primicerius; tertium, quando ex consuetudine, vel constitutione, pro dignitate habetur."

[20] Thomassinus (1619-1695), *Vetus et Nova Ecclesiae Disciplina circa Beneficia et Beneficiarios* (10 vols., Moguntiae, 1787), X, q. 1, n. 6 (hereafter cited as *Vetus et Nova Disciplina*); Wernz, *Ius Decretalium* (Vol. II, ex typographia Polyglotta, Romae-Prati, 1899), n. 240.

[21] *Dictionnaire de Droit Canonique* (3. ed., M. André, P. Condis, J. Wagner, 4 vols., Paris: Hippolyte Walzer, 1901), I, s. v. *Dignité.* Tuschus divided dignities as follows: "Dignitas in Ecclesia est triplex; prima est Papatus, qui dicitur apex dignitatis; secunda Episcopalis, quae est culmen

of course, considers only the two major dignities to which religious are promoted outside their religious institutes, namely, the episcopate and the cardinalate.

Finally, the writer thinks it unnecessary to prove that religious have been advanced to ecclesiastical dignities. One can easily enough ascertain that fact. Suffice it to say that history attests to it.[22]

---

aliarum dignitatum; tertia est dignitas simplex."—*Practicae Conclusiones Iuris,* II, Conclusio 428, n. 1.

[22] Pejška, *Jus Canonicum Religiosorum* (3. ed., Friburgi Brisgoviae: Herder & Co., 1927), p. 179.

CHAPTER II

THE LAW OF THE *CORPUS IURIS CANONICI* TO THE COUNCIL OF TRENT

I. From the year 250 to 1250

Article 1. Preliminary Notes

In the *Corpus Iuris Canonici* there is no specific title on the obligations and privileges of religious in ecclesiastical dignities. In Gratian [1] matter on this point is found in such places as deal with the question of monks in its various aspects; in the Decretal Collections [2] under the titles: *de statu monachorum, de electione et electi potestate, de vita et honestate clericorum, de postulatione praelatorum.* In them references are made to the promotion of religious to dignities in general, or to the episcopacy in particular, with special attention to their election. In this dissertation the promotion of religious to the episcopal or cardinalitial dignities exclusively is treated.

The episcopacy is of divine origin, founded by Our Lord. The Apostles, immediately appointed by Christ, ordained others to the episcopacy. After the Apostles, in the second and third centuries,

[1] The *Decretum Gratiani* was written about the year 1140; the dates of the author's birth and death are unknown.—Van Hove, *Commentarium Lovaniense,* Vol. I, Tom. I, *Prolegomena ad Codicem Iuris Canonici* (ed. altera, Mechliniae-Romae: H. Dessain, 1945), n. 343 (hereafter cited as *Prolegomena*).

[2] The *Decretales Gregorii IX* were promulgated by Pope Gregory IX (1227–1241) in the Bull "*Rex pacificus,*" 5 sept. 1234; the *Liber Sextus Decretalium* was promulgated by Pope Boniface VIII (1294–1303) in the Bull "*Sacrosanctae,*" 3 martii 1298; the *Constitutiones Clementinae* of Pope Clement V (1305–1314) were promulgated by Pope John XXII (1316–1334) in the Bull "*Quoniam nulla,*" 25 oct. 1317; the collections of the *Extravagantes Ioannis XXII* and the *Extravagantes Communes* in their present separate forms date from 1500 and 1503 respectively.—Van Hove, *op. cit.,* nn. 362, 368, 372, 373.

the clergy together with the people (*Plebe praesente et consentiente*) of the episcopal city chose the bishop, who then was confirmed in his election and thereupon consecrated by the bishops of the province. In the fourth century the election of bishops devolved entirely upon the bishops of the province. Then followed the period of Catholic Kings and Emperors who forced their way into the elections of bishops. After the eighth century the right of election was concentrated in the cathedral chapters. So it remained till the fourteenth century, when the Popes gradually reserved the appointment of bishops to themselves.[3]

The cardinalate is of ecclesiastical origin. The name *cardinal,* probably from the Latin *cardo* (hinge), was applied in the early centuries of the Church to the head priest of a church, as being incardinated in that church; also bishops for the same reason were sometimes called cardinals. In the course of time the term was used in Rome to refer to the chief priests at the ancient churches of Rome as well as to the head deacons of the seven regions of the same city. Thus in the sixth century the titles *Cardinalis Presbyter* and *Cardinalis Diaconus* appeared. Moreover, the bishops of towns in the vicinity of Rome were considered as incardinated in the cathedral church of the Pope, the Lateran Basilica, and thus in the eighth century they also were called cardinals.

The development of the office of cardinals came much later. At the time of Pope Leo IX (1049–1054) the so called Cardinal Deacons and Cardinal Priests of Rome gradually took over the Curial Offices in Rome and obtained the foremost rôle as assistants to the Pope in the government of the Church. It was this same Pope who called foreign priests outside Rome to be cardinals and so assist in the government of the Church. Pope Nicholas II (1059–1061) entrusted the election of the Pope to the cardinals, and this marked the beginnings of the action of cardinals as a college. And from the time of Pope Pascal II (1099–1118), besides the exclusive right of electing the Pope, most major matters were decided with the concurrence of the cardinals, so that from that time on they acted as a true college of cardinals. Pope Pius V (1566–

[3] Santi (1830–1885), *Praelectiones Juris Canonici juxta Ordinem Decretalium Gregorii IX* (5 vols. in 2, Ratisbonae, 1886), Lib. I, tit. VI, nn. 1-2 (hereafter cited as *Praelectiones*); Wernz, *Ius Decretalium,* II, nn. 740–750.

1572) reserved the title of Cardinal to the members of the cardinalitial college alone. Since Pope Sixtus V (1585–1590) the number of cardinals in the three ranks has been definitely established.[4]

The right of creating cardinals has always rested with the Pope alone.[5]

As to the method of presentation of this subject the writer has thought it best to trace back the law as found in the *Corpus Iuris Canonici,* and to set it down together with other laws as found elsewhere, in a topical order according to certain periods of legislation, in order thus to mark the main features in the historical development. Also other legislation that had some bearing on the subject under consideration has been used by him along with the more pertinent and direct references, in order that thus a historical synopsis of the subject matter of this treatise may duly be offered.

Article 2. The Capability of Monks to be Advanced to Clerical Offices and to the Episcopal Dignity

Very early the question arose: Are monks capable of holding clerical offices and of performing the clerical duties?[6] The reason for this doubt derived from the fact that monks originally were mere laymen.[7] In a reply to a letter from Himerius, Bishop of Tarragona, Spain, Pope Siricius (384–399) in 385 among other things touched also on this problem.[8] The Pope stated that he desired

[4] Vermeersch-Creusen, *Epitome Iuris Canonici* (5. ed., 3 vols., Mechliniae et Romae: H. Dessain, 1933–1936), I, n. 346 (hereafter cited as *Epitome*). Cf. Klewitz, "Die Entstehung des Kardinalkollegiums"—*Zeitschrift der Savigny-Stiftung für Rechtsgeschichte,* LVI, *Kanon. Abtlg.,* XXV (1936), 115-222; and especially Kuttner, "Cardinalis: The History of a Canonical Concept,"—*Traditio,* III (1945), 129–214.

[5] Wernz, *Ius Decretalium,* II, n. 265.

[6] For a historical inquiry on this point confer Bouix, *De Jure Regularium,* II, 2-9.

[7] *Thesaurus Iuris Ecclesiastici, potissimum Germanici, sive Dissertationes Selectae in Ius Ecclesiasticum* (quas . . . in ordinem digessit . . . Antonius Schmidt, 7 vols., prostat Heidelbergae, Bambergae, et Wirceburgi: Sumptibus Tobiae Goebhardt, 1772–1779), VI, Dissertatio XIV, §VI, p. 507 (hereafter cited as *Thesaurus Iuris Ecclesiastici*); *dicta* post c. 39, C. XVI, q. 1, especially §3.

[8] C. 29, C. XVI, q. 1—*Corpus Iuris Canonici* (ed. Lipsiensis 2., post Aemilii

and wished monks who were found worthy to be numbered among the clerics, and to be promoted to orders according to the required intervals of time from the minor orders upward to the episcopacy, but successively without any omission.[9] Such a statement on the part of the Pope, therefore, clearly expressed that monks were eligible not only to the clerical state, but also to the episcopal dignity, *episcopatus culmen*. Such a clear expression is all the more significant at this early time, since it appeared in the period which followed closely upon the beginnings of a religious state of life.

Emperor Justinian (527–565) in a letter directed in 535 to the saintly Epiphanius, Patriarch of Constantinople (520-535), in its first part, *Quomodo oporteat Episcopos et reliquos clericos ad Ordinationem deduci* . . . , wrote the following: " Igitur ordinandus episcopus aut ex monachis aut ex clericis sit . . . "[10] Thus, after having listed several reasons that required the candidates for the episcopacy to be men of good morals and good reputation, the Emperor seemed perhaps to have written the above quoted sentence as a conclusion, as if he implied that the candidates for the episcopacy were to be taken from either of these two groups: *aut ex monachis aut ex clericis*. In effect, then, the imperial letter ordered that candidates for the episcopacy be selected from the monks who were constituted in the religious state, as well

---

Ludovici Richteri curas instruxit Aemilius Friedberg, 2 vols., Lipsiae: Ex officina Bernhardi Tauchnitz, 1879–1881; editio anastatice repetita, 1922); Jaffé (1819–1870), *Regesta Pontificum Romanorum ab condita Ecclesia ad annum post Christum natum MCXCVIII* (ed. 2., Kaltenbrunner, Ewald, Loewenfeld, 2 vols., Lipsiae, 1885–1888), n. 255 (hereafter cited as Jaffé); Mansi (1692–1767), *Sacrorum Conciliorum Nova et Amplissima Collectio* (53 vols. in 60, Parisiis, 1901-1927), III, 660 (this work henceforth cited as Mansi).

[9] Mansi, III, 660: "Monachos quoque, quos tamen morum gravitas, et vitae ac fidei institutio sancta commendat, clericorum officiis aggregari et optamus et volumus, ita ut qui intra tricesimum aetatis annum sunt digni, in minoribus per gradus singulos, crescente tempore, promoveantur ordinibus, et sic ad diaconatus vel presbyterii insignia, matura aetatis consecratione perveniant. Nec statim saltu ad episcopatus culmen ascendant, nisi in his eadem, quae singulis dignitatibus superius praefiximus, tempora fuerint custodita."

[10] N. VI (1.7)—*Corpus Iuris Civilis* (Vol. III, ed. stereotypa quinta, *Novellae*, quas recognovit Rudolfus Schoell, opus Schoellii morte interceptum absolvit Guilelmus Kroll, Berolini: Apud Weidmannos, 1928).

as from the secular clergy who were not constituted in the religious life.[11]

In 602 Pope Gregory I (590–604) issued a letter to the priest Senator, the abbot of a monastery which had a hospice or pilgrim-house connected with it, erected some time before by Bishop Siagrius (561–600) and Queen Brunhilde (+613) in the city of Autun, France. The Pontiff confirmed the privileges granted before at the time of its erection, and permitted that the abbots be elected without the accompaniment of any simony by the King of the Franks with the consent of the monks, but forbade the abbots of the monastery to become bishops, unless they first resigned their abbatial dignity.[12]

The fact that the Pope did not allow the abbots of this monastery to be admitted to the episcopal ranks, unless they previously resigned their office of abbots, proved at least that monks could indeed be promoted to the episcopal dignity. There existed no absolute prohibition; the papal letter reflects simply a special regulation that was enacted for that monastery at Autun.

Article 3. The Permission of the Religious Superior Necessary for the Promotion of Monks to Ecclesiastical Offices or Dignities

Before promotion to any ecclesiastical office or dignity, a monk needed the permission of his religious superior. Pope Gregory I expressed it thus: "No monk can be promoted to any ecclesiastical office without the testimony or concession of his abbot." [13]

---

[11] *Thesaurus Iuris Ecclesiastici,* IV, Dissertatio I, appendix ad sectionem II, n. 1, p. 17.

[12] *Gregorii I Papae Registrum Epistolarum,* XIII, 11—*Monumenta Germaniae Historica, Epistolae* (Tom. I, ed. Paulus Ewald et Ludovicus Hartmann, Berolini: Apud Weidmannos, 1891. Tom. II, pars I; tom. II, pars II; tom. II, pars III, post Pauli Ewaldi obitum ed. Ludovicus Hartmann, Berolini: Apud Weidmannos, 1893–1899), Tom. II, pars II, 376-378 (hereafter this work will be designated with the letters *MGH*). This letter was written in November, 602; c. 39, C. XVI, q. 1; Jaffé, n. 1875.

[13] Legislation prior to the time of Pope Gregory I had established that monks could not be ordained without the consent of their abbots. For example, the Provincial Council of Agde in France (506) ruled in its 27th canon: "Si necesse fuerit clericum de monachis ordinari, cum consensu et

This was contained in a letter to Marinianus, Bishop of Ravenna (595–606), in which the Pope informed the bishop of certain privileges of monks in order to insure their liberty and freedom.[14] Apparently, reference was made not only to the promotion to sacred orders, but also to any ecclesiastical office or dignity bestowed after ordination. In either case the permission of the superior was required.

Article 4. Monks in the Clerical or Episcopal State Bound to Their Religious Profession and Obligations

Quite early the principle had been established that a monk remained a monk, even though he was advanced to the clerical state. This enunciation came from Pope Innocent I (401–417) in a letter to Victricius, Bishop of Rouen (France) in 404, in which the Pope set down various norms of ecclesiastical discipline.[15]

In the medieval interpretation, the gloss [16] to this canon definitely stated that it referred to monks in the clerical state who had been elected to secular churches as bishops.[17] Therefore a monk

---

voluntate abbatis praesumat episcopus." Likewise, the Provincial Council of Lerida, Spain, in 524 demanded in its 3rd canon: "Monachi cum abbatis voluntate debeant ordinari."—Bruns, *Canones Apostolorum et Conciliorum Saec. IV-VII* (2 vols., Berolini, 1839), II, 152; II, 21.

[14] *Gregorii I Papae Registrum Epistolarum,* VIII, 17—*MGH, Epistolae,* tom. II, pars I, 19-20. This letter was written in April, 598; Jaffé, n. 1504.

[15] Jaffé, n. 286; c. 3, C. XVI, q. 1: "De monachis, qui diu morantes in monasteriis si postea ad clericatus ordines pervenerint, statuimus non debere eos a priore proposito discedere."—Mansi, III, 1032.

[16] The *Glossae Ordinariae* originated at the time of the Decretists and Decretalists, men who carried on the canonical science in the 12th, 13th, and 14th centuries by inserting interlineal or marginal glosses as explanations of the text of Gratian and of the Decretal Collections. Ioannes Teutonicus (+1246) wrote the *Glossa Ordi ıria* for the *Decretum Gratiani*; Bernardus Parmiensis (+1263) for the *Decretales Gregorii IX*; Ioannes Andreae (1272–1348) for the *Liber Sextus* and the *Clementinae*; Zenzelinus de Cassanis (+1334) for the *Extravagantes Ioannis XXII.* There is no *Glossa Ordinaria* for the *Extravagantes Communes.* These glosses, then, show the medieval interpretation of the earlier legislation as incorporated in the various collections.—Vermeersch-Creusen, *Epitome,* I, n. 63; Van Hove, *Prolegomena,* nn. 417, 455.

[17] *Glossa Ordinaria* of c. 3, C. XVI, q. 1 s. v. *discedere—Decretum Gratiani emendatum et notationibus illustratum una cum Glossis* (Romae, 1582).

remained bound to those things which were essential to his religious state of life: to celibacy or the vow of chastity, to the vow of poverty, to the wearing of his religious garb. The monk was withdrawn from his abbot's jurisdiction, unless the church was subject to the abbot. From other observances such as fasts, silence, or vigils the monk was excused. But if a monk became a bishop, he was totally taken out from the jurisdiction of his abbot. Rufinus (+ca. 1190) explained this by saying: " . . . a jugo regulae monasticae professionis absolvuntur . . . ," as signifying particularly the obedience due to the abbot, and the observance of fasts and silence.[18]

A. THE OBLIGATION OF WEARING THE RELIGIOUS HABIT

From the general principle, namely, that when a monk had been advanced to some ecclesiastical dignity he still had to abide by his religious profession, it followed that he was obliged to wear his religious garb as a sign of his obligation.

The VIII General Council of the Church, held at Constantinople (869–870) under Pope Hadrian II (867–872), after decreeing in its last canon that the customary liturgical vestments were to be retained in each province, forbade the indiscriminate wearing of the pallium by bishops. Then it stated that monks who had merited the episcopal dignity had to retain the monastic habit and continue the observance of the religious life itself.[19]

This ruling also seemed to indicate that the testimony of a good, pious religious life in the monastery was a prerequisite before a monk could merit the episcopal honors. However, its main concern was to insist that any religious as a bishop was bound to retain his habit, and even to continue the observance of the religious status and life itself. As such the canon was a more express enactment

---

[18] *Die Summa Decretorum des Magister Rufinus* (herausgegeben von Dr Heinrich Singer, Paderborn: Ferdinand Schoeningh, 1902), ad c. 3, C. XVI, q. 1, p. 354 (hereafter cited as *Summa*).

[19] Canon 27: " . . . illos autem qui reverenter monasticam vitam sectati sunt, et episcopalem meruerunt honorem, conservare schema, et amictum monachicorum indumentorum, et ipsam beatam vitam decernimus."—Mansi, XVI, 178.

of what at least had been implied in the letter of Pope Innocent I.[20]

The XII General Council of the Church, that is, the IV General Council of the Lateran (1215), presided over by Innocent III (1198–1216), issued many decrees of a disciplinary nature designed to correct prevailing abuses. In canon 16 of this Council the extant abuses in dress among clerics in general were specifically corrected. Towards the end of the canon appear these words:

> All bishops must use in public and in the church outer garments made of linen, except those who are monks, in which case they must wear the habit of their order . . . [21]

This merely confirmed the fact that a monk in the episcopal dignity was not entirely absolved from the observance of his monastic rule.[22] From the former law it had been clear enough, but abuses probably demanded a restatement of the regulation regarding the wearing of the habit.[23]

B. THE OBLIGATION OF POVERTY

A very important and definite expression of the early law on the question of poverty in regard to the disposition of the goods of a monk who was a bishop is found in canon 36 of the Council of Altheim in Bavaria (916), which was later incorporated in the

---

[20] ". . . non debere eos [monachos] a priore proposito discedere."—*Supra*, p. 14.

[21] Schroeder (1875–1942), *Disciplinary Decrees of the General Councils, Text, Translation, and Commentary* (St. Louis, Mo.: B. Herder Book Co., 1937), p. 257 (cited hereafter as *Disciplinary Decrees*); Mansi, XXII, 1006; c. 15, X, *de vita et honestate clericorum*, III, 1.

[22] *Glossa Ordinaria* to c. 15, X, *de vita et honestate clericorum*, III, 1 s. v. *nisi monachi—Decretales D. Gregorii Papae IX suae integritati una cum glossis restitutae* (In aedibus Populi Romani, Romae, 1582); Panormitanus (Nicolaus de Tudeschis, 1386–1453), *Commentaria in Quinque Decretalium Libros* (8 vols., Venetiis, 1588), Lib. III, tit. I, *de vita et honestate clericorum*, c. 15, n. 5 (hereafter cited as *Commentaria*).

[23] Boich (+1350), after affirming that monks could be elected to a bishopric, added: "Credo tamen quod propter hoc non debeat habitum mutare."—*In Quinque Decretalium Libros Commentarius* (Venetiis, 1576), Lib. III, tit. I, c. 11, n. 3 (cited hereafter simply as Boich).

work of Gratian.[24] In the *dictum* introducing *Causa XVIII*, Gratian proposed the case of an abbot consecrated as a bishop, who before as a monk in the monastery had procured much property for the monastery. After his consecration he acquired additional property. The question arose: Could the monastery lay claim to what the monk gained after becoming a bishop, or, rather, would his church have the claim to whatever had been passed on to the monastery before his becoming a bishop, i.e., while he was still a monk in the monastery? The answer to both was in the negative, and the following canon was the basis for the negative answer:

> Statutum est et rationabiliter secundum sanctos Patres a sinodo confirmatum est, ut monachus, quem canonica electio a iugo regulae monasticae professionis absolvit, et sacra ordinatio de monacho episcopum facit, velut legitimus heres paternam sibi hereditatem postea iure vendicandi potestatem habeat; sed quicquid acquisierat, vel habere visus fuerat, monasterio relinquat, et abbatis sui, qui fuerat secundum regulam S. Benedicti, arbitrio. Postquam enim episcopus ordinatur, ad altare, ad quod sanctificatur et titulatur, secundum sacros canones quod acquirere poterit restituat.

The foregoing is the canon as found in Gratian; its wording is substantially the same as that of the Council of Altheim. But in the Council the canon concluded with the words:

> . . . salva auctoritate de propria hereditate patris sui, quam licet ei cui vult concedere; et ita distinguat omnia, ut canones diiudicant et distinguunt.

Accordingly in canon 36 of the Council of Altheim the following was established:

1. A monk raised to the episcopal state had the right in law of claiming for himself his paternal inheritance as a legitimate heir.

How, then, was this possible? A monk remained bound to his obligations as a monk in any dignity. In what way could he ac-

[24] *MGH, Leges* (5 vols., Vols. I-IV, ed. G. Pertz; Vol. V, ed. G. Pertz—G. Waitz—H. Brunner, Hannoverae, 1835–1889), II, 560; c. un., C. XVIII, q. 1.

quire things as his own? As a monk certainly he could not own anything as his own property, for whatever he received was acquired by the monastery.[25] The glossator admitted that the right to the paternal inheritance would first pass over to the monastery before the monk was advanced to the episcopate, but the right of succession occurred only after death. In reality, then, the monastery would not have the right, but only the hope of obtaining it. Accordingly, once the monk was taken out of the monastery, that hope of obtaining his inheritance was gone, for the monk was no longer a subject of that monastery. But did this really explain the reason why the monk had the right to obtain his inheritance as his own?

2. Whatever the monk had acquired as a simple monk he had to leave with the monastery at the disposition of the abbot; whatever he acquired after becoming a bishop belonged to his church.

The statement included here under number 2, though in the original text separated grammatically by means of a semi-colon from the statement contained under number 1, is nevertheless closely related to it. That relationship must be recognized and acknowledged if one is to gain a proper understanding of each of the two statements. The second statement simply qualified the first, so that the resultant import was the following. Whatever a monk received while he was still in the monastery as a subject, also his paternal inheritance, simply passed over to the ownership of the monastery; on the other hand, whatever he obtained after being made a bishop, also his inheritance, if only then he fell heir to it, passed over to the ownership of his episcopal church.[26]

Understood in this sense the canon of Altheim effected a clear demarcation, so that the principle of the monk's incapacity to own anything was upheld both prior to his episcopal advancement and after, for he was bound to his religious obligations in both cases.

---

[25] *Glossa Ordinaria* of c. un., C. XVIII, q. 1 s. v. *restituat*; c. 10, 11, C. XII, q. 1; Hostiensis (Henricus de Segusio, +1271), *In Quinque Libros Decretalium Commentaria* (5 vols. in 3, Venetiis, 1581), Lib. I, tit. XXXI, *de officio ordinandorum*, c. 7, nn. 2, 10 (hereafter cited as *Commentaria*).

[26] Rufinus, *Summa* ad dictum *Prima questio*, C. XVIII, q. 1, p. 377: "Vere acquisita in monasterio relinquenda sunt monasterio; quae vero tempore episcopalis dignitatis acquiruntur, episcopali ecclesiae relinquenda sunt."

But it was not the intent of this canon to rule out the possibility that a monk when consecrated as a bishop should enjoy the use and the administration of his inheritance as opposed to its ownership.[27]

Obviously, the foregoing explanation of the meaning of canon 36 of the Council of Altheim must be the correct one, for only in that event did the canon adequately settle the question of what the monastery or the episcopal church could claim. That was the reason, too, why Gratian invoked this canon to solve this problem. In short, even though a monk's election to the episcopate had been accepted by him and confirmed for him, as long as he had not yet transferred to his episcopal see, and therefore still abode in his monastery, the monk relinquished the ownership of the goods to the monastery. Only after he had actually taken possession of his episcopal see, did the episcopal church become vested with the right of claiming the ownership of all that he acquired thereafter.[28]

The foregoing recounts the main dispositions regarding canon 36 of the Council of Altheim as reported in Gratian. But what is to be said about the canon's last clause which was not included in Gratian? Did it in any way militate against the conclusions already drawn? This clause seemed to grant to a monk upon his consecration in the episcopate the right to dispose of his paternal inheritance by means of a last will and testament: *salva auctoritate de propria hereditate patris sui, quam licet ei cui vult concedere.* How could a monk dispose of anything by means of a last will or testament, when in fact he could not retain any ownership? [29]

The quoted clause had already been dropped by Burchard of Worms (+1025) in his *Liber Decretorum* (written about 1012), though he gave the Council of Altheim as the source of the law

---

[27] Boich definitely averred that an abbot could never give a monk the permission to own anything in his own name, and that at most he could permit him in the name of the monastery to possess things through which he could satisfy his needs. Similarly, after a monk had become a bishop and the ownership had passed over to his episcopal church, could he not *a pari* have the use and administration of the goods, though the title of ownership remained with the church?—Boich, Lib. III, tit. XXXV, c. 6, nn. 11, 12.

[28] *Glossa Ordinaria* to the dictum ante C. XVIII, q. 1, s. v. *Prima questio.*

[29] C. 7, C. XIX, q. 3; Bernardus Papiensis, *Summa Decretalium,* tit. XXII, *de testamentis et ultimis voluntatibus,* §4.

that he included in his compilation.[30] Hence it appears at least probable that canon 36 of the Council of Altheim represented rather an uncanonical practice of the tenth century, which practice was rejected as non-conformable to the law in its later interpretation.[31]

C. THE OBLIGATION OF OBEDIENCE TO RELIGIOUS SUPERIORS AND TO THE MONASTIC RULE

Canon 36 of the Council of Altheim (916) also made mention of the fact that a monk by his election to the episcopate was freed from the bond of the monastic rule. The *Glossa Ordinaria* singled out in particular the obedience to the abbot, and the monastic rules about fasts, vigils, silence, etc., as matters in which this freedom was gained.[32] However, the bond of the monastic rule was not loosed in every regard.[33] The fact remained that, when a monk had been promoted to the ecclesiastical dignity of the episcopacy, he was still bound to observe the monastic rule in those things which in no way hindered the administration of his episcopal office or duties. Thus, whatever factors could be of aid in the fulfillment of the duties of his episcopal charge remained in full force for the monk, such as the vows of poverty and of chastity, as well as other religious observances commanded by the rule.[34]

Concerning the vow of obedience, the monk in the episcopal dignity was withdrawn from the obedience due to his abbot, for he was no longer a subject. Nevertheless the vow of obedience continued to bind such a monk at least virtually. In other words, in

---

[30] Lib. I, cap. CCXXXI—Migne, *Patrologiae Cursus Completus, Series Latina* (221 vols., Parisiis, 1844–1864), CXL, 615 (hereafter this work will be designated with the letters *MPL*).

[31] Ivo of Chartres (+1116) in his *Decretum* (written about 1094) also quoted this canon of the Council of Altheim without including the last clause.—Lib. V, cap. CCCXLIII; *MPL*, CLXI, 426.

[32] *Glossa Ordinaria* to c. un., C. XVIII, q. 1 s. v. *absolvit.*

[33] Rufinus, *Summa* ad c. 1, C. XVIII, q. 1, p. 377.

[34] St. Thomas (1225-1274), *Summa Theologica,* IIa, IIae, q. 185, art. 8, *in corpore articuli.—S. Thomae Aquinatis Doctoris Angelici Summa Theologica diligenter emendata, de Rubeis Billuart et aliorum notis selectis ornata* (6 vols., Augustae Taurinorum: Typographia Pontificia; Vol. IV, 1886).

virtue of the vow which he had taken, his obedience became due to any of the superiors set over him in his new episcopal status. The reason was that essentially a monk remained bound to his religious profession. Only circumstantially was he withdrawn from the obedience due to his religious superiors, inasmuch as he in no way continued as a subject of theirs once he was promoted to the episcopal dignity. However, at his return to the monastic way of life he again became bound by his vow of obedience as before.[35] Apart from the question of his vows, if a conflict existed between his religious observances as according, on the one hand, with his monastic rule, and as called for, on the other hand, by his episcopal status, then any hindrance which the former implied for the latter warranted a freedom from compliance with them.[36]

Furthermore, when a monk had attained the episcopal dignity, or any other dignity, he was allowed to act as sponsor at baptism.[37] A simple monk was strictly forbidden to act as sponsor.[38] But once he was promoted to a dignity in the Church, he was no longer subject to the same prohibition.

II. From the Year 1250 to the Council of Trent (1545-1563)

Thus far, as has been seen, most of the historical references have employed the term *monachi;* in the following period, beginning roughly about the year 1250, that term gave way to the use of the term *religiosi*. It is for this reason that a line of division seems properly indicated in the discussion.

Article 1. Preliminary Remarks on Election in General

In the period from the year 1250 to the Council of Trent (1545–1563) significant legislation appeared on the election of religious to prelacies or to dignities outside their Orders or institutes. But before particular consideration be given to this legislation, a sum-

---

[35] St. Thomas, *op. cit.*, IIa, IIae, q. 185, art. 8, *ad tertium*; IIa, IIae, q. 88, art. 11, *ad quartum*; cf. Bouix, *De Jure Regularium*, II, 67–69.

[36] St. Thomas considered the wearing of the religious garb by a religious in the episcopal dignity as a sign of his obligation to the observance of his rule of life.—*Op. cit.*, IIa, IIae, q. 185, art. 8, *in corpore articuli*; cf. Santi, *Praelectiones*, Lib. III, tit. XXXV, nn. 10-14.

[37] Dictum post c. un., C. XVIII, q. 1; Rufinus, *Summa, in eodem loco*, p. 377.

[38] Ferraris, *Prompta Bibliotheca*, s. v. *Baptismus*, I, art. 7, n. 41.

mary review of the law regarding election, confirmation, and postulation seems in order.[39]

Election is a method of ecclesiastical appointment. It may be defined as the selection—made according to prescribed canonical norms—of a person with the requisite qualities for some vacant office or pastoral dignity in the Church.[40] The definition is taken in a strict and proper sense to distinguish it from others taken in a wide sense, which sometimes signified any sort of appointment or approbation, such as presentation, nomination, postulation and direct assignment.

An election, then, is a true canonical act. It must be noted that the assembled voters who perform this act of election do not at all confer the office, but simply issue the call to the office. Hence the one chosen has a strict claim (*ius ad rem*) to confirmation by the competent and legitimate superior, who thereby completes the canonical act of the conferral of office. In order to bring out the characteristics of a true election, it is helpful to see how elections differ from free appointment (*libera collatio*), from presentation, and from nomination.

1. Election differs from free appointment:
   An election is usually the act of subjects who select their superior, while a free appointment is always the act of a superior. Moreover, in an election the one chosen has a claim to be confirmed (*ius ad rem*), but he cannot perform any acts of his office before his confirmation; in a free appointment the person has the full title to the office (*ius in re*) and can perform all acts of the office at once. In other words, the person is named by the superior, and the title to the office

[39] Cf. Parsons (1911–1945), *Canonical Elections*, The Catholic University of America Canon Law Studies, n. 118 (Washington, D. C.: The Catholic University of America Press, 1939), pp. 1–7.

[40] "Electio est alicuius personae idoneae ad dignitatem, vel fraternam societatem, servata forma, canonice facta vocatio."—Hostiensis (+1271), *Summa Aurea* (Venetiis, 1570), tit. *de electione et electi potestate*, §*Quid sit electio*, n. 1. "Personae idoneae ad Ecclesiae vacantis pastoralem dignitatem canonica vocatio."—Laymann (1574–1635), *Quaestiones Canonicae de Praelatorum Ecclesiasticorum Electione, Institutione et Potestate ex lib. I Decretalium* (Dilingae, 1627), Quaestio XIII (hereafter cited as *Quaestiones Canonicae de Electione*).

is granted and confirmed in one and the same act of this superior. Such an inseparable association does not obtain in the case of an election.

2. Election differs from presentation:
An election is accomplished by an assembly through the use of votes; a presentation, however, is ordinarily the act of an individual who enjoys a right of patronage granted to him by the Church. Moreover, an election is the final choice of a single candidate, whereas a presentation is oftentimes an alternate proposal of several candidates. Besides, before the competent superior is approached for a confirmation of the election, the outcome of the election must be made known to the one elected for the sake of ascertaining whether he accepts or declines the expressed will of the electoral body. Such a previous notification to the potential candidate is not necessary in the act of presentation, for it is directed at once to the superior, and the presented candidate has no claim whatever to the office.

3. Election differs from nomination:
By nomination here is meant not the proposal of the names of candidates before the actual balloting, as is done in elections, but rather the presentation of candidates as explained above. However, nomination and presentation differ in this that the former is usually the act of a religious superior who designates a cleric for some office, while the latter is regularly the act of a lay patron who submits a similar proposal. As in the act of presentation, the nominated cleric obtains no claim to the office.[41]

Postulation can be considered as a form of election, for in relation to election it was introduced as a subsidiary element or suppletory factor. Postulation is a petition directed to a superior concerning the promotion to some dignity or prelacy of some person who in accord with the common observance or norm cannot be lawfully elected in view of some deficiency or impediment.[42] The

[41] Laymann, *op. cit.*, Quaestiones XIV-XVI.

[42] " Postulatio est quaedam gratiae petitio a superiore facta, de promovendo aliquem ad praelationem, ad quam de iure communi propter defectum ali-

aim, then, of postulation is to obtain from the superior a dispensation from some existing disqualification in law on the part of the one postulated. Thus, any person who is barred from being elected because of some disqualification established by law can be postulated. But if this disqualification of the person has resulted from his own criminal act, then the possibility of his postulation no longer obtains.

Postulation was characterized as solemn or simple. The definition as previously given points to solemn postulation. Simple or non-solemn postulation merely signified the superior's supplied permission and consent in cases in which the one chosen could not have been promoted without the permission of his proper superior. This is requisite, as will be seen later, in cases in which religious were by means of an election promoted to any dignity outside their religious institute.[43]

The difference between postulation and election lies in this that in a postulation the voters do not actually elect a candidate. They simply submit an electoral petition to ask the superior to make the appointment. The whole matter depends entirely on the good will of the superior who may choose to give or to withhold the dispensation. There is no question of justice here, for the one who has been postulated holds no claim at all, while the one who has been elected enjoys a full claim, and accordingly can with a full right anticipate a subsequent necessary act of confirmation in office, as long as nothing on the side of the law or on the part of his own person militates against the requisite fitness for the office.

Confirmation, as has been said, is a requirement for the completion of the canonical act of election, and is wholly the act of the superior. Furthermore, it involves the question of justice, so that the superior must confirm the one elected, if he is found fit, for he has a strict claim to the office. The superior ordinarily is the next immediate superior to whom the dignity or the office is subject.

---

quem, vel impedimentum, eligi seu promoveri non poterat."—Panormitanus, *Commentaria*, Lib. I, tit. *de postulatione praelatorum*, §*Quid sit postulatio*, n. 1. "Postulatio est alicuius personae ad praelaturam, seu dignitatem erga Superiorem destinata petitio, ut eam dispensative admittere velit."—Laymann, *op. cit.*, Quaestio I.

[43] Santi, *Praelectiones*, Lib. I, tit. V, n. 3.

Before the confirmation the one chosen cannot, under threat of privation of all rights to the office *ipso iure,* perform any of the jurisdictional or administrative acts warranted by the office, whether in spiritual or in temporal things.[44]

Article 2. The Eligibility of Religious to Prelacies or Dignities Outside Their Institutes

Important legislation, chiefly concerned with the election of religious to prelacies or dignities outside their Orders or institutes, was incorporated in the *Liber Sextus* by Pope Boniface VIII (1294–1303).[45]

Pope Clement V (1305–1314), perhaps in the Council of Vienne (1311–1312), also settled several points about the election of religious to ecclesiastical dignities.[46]

It was Clement V who declared that the religious of one religious Order or profession were ineligible to any prelacy in another religious Order or profession.[47] Thus it was forbidden that a religious of one Order be elected as Abbot, Prior, Master, Minister, Guardian, etc.[48] in some other Order, since it was unreasonable that men of a differing religious profession or of dissimilar religious

---

[44] Laymann, *op. cit.,* Quaestiones CVI, CVII, CXII. For the special developments of election in the *Liber Sextus* and the later Decretals, cf. Parsons, *Canonical Elections,* pp. 64–69.

[45] C. 27, 28, 36, *de electione et electi potestate,* I, 6, in VI°.

[46] Mansi, XXV, 402: "Constitutiones autem hujus synodi [Viennensis] separatim excusae reperiuntur in jure canonico, et Clementinae inscribuntur. . . ." The official acts of the Council of Vienne have been lost, a few fragments excepted. In the five books of the *Clementinae* no more than twenty decrees have certainly proceeded from the action of the Council; the rest of the decrees in the *Clementinae* marked as deriving from this Council are more probably the legislation of Clement V issued before and after, or even during the Council, but without its concurrence.—Schroeder, *Disciplinary Decrees,* pp. 367, 370, 371.

Of the 3 canons referred to in the following pages Schroeder includes only one (c. 1, *de electione et electi potestate,* I, 3, in Clem.) in his added list of the canons under the category of fairly certain and probable conciliar enactments of the Council of Vienne.—*Op. cit.,* p. 413.

[47] C. 1, *de electione et electi potestate,* I, 3, in Clem.

[48] *Glossa Ordinaria* to this same canon s. v. *praelatum—Liber Sextus D. Bonifacii Papae VIII suae integritati una cum Clementinis et Extravagantibus, eorum glossis restitutis* (In aedibus Populi Romani, 1582).

garb should live together in one and the same monastery. If nevertheless such an election was performed contrary to this rule, the whole procedure was invalid and without any effect.

This prohibition, as is evident, had reference only to non-episcopal dignities within religious institutes, and not at all to the episcopal or other dignities outside the religious pale, for the canon ended with the words: "Per hoc autem, quin religiosus in episcopum saecularis vel cuiuslibet regularis ecclesiae licite possit eligi, non intendimus prohibere." Therefore, any religious of any Order or profession could be chosen for any secular or regular church, even of a different religious group.[49] Some of the commentators on the Decretals point to this last part of the canon in the *Clementinae* as being the basis in common law for the eligibility of religious to the episcopal dignity.[50]

One should not deem the episcopal state and the religious state as irreconcilable. In fact, there is nothing in the episcopal state as such that is repugnant or opposed to the religious state of life. Through his profession a religious has the bounden duty of following the evangelical counsels, and of striving for perfection. But the episcopacy is considered to be the height of perfection, an advancement, a step higher. Therefore, the two states are not exclusive of each other, yet the episcopacy is the more perfect. Hence the two can, without incongruity, be joined in the person of a religious.[51]

Pope Clement V also inveighed against the custom of installing religious, especially Mendicants, as bishops over cathedral churches in territories of the infidels, where there were no clergy and no christian subjects.[52] Provision for such churches could be made

---

[49] *Glossa Ordinaria* to this same canon s. v. *cuiuslibet.*

[50] Boich, Lib. III, tit. XV, c. 11, nn. 3, 5; Schmalzgrueber (1663–1735), *Jus Ecclesiasticum Universum* (5 vols. in 12, Romae, 1843–1845), Lib. I, tit. VI, n. 90, 2 (hereafter cited simply as Schmalzgrueber); Wernz, *Ius Decretalium,* III, n. 666, II.

[51] Thomassinus, *Vetus et Nova Disciplina,* Pars I, Lib. III, cap. XVII, n. 13; St. Thomas, *Summa Theologica,* IIa, IIae, q. 184, art. 7; Suarez (1548–1617), *De religiosis* (*Opera Omnia,* ed. nova a Carolo Berton, 26 vols.; Vol. XVI, Parisiis, 1860), Tractatus Octavus, Liber III, Caput XVI, n. 1, pp. 396, 397.

[52] C. 5, *de electione et electi potestate,* I, 3, in Clem.

solely with the special permission of the Supreme Pontiff. Pope Clement's decretal absolutely prohibited that any religious be made bishops over those churches, that a religious seek permission to be admitted to this dignity, and that any superior presume to give permission. In case a religious out of ambition nevertheless did obtain unlawful permission from his superior and even was consecrated a bishop, then, by way of punishment, he gained nothing from it and was not to be honored as a bishop.[53] Such a religious was also commanded to return to his monastery and for the future he could never aspire to any dignity. Any contrary custom [54] was strictly reprobated.

One cannot construe from this legislation that religious were as a result ineligible to bishoprics. The legislation rather intended to preclude occasions of detracting from the high honor and regard for the episcopal office, for often enough bishops in such churches without any clergy or without a designated Christian laity necessarily were forced to resort to wandering about and to begging for alms. These bishops were in fact no more than titular bishops, and precisely that status was ruled out by the law.[55]

Pope John XXII (1316–1334) restricted the postulation of seculars to a cathedral church, and also of religious professed in any Mendicant Order to inferior churches outside their Order, until they had at least attained the twenty-seventh year of age.[56] And if the postulation of a person under the age of twenty-seven was carried out *scienter,* the whole process had no meaning whatsoever, for the whole action was null and void. Severe penalties were levied against the offenders, the postulators and the one postulated. As far as religious were concerned, it was only an enactment against the postulation of Mendicants to inferior or minor dignities

---

[53] However, such a religious would have received the episcopal character through the consecration.—*Glossa Ordinaria* of c. 5 s. v. *vel aliquod.*

[54] *Glossa Ordinaria* to this same canon s. v. *superiorum.*

[55] Thomassinus, *Vetus et Nova Disciplina,* Pars I, Lib. I, cap. XXVII, n. 2.

[56] C. un., *de postulatione praelatorum,* I, 2, in Extravag. com.; Reiffenstuel (1642-1703), *Jus Canonicum Universum* (5 vols., Parisiis: Apud Ludovicum Vivès, 1864–1870), Lib. I, tit. V, n. 58 (hereafter simply cited as Reiffenstuel).

outside their Order.[57] Likewise the law did not appear to exclude Mendicant or non-Mendicant religious from election or postulation to the major dignities.

Some stringent measures had been passed against religious as titular bishops, especially in places where they were quite numerous and troublesome.[58] Thus, in the German Empire in the Council of Salzburg, in 1420, during the Pontificate of Pope Martin V (1417–1431), these bishops were excommunicated for refusing to wear their religious garb under the pretext of exemption, and probably for other abuses as well. Other bishops were warned under the threat of suspension *ab ingressu ecclesiae* not to have any dealings with these titular bishops, and not to allow them to pontificate in their churches, unless they led a good life and possessed a good reputation.[59] Such severe steps on the part of this particular Council must not be viewed as discriminatory against religious as bishops, but must rather be looked upon as an apt means adopted to put an end to any and every abuse.[60]

A. THE NECESSITY OF RELIGIOUS PROFESSION

Before a religious could be elected to the abbatial dignity or any other prelacy in a religious institute, he had to be a religious who had been expressly professed in the Order, and not merely a member by a tacit profession; otherwise the election was invalid.[61] But at once an exception was made, inasmuch as a religious only tacitly professed could, for example, by wearing the habit of the religious Order and by following the religious life without ever having taken a formal or express profession, be promoted to the episcopal dignity in a secular or regular church.[62] In fact, the exception was explicitly made for novices who had made not even a tacit profession.[63]

---

[57] Schmalzgrueber, Lib. I, tit. VI, n. 90, 3.

[58] The reference was possibly to the bishops mentioned in c. 5, *de electione et electi potestate,* I, 3, in Clem.; *supra,* pp. 26, 27. Cf. Thomassinus, *Vetus et Nova Disciplina,* Pars I, Lib. I, cap. XXVII, nn. 4-6.

[59] Canon 17—Mansi, XXVIII, 992.

[60] Thomassinus, *op. cit.,* Pars I, Lib. I, cap. XXVII, n. 5.

[61] C. 28, *de electione et electi potestate,* I, 6, in VI°.

[62] *Glossa Ordinaria* to this canon s. v. *nullus religiosus.*

[63] *Glossa Ordinaria* to this same canon s. v. *novitii*; Schmalzgrueber, Lib. I, tit. VI, n. 90, 2.

B. THE SUPERIOR'S PERMISSION BEFORE CONSENT TO AN ELECTION

A religious could not consent to an election of himself to any prelacy or dignity outside his own monastery or church without the prior consent of the immediate superior; otherwise, the consent given by a religious on his own authority was *ipso facto* null, and the election invalid.[64] It was the superior who gave the permission to the religious to furnish his consent when elected, since of himself the religious could not signify his acceptance of the election. It was likewise the superior who granted the religious the requisite permission to leave the monastery in order to take up his new duties. For the granting of these permissions the superior was not obliged to seek the consent of the religious chapter; he was authorized to act without the concurrence of others (*sine conventu aliorum*).[65] In a way the transfer of a religious to a prelacy outside the Order could have been deemed a species of alienation, so that for it as for any other kind of alienation the superior would have needed the consent of the religious chapter. But Pope Boniface VIII (1294–1303) clearly decided the issue in favor of the sole permission of the superior.[66]

The legislation just mentioned did not directly refer to the question of religious who were promoted to ecclesiastical dignities outside the religious state of life; rather it referred to the election of a religious of one monastery to a prelacy in another. Nevertheless, since the phrase " . . . ad praelationem aliquam extra suum monasterium vel suam ecclesiam . . . " was very general, it could very well be understood as including any other dignity outside the religious state, and hence the law was considered applicable in such manner that the superior's permission was required in either of the two eventualities.

The *Liber Sextus* reported the following case: [67] An abbot ruling over a monastery immediately subject to the Apostolic See had been elected to the bishopric of the city. Before this exempt abbot could signify his acceptance of the election, he had first to procure

[64] C. 27, *de electione et electi potestate,* I, 6, in VI°.

[65] *Glossa Ordinaria* to this canon s. v. *si religiosus*; Hostiensis, *Commentaria,* Lib. I, c. 6, tit. V, *de postulatione praelatorum,* n. 6.

[66] Laymann, *Quaestiones Canonicae de Electione,* Quaestio CXCVIII.

[67] C. 36, *de electione et electi potestate,* I, 6, in VI°.

the permission or confirmation of the Apostolic See, or of the apostolic legate *a latere,* if there was one present in that province. The election of itself did not imply for him the permission to give his consent, since as a religious that permission for him could come only from the immediate superior—in this case the Holy See.[68] But if the abbot of a non-exempt monastery, i.e., one not immediately subject to the Holy See, was elected to the episcopal dignity, then the requisite permission of the abbot's immediate superior—in this case the proper bishop—had to be furnished.[69]

Pope Benedict XI (1303–1304) proposed a solution to a further problem concerning the consent to be given by religious when they were elected to dignities.[70] While this Pope's legislative enactment dealt only in general with the election of religious to office, yet it certainly did not abstract from the election of religious to ecclesiastical dignities. The content of the legislation was the following: If a religious, when apart from his superior's permission he could not on his own authority give his consent to an election, had not obtained that permission after receiving the notification of his election, or if the electors had not obtained it for the religious within a reasonable length of time to be fixed according to the presence or absence of the superior, then the electors could proceed to a new election according to the norm of the II General Council of Lyons (the XIV General Council of the Church in 1274).[71] The religious,

[68] Laymann, *Quaestiones Canonicae de Electione,* Quaestio CVII.

[69] Reiffenstuel, Lib. I, tit. 5, n. 53.

[70] C. 2, *de electione,* I, 3, in Extravag. com.

[71] Canon 5 of the II General Council of Lyons, held under Pope Gregory X (1272-1276), prescribed that the electors had to make known the result of the election to the one elected as soon as possible. Then the canon continued: ". . . the one elected, however, is bound to declare his intention within one month from the time of such notification. If on the expiration of that time he has failed to do so, he is *eo ipso* deprived of the right which came to him from the election, unless his position be such that he cannot by reason of a prohibition or some provision of the Apostolic See accept the election without the permission of his superior. In which case he or his electors must endeavor to seek and obtain permission from his superior with such haste as the presence or absence of the superior may require. Otherwise, if the time has expired, even with the allowance made for the presence or absence of the superior, and permission has not been obtained, then the

if he had failed to receive permission, *ipso iure* remained without the acquisition of all the rights that could have accrued from the election.

It was evident that a religious needed the previous permission of his superior to give his consent when elected to some dignity in the Church. The permission could not simply be a general permission. Pope Clement V declared that a general permission granted by a superior to his religious subject to enable him to give his consent when elected to a benefice or a dignity was for the future entirely without force, for such a practice would only open the way to unbridled ambition.[72] No doubt such a practice stands thoroughly condemned by this law, which contemplated in its prohibition any and every form of election or assignment to office,[73] and also any and every permission granted for giving consent to an election performed in the past, of which election the superior was himself perhaps ignorant.[74] Positively expressed, this legislation demanded a special permission from the superior in each single instance in order to allow his subject to consent to a definite and certain election.

C. THE EFFECTS OF NON-UNANIMOUS ELECTIONS FOR MENDICANTS AND OF ELECTIONS UNDERTAKEN BY A MINORITY FOR NON-MENDICANTS

Special regulations appeared concerning elections that were attended with dissension among the electors or undertaken by a minority of the electoral body. Pope Boniface VIII in 1297 stated the effects of these non-unanimous elections in reference to Mendicants, and the effects of elections undertaken by a minority of the voters in reference to non-Mendicant religious.[75] Any religious

---

electors are free to proceed to a new election . . ."—Text quoted from Schroeder, *Disciplinary Decrees*, p. 338. Cf. Mansi, XXIV, 87.

[72] C. 8, *de electione et electi potestate*, I, 3, in Clem.: "Quum concessa religioso a superiore suo licentia, ut electioni vel provisioni, si quam de ipso contigerit fieri, suum dare possit assensum, ambitionis vitio viam paret: nullius eam existere volumus firmitatis."

[73] *Glossa Ordinaria* to this canon s. v. *provisioni*.

[74] *Glossa Ordinaria* to this same canon s. v. *nullius*.

[75] Potthast (1824–1898), *Regesta Pontificum Romanorum inde ab anno*

of a Mendicant Order who had not been elected unanimously to any dignity outside the administration of his Order acquired no right to that office, nor could he consent to that election even with the permission of his superior; other religious who were not Mendicants likewise obtained no right to the office when only a minor part of the electors took part in the election. In both cases the consent to the election as well as the election itself was null and void.[76]

The afore-mentioned legislation about elections which lacked unanimity among the electors was, of course, something entirely special to the Mendicant Orders.[77] Still in no way did it preclude the possibility of the election of a Mendicant to some dignity outside his Order, as long as the election was a canonical election marked by unanimity, i.e., without division among the electors.[78]

Any religious could validly give his consent when elected to an ecclesiastical dignity outside the Order or institute if he had the explicit permission of his superior, provided that the majority had elected him. So far, then, this was but a restatement of the general rule.[79] But a distinction had to be made between religious, that is, the non-Mendicant and the Mendicant:

1. A non-Mendicant religious could consent to his election with his superior's permission, even though some had opposed him as a candidate or had voted against him in the election, provided only that the majority had elected him.

---

post Christum natum MCXCVIII ad annum MCCCIV (2 vols., Berolini, 1874–1875), n. 24491 (hereafter cited as Potthast); c. 24, *de electione et electi potestate,* I, 6, in VI°.

[76] Laymann, *Quaestiones Canonicae de Electione,* Quaestio CXCII.

[77] *Glossa Ordinaria* to c. 24, *de electione et electi potestate,* I, 6, in VI°, s. v. *Mendicantium.*

[78] Laymann furnished examples of what was meant by "discordant" elections.—*Op. cit.,* Quaestio CXCIII. Reiffenstuel commented on c. 24, *de electione et electi potestate,* I, 6, in VI°, in Lib. I, tit. 6, nn. 317, 318. Later, in *Adnotatio XXXV* to this place in his work, he reported that Mendicants could be elected or also postulated to dignities outside the Order, provided that the election or postulation reflected a unanimous vote. But in relying on the authority of others he also stated that even this seemed to have been forbidden by the Decretal *Calumniis* of Pope John XXII, which was never included in the *Corpus Iuris Canonici.*

[79] C. 27, *de electione et electi potestate,* I, 6, in VI°; *supra,* p. 29.

2. A Mendicant could give his consent to his election with his superior's permission only when and if the election had been *in concordia* or unanimous.[80]

If a Mendicant had already been appointed to the episcopal dignity, but afterwards was elected to an archiepiscopal see, could he then of himself give his consent when the election had actually been effected by a majority? Or was he still bound to the rule of a concordant election, and did he still need to seek his superior's permission? The glossator answered in the negative to the first question, based on the fact that such a religious in the episcopal dignity must still be considered a true Mendicant, despite the fact of his prior promotion to the episcopal state.[81]

Schmalzgrueber (1663–1735) proposed a similar case, but his answer was in the affirmative, based on the fact that a religious in an ecclesiastical dignity such as that of a bishop or of a cardinal was withdrawn or freed from the monastic rule, though of course he remained a religious. Therefore, since he was no longer a subject, he did not need the superior's permission for giving his consent when later elected to another or a higher dignity; and since he had been freed from the monastic rule, he was not bound to the regulation of a unanimous election; for him the election by a majority sufficed, since the legislation of Pope Boniface referred specifically to those under the Mendicant Rule.[82]

Pope Clement V determined the significance of a non-unanimous election of Mendicant religious to dignities outside their Order, and the meaning of a minority in the election of non-Mendicant religious to any prelacy,[83] as had been established by Pope Boniface VIII.[84]

A fictional case to explain the tenor of the legislation is readily at hand.[85] Let it be supposed that a Mendicant were elected to some dignity outside his Order by an electoral college of ten.

---

80 Schmalzgrueber, Lib. I, tit. VI, n. 90, 2 ss.

81 *Glossa Ordinaria* to c. 24, *de electione et electi potestate,* I, 6, in VI°, s. v. *Mendicantium.*

82 Lib. I, tit. VI, n. 90, 5. Cf. Laymann, *Quaestiones Canonicae de Electione,* Quaestio CXCIV.

83 C. 6, *de electione et electi potestate,* I, 3, in Clem.

84 C. 24, *de electione et electi potestate,* I, 6, in VI°; *supra,* pp. 31, 32.

85 Cf. Laymann, *Quaestiones Canonicae de Electione,* Quaestio CXCVI.

Eight vote for him and two vote for another. Such a result would imply a discordant election, i.e., one not unanimous, and accordingly the Mendicant who had received the eight votes would not be elected. The Mendicant could not claim that he had been elected unanimously for the reason that the two who had voted against him were actually excommunicated or suspended at the time of the election, and thus had no voice in the election.[86] In consequence their two votes, it might have been argued, by a fiction of the law could be considered as contained among the eight votes cast for him. This, then, would bring about a unanimous election. It was against this line of argumentation that Pope Clement V definitely established that such an election, only fictitiously unanimous, did not fulfill the requirements of a concordant election. It was required that a Mendicant be elected by all the electors *in facto,* and not simply *in fictione vel iuris effectu,* even thought it was to be acknowledged that excommunicates had no voice in the election.

Article 3. The Obligation of the Vow of Poverty for Religious Promoted to Prelacies Outside Their Institutes

The obligation of the vow of poverty in itself was clear. Yet particular legislation for certain Orders appeared. Thus, Pope Alexander IV (1254–1261) specifically obliged the Friars Minor Conventual, if they were promoted to the episcopal dignity, to cede their books to the Order, as well as other goods which they held at the time of their promotion.[87]

A similar obligation was put on the members of the Order of Preachers by Pope Clement IV (1265–1268). The members of this Order, if they were advanced to any prelacy outside their Order, had to give back to the monastery whatever they had received from the Order itself before they entered upon their new office.[88]

---

[86] *Glossa Ordinaria* to c. 6, *de electione et electi potestate,* I, 3, in Clem. s. v. *quae in facto, non in fictione.*

[87] Const. "*Ex parte vestra,*" 5 dec. 1255—*Bullarum Diplomatum et Privilegiorum Sanctorum Romanorum Pontificum Taurinensis Editio, auspicante Cardinali Francisco Gaudè* (25 vols., Augustae Taurinorum, 1857–1872), III, 628 (henceforth cited *BRT*).

[88] Const. "*Providenti,*" 9 iun. 1268—*BRT,* III, 799.

Article 4. The Obligation of Wearing the Religious Habit

Earlier legislation had always insisted that those religious who had been promoted to some dignity in the Church were still obliged to wear their religious habit. The Supreme Pontiff could relax this rule in particular cases. For example, in 1519 Pope Leo X (1513–1521) permitted the Canons Regular of Saint Augustine who had been raised to the episcopal dignity to conform their habit to the form of dress used by secular clerics in the episcopal dignity.[89] Certainly this had to be considered as a very particular concession granted to the Canons Regular of Saint Augustine, since religious were not at liberty to alter their religious garb for the sole reason that they had been promoted to the episcopal dignity outside their Order.

In summary, then, this whole period from the beginnings of the religious life to the Council of Trent evolved, as it were, certain fundamental principles as a basis for measuring and determining the obligations and privileges of religious who had been promoted to ecclesiastical dignities outside their proper Orders or institutes. They were the following:

1. Religious could be promoted to ecclesiastical dignities outside their Order or institute.
2. A religious, though he had been promoted to a dignity, still remained a religious. He continued subject to the observance of his rule in all things essential to his religious state of life. He was freed from the observance of his rule in only those things which were not essential, but solely on the condition that they were incompatible with the duties or status of his dignity.
3. The permission and testimony of the religious superior was a means requisite for the election itself.

From these principles flowed the other regulations regarding the signifying of acceptance on the part of a religious when elected to dignities, concerning the disposition of his goods, and pertaining to his obligation of retaining the use of the religious habit.

[89] Const. "*Dudum,*" 1 sept. 1519—*BRT*, V, 729.

CHAPTER III

THE LAW FROM THE COUNCIL OF TRENT TO THE CODE OF CANON LAW

Article 1. Preliminary Notes

Before considering the historical developments in the law regarding the obligations and privileges of religious when promoted to the episcopal or cardinalitial dignities outside their proper religious organizations in the period from the Council of Trent (1545–1563) to the Code of Canon Law (1918), one must note at the outset that throughout this period there were few cases in which there was any question of needed consent on the part of religious when elected to these two dignities outside the Order. The reason was that since the fourteenth century the Popes had begun to reserve to themselves the canonical appointment of anyone to the episcopate.[1] Thus the former law under which bishops were elected by the cathedral chapters had given way to the free bestowal by the Supreme Pontiff himself; hence it followed that the permission of a religious superior, required in the past to be given to his religious subject to enable him to consent to an election in which he had been chosen to the episcopal dignity outside the Order, was not at all required when the Pope himself appointed the religious.[2] Only in such cases in which election to the episcopacy was still permitted as a legitimate way for the promoting of anyone to that dignity was the superior's permission necessary for his religious subject, just as it had been in the former law.

[1] Wernz, *Ius Decretalium,* II, n. 750: "Ex saeculo decimo quarto Romani Pontifices sibi coeperunt reservare provisionem canonicam Episcoporum, atque exinde ius commune Decretalium, quo libera electio Episcoporum fuit Capitulis cathedralibus concessa, paulatim ob iustas causas commutatum est in novam disciplinam liberae collationis Episcopatuum per Romanum Pontificem. Quacum innovatione etiam illa coniuncta est, quod Romani Pontifices sibi saltem reservarent confirmationem electionis Episcoporum, ubi libera collatio non fuit introducta."

[2] Reiffenstuel, Adnotatio XXXV ad Lib. I, tit. VI, nn. 317, 318.

Promotion to the cardinalate had always exclusively and entirely depended on the free bestowal of the Pope.[3] In the event of such a promotion there was never any need for the consent of the religious superior; such consent could not occupy any helpful or useful place in an act which belonged entirely to the Pope as peculiarly his own.

The legislation during the post-Tridentine period was mainly a vigorous restatement, an added confirmation, or an adapted extension of the former law, and thus contributed to a further development in the application of the law. The sources of the legislative enactments of this period were especially the Constitutions and Letters issued by the Supreme Pontiffs, and the decisions and the responses furnished by several of the Sacred Roman Congregations.

Article 2. The Capability of Religious to be Promoted to the Cardinalitial or Episcopal Dignities

Pope Sixtus V (1585–1590) in his Constitution "*Postquam,*" which he issued on Decemer 3, 1586, was primarily concerned with the status of cardinals, their number and their rank, their requisite age and other needed qualifications. After establishing the number of members composing the cardinalitial college, the Pope continued in the next paragraph stating that among the 70 cardinals there should not be wanting, besides the doctors of law and men well versed in the laws of the Church, outstanding men who were Masters of Theology, to be selected from the regular and Mendicant Orders, to the number of at least four, but not in smaller number.[4]

This clearly evinced the fact that regulars could be raised to the cardinalitial dignity, since the Supreme Pontiff expressed his desire that regulars also be numbered in the college of cardinals.

Indeed, regulars could also become bishops. However, that they should not be indiscriminately advanced to the episcopal dignity was indicated in the Letter "*Acceptis*" of Pope Clement XIII

[3] Wernz, *op. cit.*, II, n. 625.

[4] §9: "Inter hos septuaginta cardinales, praeter egregios utriusque iuris aut decretorum doctores, non desint aliquot insignes viri in sacra theologia magistri, praesertim ex regularibus et Mendicantium Ordinibus assumendi, saltem quatuor, non tamen pauciores."—*BRT,* VIII, 812.

(1758–1769), sent to the noble Prince of Montmorency, France, who had requested that a certain professed member of the Carmelites be consecrated as a bishop.[5] The Pope refused the request for the reason that merely the good character, reputation and learning of a regular was not sufficient in itself for his promotion to the episcopal dignity. Rather, the necessity of a church or the great utility for a church was required as a condition for the admission of regulars to the episcopate.

The attack of the Synod of Pistoia in Italy against the compatibility of the religious or monastic state of life with the care of souls in pastoral work and offices was not countenanced in the Church. Pope Pius VI (1775–1799) condemned Proposition 80 of this Synod in his famous Bull *"Auctorem Fidei,"* on August 28, 1794. The Synod had proposed three fundamental rules for the reform of regulars. The first of these (Proposition 80) declared that the regular or monastic state by its very nature was incompatible with the care of souls and its attendant pastoral offices and duties, and that therefore the monastic state could have no part in the ecclesiastical hierarchy without opposition to the very fundamental principles underlying it. The Pope roundly condemned this statement as false, pernicious, and injurious, and also as contrary to the ancient and approved custom of the Church as well as the enactments of Popes, particular reference being made to the early letter of Pope Siricius to Himerius of Tarragona, Spain.[6]

---

[5] *Bullarii Romani Continuatio Summorum Pontificum* (9 vols. in 10, Prati, 1840–1856), I, 428. This letter was written on Jan. 2, 1761.

[6] §54: "Regula 1, quae statuit universe et indiscriminatim: *statum regularem, aut monasticum natura sua componi non posse cum animarum cura, cumque vitae pastoralis muneribus, nec adeo in partem venire posse ecclesiasticae hierarchiae, quin ex adverso pugnet cum ipsiusmet vitae monasticae principiis.*

Falsa, perniciosa, in sanctissimos Ecclesiae patres, et praesules, qui regularis vitae instituta cum clericalis ordinis muneribus consociarunt, iniuriosa, pio, vetusto, probato Ecclesiae mori, Summorumque Pontificum sanctionibus contraria: quasi monachi quos morum gravitas, et vitae, ac fidei institutio sancta commendat, *non rite, nec modo sine religionis offensione, sed et cum multa utilitate Ecclesiae* clericorum officiis *aggregentur.*

Ex s. Siricio epist. decret. ad *Himerium Tarracon.*, c. 13."—*Codicis Iuris Canonici Fontes,* cura Emi Petri Card. Gasparri editi (9 vols., Romae [postea Civitate Vaticana]: Typis Polyglottis Vaticanis, 1923–1939; Vols.

ARTICLE 3. THE ATTESTATION OF THE SUPERIOR TO THE REQUISITE QUALITIES OF A RELIGIOUS TO BE ADVANCED TO THE EPISCOPACY

The Fathers of the Tridentine Council (1545–1563) did not devote any special section to the obligations and privileges of religious in ecclesiastical dignities. However, in the twenty-second session of the Council in the section *de reformatione,* chapter two concerned itself with those who were to be promoted to cathedral churches. Mention was made of regulars. The chapter stated that a candidate for appointment to a cathedral church needed the necessary qualifications with regard to parentage, age, morals, and the other requisite characteristics in his life; and that he must have been in sacred orders for at least six months. Moreover, he had to possess the required learning and knowledge to enable him to discharge the obligations and duties of his office, and therefore must have attained the degree of Master or Doctor or Licentiate in Sacred Theology or in Canon Law at some recognized university. If the candidate was a regular, the certification as to the presence of these qualifications had to be furnished by the superiors of his Order.[7] It was, then, an obligation that rested upon the superiors to attest to the requisite qualities of the religious; indeed, it was a grave and serious obligation, as the last part of the chapter indicated.[8]

Pope Gregory XIV (1590–1591) defined that the supreme superiors in the religious organization were the superiors obliged to attest to the requisite qualifications of a religious who was to be

---

VII–IX, ed. cura et studio Emi Iustiniani Card. Serédi), n. 475 (hereafter cited as *Fontes*); italics of §54 are the same as found in *Fontes,* n. 475. The mentioned letter of Pope Siricius was included by Gratian in his *Decretum* as c. 29, C. XVI, q. 1.

[7] Conc. Trident., sess. XXII, *de ref.,* c. 2—*Canones et Decreta Sacrosancti Oecumenici Concilii Tridentini* (ed. novissima, Romae, 1882), pp. 142–143; Schroeder, *Canons and Decrees of the Council of Trent, Original Text with English Translation* (St. Louis, Mo.: B. Herder Co., 1941), p. 153.

[8] In pointing out who these superiors were according to this same chapter of the Council of Trent, Fagnanus (1598–1678), referred to the Constitution "*Onus*" of Pope Gregory XIV, May 15, 1591.—*Commentarium in Librum Decretalium* (3 vols., Venetiis, 1709), Lib. I, tit. *de renuntiatione,* cap. X *nisi cum pridem,* n. 69.

promoted to a cathedral church according to the provisions of the Council of Trent, as above mentioned.[9] This ruling was found in the Pope's Constitution "*Onus,*" of the 15th of May, 1591, which recounted at length the method to be employed for the promotion of bishops to cathedral churches.[10]

Article 4. The Obligations of Religious Profession and of the Rule for a Dignitary Religious

The momentous Constitution "*Custodes*" of Pope Benedict XIII (1724–1730) on March 7, 1726, may be considered as the crystallization of much of the former legislation that dealt with the obligations of regulars who had been consecrated bishops. Its title, "De Episcopi regularis habitu et obligationibus," at once showed its import. At the very beginning of the Constitution Pope Benedict XIII pointed out that professed members chosen from religious institutes of regulars, monks or Mendicants who had received the episcopal dignity were under obligation to follow the customs of their respective Orders, especially in regard to their manner of dress.[11]

In confirmation of this provision the Pontiff recalled the more important decrees of former Councils, and of former Popes, in which it had been declared again and again that monks or regulars in the episcopal or cardinalitial dignities had to observe all the obligations of their religious state of life which in no way were prejudicial or repugnant to their dignity.[12] In consequence, these religious, the Constitution declared, were not exempted from keeping the prescriptions of their rule, in so far as that was compatible with their dignity or office; besides, they were bound to wear their religious garb and tonsure as before:

> " . . . statuimus atque sancimus, ut ex Monastico, Regulari, et Mendicantium instituto ad Episcopalem, seu quamcumque aliam dignitatem, etiam S. R. E. Cardinalatum, iam evecti, et in posterum evehendi, universis, et singulis suae regulae officiis, et obligationibus, quae Pontificale,

[9] Conc. Trident., sess. XXII, *de ref.*, c. 2.

[10] §9—*BRT*, IX, 422.

[11] §1—*Fontes*, n. 291.

[12] §4—*Fontes*, n. 291.

> sive cuiuscunque alterius dignitatis, aut Cardinalatus, officium minime impediant, perpetuo subsint, et proinde sui monastici Ordinis, sive alterius regulae Mendicantium, insignia, et propria indumenta lanea, suoque peculiari colore distincta, rasilem quoque, et ad cutis planitiem in summo vertice, vel eo gyro, et forma expressam coronam praeferant, quibus antea, cum intra eorundem regularium Ordinum claustra Deo militarent, ex solemni sua professione, insignia induere, et coronam praeferre tenebantur, a cuius professionis obligationibus per munus Episcopale neutiquam absolvuntur, aut ullo pacto eximuntur." [13]

The Pope exacted strict obedience, otherwise the punishment of suspension *ab exercitio pontificalium,* reserved for its absolution to the Holy See, was incurred *ipso facto.*[14]

A further question was raised: Was a bishop regular obliged *sub gravi* or *sub levi* to observe his religious rule of life? This question was proposed to the Sacred Congregation of Bishops and Regulars for a definite and clear answer. The Congregation referred the whole matter to two consultors, who offered a written report. On the basis of these reports the Congregation replied in 1864 that a bishop regular was certainly obliged to observe all the rules of his Order which determined the matter of the vow of poverty, as well as all other rules and observances not conflicting with his episcopal dignity or office.

The bishop regular could himself pass prudent judgment whether conflict or harmony existed between his religious duties and observances on the one hand, and his episcopal dignity on the other. Regarding the nature of the obligation as binding *sub gravi* or *sub levi,* the question had to be decided according to the proper rule or constitutions to which the religious had obliged himself by his religious profession. This resolution of the Congregation of Bishops and Regulars was approved and confirmed by Pope Pius IX (1846–1878).[15] Though this response was restricted to bishops

---

[13] §5—*loc. cit.*

[14] §6—*loc. cit.*

[15] S. C. Ep. et Reg., *Alexien.,* 6 maii 1864: "Haec omnia sedulo diligenterque perpensa sunt in Congregatione generali habita die 6 Maii 1864, proposito dubio:

'Se, e come il Vescovo Regolare sia obligato alla Regola professata?'

regular, its import rightly could be extended to bishops religious who in their institutes had been professed with simple vows.[16]

A. THE VOW OF POVERTY

Since it was clear that a religious in the episcopal dignity, or in the cardinalitial dignity for that matter,[17] was still bound by his religious profession, there were cases about the acquisition and disposition of goods, which in relation to the vow of poverty on the part of these religious dignitaries entailed obligations of binding force. Such a case brought before the tribunal of the Sacred Roman Rota concerning the acquisition of inheritances by regulars elicited the following statements about regulars who had become bishops, as found in the argumentation preceding the solution of this case by the Rota on May 24, 1619:

1. A regular who had been promoted to the episcopacy could claim for himself any inheritance that fell to him after assuming the episcopacy; he acquired the usufruct of that inheritance just as any secular. His church, however, acquired the ownership, since the regular was still under the vow of poverty. The authority cited was c. un., C. XVIII, q. 1, of Gratian, and the *Summa Theologica* of Saint Thomas, IIa, IIae, q. 185, art. 8.[18]

Cui Emi Patres, referente Emo Quaglia Praefecto, rescripserunt: Affirmative ad praescriptum Constit. Bened. XIII, incipien. *Custodes:* nempe Episcopus Regularis tenetur observare regulas suae Religionis, quae materiam voti paupertatis determinant; item tenetur alias regulas et observantias Dignitati et Officio episcopali non repugnantes eadem obligatione gravi vel levi observare, qua tenebatur antequam assequeretur dignitatem episcopalem, ita tamen ut in peculiaribus casibus prudenter iudicium ferre possit utrum cum dignitate et officio episcopali illae conveniant.

Et facta de praemissis relatione SSmo D. N. Pio PP. IX in audientia habita eadem die, Sanctitas Sua resolutionem S. C. benigne approbavit, et confirmavit."—*Fontes,* n. 1990.

[16] The *votum* of one of the consultors on this question is reported in the *Acta Sanctae Sedis.* He presented as one of his conclusions in the report the fact that the above mentioned response applied also to religious with simple vows, when they had been raised to the episcopal status.—*Acta Sanctae Sedis* (41 vols., Romae, 1865–1908), I (1865–1866), 446, n. VI (hereafter signified by the letters *ASS*).

[17] Suarez, *De religiosis,* Tractatus Octavus, Liber III, Caput XVIII, n. 4.—Opera Omnia, XVI, 415.

[18] S. R. R. *Urgellen. Haereditatis,* 24 maii 1619, *coram R. P. D. Pirovano,*

2. A member of the Friars Minor (whose community, by its organic law, could not own property even in common) when made bishop could regain for himself by the authority and permission of the Supreme Pontiff the right of succession to inheritances of any intestate estate or of testamentary wills that came to him after his promotion. But his vow of poverty was to be upheld. Therefore the Friar Minor in the episcopal dignity acquired for himself only the use and usufruct, while his church obtained the ownership.[19]

A further elucidation on the question of what goods or property a regular could claim when he had become a bishop came from the Sacred Congregation of the Council in 1631. The Congregation definitely stated that a bishop regular regained for himself at least the use and usufruct even of those goods or properties which he had renounced at his entry into the Order, but solely on the condition that these same goods or properties had not yet been acquired by others, i.e., not claimed by the party in whose favor the renunciation had been made.[20]

In answer to several *dubia* about the right of succession to inheritances by regulars who were incapable of ownership as a result of their renunciation of all ownership before profession, the Sacred Congregation of the Council gave corresponding replies. A dignitary regular who by profession in an Order had become incapable of ownership of property nevertheless acquired the right of succession to any inheritance which fell to him after his promotion to the episcopal status.[21] He acquired thereby the ownership for

dec. CXV, nn. 3-5, 8, 18—*Sacrae Rotae Romanae Decisiones Recentiores* (19 partes in 25 vols., Romae, 1623–1703), Tomus Secundus Partis Quartae Recentiorum, 143–144.

[19] *Ibidem*, nn. 22–24.

[20] S. C. C., *Nullius*, 11 ian. 1631—Pallottini, *Collectio omnium conclusionum et resolutionum quae in causis propositis apud Sacram Congregationem Cardinalium S. Concilii Tridentini Interpretum prodierunt ab eius institutione anno MDLXIV ad annum MDCCCLX, distinctis titulis alphabetico ordine per materias digesta* (17 vols., Romae, 1868–1893), s. v. "Episcopus," §I, nn. 21, 22.

[21] It was clear that inheritances coming to regulars before their promotion to the episcopacy, i.e., while they were simple religious in the Order, passed over to the party in whose favor the renunciation had been made at the

the utility of his church, and the usufruct for his own benefit and use. According to the prescriptions of the Council of Trent the renunciation of all ownership of goods was to be made before profession in favor of someone else, a brother for instance. But such a renunciation was no impediment to the right regained by a regular upon his promotion to the episcopal dignity, provided only that the inheritance had not been duly claimed and acquired, before the regular had attained the episcopal dignity, by the party in whose favor the renunciation had been made.[22]

There were also several decrees, issued by the Sacred Congregation for the Propagation of the Faith in 1716, concerning the disposition of goods acquired during their time in the missions by missionaries or bishops regular, vicars and prefects apostolic, subject to this Congregation.[23] With the approbation of Pope Clement XI (1700–1721) the Sacred Congregation ruled that after the death of the missionaries or bishops regular all the goods acquired during their activity in the missions (*spolia*) were to be placed in possession of the Sacred Congregation for the Propagation of the Faith. In fact, all these things belonged to the Sacred Congregation, and were to be employed for the utility of the missions; they could not be claimed by the religious Order.[24]

---

time of profession, whether this party was the Order or monastery itself or some other person. In other eventualities, of course, the old principle held: "Quidquid acquirit monachus monasterio acquirit."

[22] S. C. C., *Neapolitana,* 7 dec. 1639: "Quaeritur:

1. An Regularis professus incapax bonorum ad Episcopatum assumptus recuperet ius succedendi quoad haereditates post assumptum Episcopatum sibi delatas.

2. An eidem obstet cessio, et renuntiatio huiusmodi haereditatum facta ad favorem fratris ad praescriptum Sacri Concilii Tridentini, cap. 16, Sess. 25, *de regul.*

Sacra, etc. ad 1. respondit recuperare ius succedendi ad haereditates post adeptum Episcopatum ad utilitatem suae Ecclesiae sibi delatas quoad proprietatem, et ad proprium commodum quoad usum fructum.

Ad 2. Eidem non obstare supradictam cessionem et renuntiationem quoad haereditates, quae non sint alteri ante adeptum Episcopatum acquisitae."—*Fontes,* n. 2613.

[23] S. C. de Prop. Fide, 4 mart. 1716; (C. G.), 10 nov. 1716; *Fontes,* nn. 4500, 4501. Cf. Berutti, *Institutiones Iuris Canonici* (6 vols., Vol. III, Taurini, Romae: Marietti, 1936), III, *De Religiosis,* n. 140, A, b (hereafter cited as *De Religiosis*).

[24] S. C. de Prop. Fide, (C. G.), 22 dec. 1716—*Fontes,* n. 4502.

In 1722 the following case was submitted to the Sacred Congregation of the Council: A certain Thomas de Adamis, a solemnly professed member in the Congregation of the Canons Regular of the Lateran, received a parish and was duly and legitimately installed as pastor. An argument broke out between him and the religious of his congregation concerning his obligation of wearing the habit, and especially concerning the regaining of the goods which he had renounced at his profession. Appealing to the former law, the Sacred Congregation of the Council obliged him to wear his religious garb, but, on the basis of certain responses rendered by the Sacred Congregation to questions of a similar nature, upheld his right of regaining at least the use of the goods which he had renounced at his profession.[25]

Then a further argument centered about the ownership of all the goods which he had obtained after becoming a pastor. His brothers in religion asserted that the ownership rested with the religious society of which he was a member by virtue of his former profession. Hence it was asked of the Sacred Congregation whether all the goods thus acquired belonged to this Thomas or to his parish church. The Sacred Congregation simply answered: " Non spectare ad Thomam, et amplius."

In the discussion of the case, c. un., C. XVIII, q. 1, of Gratian was adduced. Based on that reference, the following statement was offered: " Iuxta receptiorem sententiam Religiosus ad Episcopatum promotus remanet obstrictus voto Paupertatis, et proprium habere non potest." Thence followed the logical inference that whatever obtained as doctrine and consequent practice regarding monks who succeeded to inheritances when they had become bishops applied equally to canons regular in any secular benefice.[26]

Religious when once promoted to an ecclesiastical dignity could not claim goods or property from their own Order or monastery. Pope Benedict XIII (1724–1730) prohibited all regulars, no matter to what ecclesiastical dignities they had been raised, to take

[25] Cf. S. C. C., *Neapolitana,* 7 dec. 1639—*Fontes,* n. 2613. *Supra,* pp. 43, 44.

[26] S. C. C., *Firmana, Renunciationis,* 23 maii 1722—*Thesaurus Resolutionum S. C. Concilii* (167 vols., Urbini, 1718–1749, Romae, 1843–1908), II, 340-343.

along with them anything from their own monasteries.[27] Thereby the prescriptions of Pope Alexander IV (1254–1261) for the Friars Minor Conventual, and of Pope Clement IV (1265–1268) for the Dominicans were not only confirmed,[28] but were also extended by Pope Benedict XIII to all Orders regular, except with regard to those things concerning which his own Constitution, "*Postulat humilitatis nostrae,*" had made contrary provision.[29] These exceptions were briefly stated by the Pope: *exceptis dumtaxat scriptis, propriis indumentis et breviario.*[30]

Again, in 1725, the Sacred Congregation for the Propagation of the Faith reiterated the provision that was to be observed as a general rule in China, namely, that all goods acquired by bishops, vicars apostolic and missionaries subject to the Sacred Congregation should be delivered over entirely and faithfully to the Procurator of this same Congregation in China, since the *spolia,* if thus acquired, belonged to the said Congregation.[31]

An earlier decree of the Sacred Congregation for the Propagation of the Faith, under the date of December 22, 1716, and approved by Pope Clement XI,[32] was renewed and confirmed by this same Congregation on August 17, 1772, with the approbation and confirmation of Pope Clement XIV (1769–1774).[33] Thus the Sacred Congregation once again asserted its right to all the goods obtained by missionaries or bishops regular or vicars apostolic in mission territories during their activity there. These so called *spolia* did not revert to the religious Order under the old rule of *quidquid acquirit monachus monasterio acquirit.*

---

[27] Const. "*Postulat humilitatis nostrae,*" 4 mart. 1725—*BRT,* XXII, 129-133.

[28] *Supra,* p. 34.

[29] §§3 and 4—*BRT,* XXII, 130.

[30] §5—*loc. cit.* Cf. Prümmer (1866–1931), *Manuale Iuris Canonici in Usum Scholarum* (3. ed., Friburgi Brisgoviae: Herder & Co., 1922), Q. 249, n. 2 (hereafter cited as *Manuale*).

[31] S. C. de Prop. Fide (C. P. pro Sin.), 28 sept. 1725: "Sit regula generalis, et perpetuis deinceps temporibus omnino servanda, scilicet, quod spolia Episcoporum, Vicariorum App. et missionariorum S. Congregationis ad eam pertineant, at ad Procuratorem pro tempore eiusdem S. C. in Sinis morantem fideliter atque integerrime transmitti debeant."—*Fontes,* n. 4505.

[32] *Supra,* p. 44.

[33] *Fontes,* n. 4557.

B. THE FOURTH VOW OF NOT SEEKING OR ACCEPTING DIGNITIES

Pope Urban VIII (1623–1644) took cognizance of the question of a fourth vow, that of not seeking or accepting any dignity outside the Order, as taken in some religious Orders.[34] The Pope declared that regulars who besides the usual three vows of religion had taken also a vow of not seeking or accepting any dignity outside their Order were in no way freed from that vow if they transferred to another religious Order whose members did not take such a vow, and likewise that freedom from the vow was in no way gained through deprivation of the wearing of the religious habit or through a dismissal from the religious institute.[35] Furthermore, neither ecclesiastical judges nor cardinals, not even legates *a latere* or apostolic nuncios, had any faculty or power to render a contrary decision.[36]

Pope Urban VIII, who earlier had insisted on the binding force of the fourth vow, namely, of not seeking or accepting any dignity or superiorship outside the religious Order,[37] again dealt with the question of this fourth vow, in particular with the question of a possible dispensation from it, in his Constitution "*Honorum*" of February 24, 1643. The vow of not seeking or accepting any dignity or prelacy outside the religious Order was qualified by the phrase, "unless they (the religious) were constrained or obliged [to accept] by the precept of him who in law could command them."[38]

This provision, the Pontiff explained, signified that no regular superior, not even the supreme superior, neither the chapter of the Order, nor the apostolic nuncio, nor the Cardinal Protector nor any other cardinal or legate of the Holy See had the right to oblige a regular, if he was bound by this vow, to accept a dignity outside the Order. The capacity to impose such an obligation rested with the Pope alone. None of those named could dispense from that vow or relax its rigor; the granting of any and every dispensation

[34] Const. "*Cum sicut accepimus,*" 21 maii 1635—*Fontes*, n. 216.

[35] §3—*Fontes*, n. 216.

[36] §5—*Fontes*, n. 216.

[37] *Supra*, p. 47.

[38] §2: "*nisi coacti vel adstricti fuerint praecepto eius, qui sibi iure praecipere potest.*"—*Fontes*, n. 227.

in this matter was entirely reserved to the Supreme Pontiff.[39] But if a regular under such a vow was appointed to some dignity by the Pope himself and commanded to accept, then no special dispensation was any longer necessary. The very appointment or command of the Pope implicitly included the dispensation.

C. THE WEARING OF THE RELIGIOUS GARB

Religious when promoted to an ecclesiastical dignity were obliged to retain their religious habit and form of dress. There were instances, of course, in which the Popes in some way derogated from this established rule, but not entirely. Thus Pope Gregory XIV (1590–1591) granted the right of wearing the red biretta to certain cardinals chosen from the Orders of regulars, but he did not grant any permission to alter their religious form of dress in other ways.[40] Hence, regulars promoted to the cardinalitial dignity were still under the obligation of keeping their religious habit and form of dress.

In answer to a presented case the Sacred Congregation of Rites affirmed that a regular who had become a bishop had to use a *cappa pontificalis* of the same color as his proper religious habit; in the event of a refusal, apt penal remedies could be invoked to compel him to conform.[41]

Pope Benedict XIII in his Constitution *"Custodes"* emphatically stated that religious, when promoted to the episcopal, the cardinalitial, or any other dignities, had to retain their religious habit, i.e., the woolen habit with the color proper to the Order;

---

[39] *Loc. cit.*

[40] Const. *"Sanctissimus,"* 9 iun. 1591: "Sanctissimus D. N. Romae in aedibus Hortorum Quirinalium, . . . dedit rubra bireta infrascriptis DD. Cardinalibus ex Ordinibus regularium, quae perpetuo deferrent more aliorum, habitu in caeteris nihil immutato."—*BRT*, IX, 433.

[41] S. R. C., *Calaritana,* 12 ian. 1636: "Regulares promotos ad Episcopatus debere uti cappa pontificali coloris propriae Religionis: et ideo in casu proposito Archiepiscopum Calaritanum Regularem Ordinis B. Mariae de Mercede Redemptionis Captivorum, non posse uti cappa pontificali alterius coloris, quam suae propriae Religionis: et renuentem, opportunis remediis coercendum."—*Decreta Authentica Congregationis Sacrorum Rituum ex actis eiusdem collecta eiusque auctoritate promulgata sub auspiciis SS. D. N. Leonis Papae XIII* (5 vols. et 2 Appendices, Romae: Typis Polyglottis Vaticanis, 1898–1927), n. 628 (hereafter cited as *Decreta Authentica*).

therefore they could not exchange their woolen habit for the silken robes of the dignitary status, though it was permissible for them to conform their religious garb in form and cut to that used by secular prelates.[42]

The Apostolic Letter "*Biennium*" of Pope Benedict XIV (1740–1758) may also be adduced as further testimony regarding the obligation of monks or regulars in ecclesiastical dignities to wear their religious habit.[43] The letter was addressed to Joachim, named Portocarrero, Cardinal Priest of the Holy Roman Church, and was concerned about defining the proper habit of the members in the Military Order of the Knights of Saint John of Jerusalem. The Pope stated that the members of this Order were to be considered as true regulars, and hence as meriting the title "*Fratres.*" Therefore, inasmuch as monks or regulars who were promoted to the episcopate or to the cardinalate were obliged to wear their proper religious habit, the same rule applied to the members of this Order. Their religious habit was distinguished by a cross of white cloth sewed on their external clothing. That religious badge was to be worn publicly by the member who had been advanced to ecclesiastical dignities.[44]

In 1867 Pope Pius IX (1846–1878) granted to all patriarchs, archbishops and bishops of the Catholic Church the use of the violet skull cap.[45] And the next Pope, Pope Leo XIII (1878–1903), on the occasion of the fiftieth anniversary of his ordination to the priesthood, granted to the same the use of the violet biretta.[46]

---

[42] §5—*Fontes*, n. 291.

[43] *Benedicti XIV Bullarium* (3 vols. in 4, Prati, 1845–1847), III, Pars I, 456. The letter was dated Oct. 13, 1745.

[44] §§2-4—*loc. cit.*

[45] Litt. ap. "*Ecclesiarum,*" 17 iun. 1867: ". . . Itaque auctoritate Nostra Apostolica harum litterarum vi omnibus, et singulis Catholicae Ecclesiae Patriarchis, Archiepiscopis, et Episcopis tam praesentibus, quam futuris concedimus, atque indulgemus, ut ipsi in posterum a primis tamen vesperis proxime futuri festi Sanctorum Apostolorum Petri et Pauli pileoli violacei coloris uti libere ac licite possint, et valeant. . . ."—*Fontes*, n. 545.

[46] Litt. ap. "*Praeclaro,*" 3 febr. 1888: ". . . Quare hisce litteris Apostolica Auctoritate Nostra perpetuum in modum concedimus ut universi Patriarchae, Archiepiscopi et Episcopi birreto violacei coloris hoc futurisque temporibus uti libere et licite possint et valeant. Hoc ita illis proprium volumus

Certainly, religious constituted in these dignities could also partake of these privileges, since they were granted to all patriarchs, archbishops and bishops without any distinction.

D. THE RECITATION OF THE DIVINE OFFICE

Though a religious when promoted to an ecclesiastical dignity still remained a religious, i.e., still was bound to observe his rule as far as possible in his new office, this did not oblige him in his dignitary status with reference to the recitation of the divine office. A reply of the Sacred Congregation of Rites, given on June 11, 1605, to some proposed doubts, confirmed the fact that a religious upon being promoted to the episcopacy was freed from the observance of his rule in regard to the recitation of the divine Office and also the celebration of feasts.

A professed member of the Hermits of Saint Augustine had been raised to the episcopal dignity in the Indies. The Sacred Congregation was then asked the following questions to which it issued the following replies:

1. Was that bishop religious bound to say the Office according to the form as followed in his own Order, or according to the form as determined for the respective diocese by the Holy See? The Sacred Congregation answered that he was to say divine Office in accordance with the rite of the diocese.
2. What feast was that bishop to celebrate when on one and the same day a feast of a saint of the diocese concurred with a feast of a saint of his Order? The answer again was that the bishop was to celebrate the feasts according to the calendar of the diocese.
3. Did chaplains, whether secular or religious, who recited the divine Office together with the bishop, have to follow the form of the Office as used by the bishop? The Sacred Congregation answered in the affirmative.[47]

The Sacred Congregation of Rites had issued a decree on September 27, 1659, about the veneration of the beatified. Almost a

---

ut alius qui episcopali dignitate non sit insignitus eiusmodi ornamento nullatenus potiri queat . . . "—*Fontes*, n. 597.

[47] *Decreta Authentica*, n. 181.

year later this same Congregation had to clarify the import of this decree. Among the *dubia* referred to the Congregation was one that dealt with bishops regular. The question was asked whether regulars in the episcopal dignity, when they enjoyed all the privileges of their Order by apostolic indult in so far as these privileges were compatible with their rank, could recite the Office of the beatified of their Orders, celebrate their Masses in the cathedral churches, or erect altars in their honor. The answer was in the negative.[48]

E. THE RETURN TO RELIGIOUS LIFE IN THE PROPER INSTITUTE

Pope Alexander VII (1655–1667) in his Constitution "*Quia Ecclesia*" of July 26, 1662, reminded bishops of their obligation of residence, especially at the cathedral churches erected among the schismatics. According to the precepts of the Council of Trent, bishops were not to be absent from their dioceses over a period of six continuous months, unless some just and reasonable cause intervened, such as Christian charity, urgent necessity, due obedience, etc.[49] Also bishops regular were bound by this law of residence. But since a bishop regular was not freed from the obligations of his rule by the fact of his promotion to the episcopacy, he was obliged to return to his cloister if he was actually not residing in his diocese, regardless of whether this absence from the diocese was the result of his own fault, or the consequence of some just and legitimate impediment, unless the Holy See made other provision for him.[50]

The Sacred Congregation for the Propagation of the Faith on June 17, 1715, approached Pope Clement XI (1700–1721) to obtain a renewal of the enacted decrees of Pope Alexander VII, and an extension of the same to all regulars in future to be promoted by

[48] S. R. C., *Declaratio Decreti*, 17 apri. 1660, ad 5: "An Episcopi Regulares qui ex indulto Sedis Apostolicae gaudent privilegiis suae Religionis, de quibus sunt capaces pro eorum conditione, possint de Beatis suae Religionis recitare Officium et in propriis cathedralibus Missam celebrare, et altare Beatis praedictis erigere?

S. R. C. respondit: ad 5: Negative."—*Decreta Authentica*, n. 1156.

[49] Conc. Trident., sess. VI, *de ref.*, c. 1; sess. XXIII, *de ref.*, c. 1.

[50] *Fontes*, n. 238.

the Holy See at the nomination or supplication of the Sacred Congregation to the offices of vicar apostolic and of administrator or visitator of some church, whenever the appointee was endowed with the episcopal character. The Pope gave his approval.[51]

In regard to the obligation of returning to the cloister, Pope Benedict XIII in his Constitution "*Custodes,*" which approved and confirmed the decrees of Popes Alexander VII and Clement XI,[52] insisted that regulars when made bishops or vicars apostolic in places across the ocean, or administrators, or visitators of churches, had to return to their former monasteries to live their religious way of life with their brethren whenever they did not actually reside at the churches or places assigned to them, when they had resigned from them, when they had fulfilled their offices, or when they were impeded in any way from exercising their episcopal office.[53]

In the tenth paragraph of his Constitution the Pope again ordered these religious to return to their cloisters, unless they had received an apostolic faculty to remain outside the cloister:

> ". . . decernimus, volumus et praecipimus, ut Monachi, Mendicantes, et cuiuscunque alterius instituti Regulares, specialissima etiam mentione digni, qui Episcopatu sibi pridem collato quacunque de causa se in posterum abdicare permissi fuerint, claustra suae Religionis repetere omnino teneantur, et debeant, iis tantum exceptis, qui a Nobis, sive a Romanis Pontificibus antecessoribus, aut successoribus nostris obtinuissent, vel obtinebunt facultatem expressam vivendi extra claustra, sacro alicui muneri, quod cum vita claustrali exerceri non posset . . ."

Any recalcitrants who in this matter refused obedience incurred *ipso facto* a suspension *a pontificalibus;* and further, if they remained contumacious for a year by not returning to the cloister, they likewise incurred the suspension *a divinis.*[54]

---

[51] *Fontes,* n. 4497.

[52] *Supra,* p. 51.

[53] §7—*Fontes,* n. 291.

[54] §11—*loc. cit.*

Article 5. The Incapability of Dignitary Religious to be Elected to Dignities or Offices in Their Proper Institutes

Pope Paul IV (1555–1559) was the first to prescribe that archbishops or bishops religious, when once consecrated, were perpetually incapable of being chosen to any dignities or offices or superiorships in their proper Orders, even though they had been legitimately freed from the church over which they had previously ruled as bishops, and had returned again to their monasteries.[55] The Pope issued a strict and grave prohibition, indeed, for whoever knowingly elected such dignitary religious to any office in the religious institute were thereby deprived automatically of their electoral right in both the active and the passive sense.[56]

Article 6. The Privilege of Dignitary Religious at Their Return to the Proper Institutes to Choose Their Place of Residence

To bishops regular who returned to their own monasteries Pope Benedict XIII in his Constitution "*Custodes*" granted the privilege of selecting any monastery in the province, where they conveniently and devoutly could carry out their religious life:

> "Huiusmodi autem Episcopis, tam pio disciplinae regularis instinctu ad suos redeuntibus, Apostolica largitate concedimus, ut in sua Provincia quodcunque Ordinis sui Coenobium, et Monasterium, ubi commode et religiose degere possint, sibi pro libitu eligant, ideoque volumus, et praecipimus, ut illorum Praesides et Superiores regulares

---

[55] Const. "*In sacra,*" 19 iul. 1559, §2: "Nos . . . providere volentes, Motu proprio, et ex certa nostra scientia volumus, et Apostolica auctoritate statuimus, et ordinamus, quod nullus cuiusvis Ordinis, seu Religionis professor, Episcopus seu Archiepiscopus postquam munus consecrationis huiusmodi susceperit (etiam si a vinculo Ecclesiae, cui praefuerat, per Sedem eamdem absolutus, eique, quod in suo Ordine remanere, et ad dignitates, ac officia, et superioritates huiusmodi assumi, eaque obtinere posset, per Sedem eamdem, seu illius auctoritate concessum foret), ad dignitates, aut officia, seu superioritates huiusmodi, cuiuscumque qualitatis existant, et quavis nomine nuncupentur, eligi, seu assequi, aut obtinere nullatenus possit, et ineligibles, ac ad ea obtinenda inhabilis existat."—*Fontes,* n. 95.

[56] §4—*Fontes,* n. 95.

> congruas eis et honestas cellulas in Coenobiis, et Monasteriis ab eisdem electis, assignent." [57]

This free choice, then, was a privilege conceded to the dignitary religious by the Supreme Pontiff. It constituted an entirely new concession when it was issued on March 7, 1726.

By way of summary, then, it may be stated that in the period from the Council of Trent to the Code of Canon Law the legislation of the former period from the beginnings of a religious state of life to the Council of Trent was restated and confirmed:

1. The religious state and the episcopal and cardinalitial state could be combined in the person of a religious.
2. A religious remained bound as a religious to the observance of his vows and the other religious practices of his rule or constitutions in so far as these were, in his discretion, not in conflict with the duties and status of the dignity attained. Accordingly, a religious who had been promoted to an ecclesiastical dignity, such as that of bishop or cardinal, had to wear his proper religious habit except when privileges conceded him some modification. On the other hand, by his promotion he was freed from the jurisdiction of his religious superiors and from the religious or monastic rule in the matter of the recitation of the divine Office, in the celebration of feasts, etc.
3. A regular when advanced to the episcopacy or the cardinalate regained the right of succession to inheritances which fell to him after his promotion, but only these, despite the cession and renunciation of all goods at his profession in the Order, as long as these goods had not yet actually passed by title of a vested right to a third party. But in such instances the regular did not obtain the ownership; that passed to the church, or in mission countries to the Sacred Congregation for the Propagation of the Faith. The dignitary regular could lay claim only to the use and usufruct. Of course, goods acquired by the regular before attaining the episcopal dignity, i. e., before the promotion itself, remained with the

[57] §8—*Fontes*, n. 291.

Order; the regular could claim at his promotion only his manuscripts, personal clothing, and breviary.

Besides the approbation and confirmation of the former law, the period from the Council of Trent to the Code of Canon Law also produced new legislation on the question of religious promoted to the episcopal and cardinalitial dignities:

1. The degree of obligation of the rule or constitutions, whether *sub levi* or *sub gravi,* depended on the determination of the proper rule or constitutions.
2. A fourth vow, namely, of not seeking or accepting dignities outside the Order, as pronounced in some Orders, required a dispensation obtainable from the Supreme Pontiff alone. Moreover, the Pope alone could command acceptance of such dignities. If he did so, then no explicit grant of a dispensation was necessary.
3. If a religious in the episcopal dignity could not or did not take up his residence as required, if he had fulfilled the offices or tasks assigned, or if he had resigned the office, he then was under strict obligation to return to the cloister or to his own monastery.
4. On the occasion of his return to his confrères in religion he could freely select any monastery of the province. There he was to continue his life as a religious among his brother religious.
5. After his promotion to any dignity outside the Order or institute, the dignitary religious was perpetually incapable of being elected to any dignities, offices, or superiorships in the religious institute, even after his return to his own confrères in religion.

PART TWO
CANONICAL COMMENTARY

GENERAL INTRODUCTION

The Second Book of the Code of Canon Law, entitled *De Personis,* treats of religious in its second part, comprising nine Titles: Title IX to Title XVII. Under the general caption of Title XIII: *De obligationibus et privilegiis religiosorum* falls Chapter III: *De obligationibus et privilegiis religiosi ad ecclesiasticam dignitatem promoti vel paroeciam regentis.* That chapter encompasses the canonical legislation of the matter of this dissertation: The Obligations and Privileges of Religious Promoted to the Episcopal or Cardinalitial Dignities. Canons 626–629 are the respective canons upon which this canonical commentary is based.

Canon 626 defines what is to be observed in the lawful promotion of religious to dignities, offices or benefices which as such are incompatible with the religious state of life. This canon, more or less introductory to the subsequent canons, offers general rules and sets forth certain principles to be followed in the promotion of religious to dignities, offices or benefices. Canons 627 and 628 list the obligations of religious in the episcopal or cardinalitial dignities in relation to their proper religious state. These two canons—in opposition to canon 626, which is general—embody special norms for cardinals and bishops religious in particular. Finally, canon 629 is concerned with the abdication or dismissal from the office or dignity.[1]

This dissertation is limited to the consideration of the promotion

[1] Confer the following: Blat, *Commentarium Textus Codicis Iuris Canonici* (7 vols., Romae: Ex Typographia Augustiniana; Vol. III, *Ius De Religiosis et Laicis iuxta Codicis Ordinem,* ed. 3., 1938), n. 597 (hereafter cited as *Ius de Religiosis*); Berutti, *De Religiosis,* p. 304: *Ratio Ordinis*; Chelodi (1880–1922), *Ius Canonicum De Personis* (ed. 3. curavit Pius Ciprotti, Vicenza: Societa Anonima Tipografica, 1942), n. 284 (hereafter cited as *De Personis*); Claeys Bouuaert-Simenon, *Manuale Juris Canonici* (3 vols.; Vols. I. III. 3. ed., 1930; Vol. II, 1931, Gandae et Leodiensi: Prostat Apud Auctores), I, n. 682; Schaefer, *De Religiosis ad Normam Codicis Iuris Canonici* (3. ed., Roma: Typis Polyglottis Vaticanis, 1940), nn. 494, 496 (hereafter cited as *De Religiosis*).

of religious to the two major dignities of the cardinalate and episcopate—dignities outside the scope of the religious institute.[2] The writer desires to call to mind that the obligations and privileges to be dealt with here are not those connected with these two dignities as such. Those matters are found in the canons of the Code dealing properly with the cardinalate and episcopate (canons 230–242 and canons 329–350). Rather, of concern here are the special obligations and privileges of cardinals and bishops religious as religious, which exist over and above the obligations and privileges reported in the respective canons of the Code with respect to cardinals and bishops for all promoted to those ecclesiastical dignities, whether they are religious or secular.[3] The grounds for the special obligations and privileges of the religious dignitary are to be found in the inter-relations of the dignitary status and the religious state; moreover, it must be realized that religious after having been advanced to the cardinalate or episcopate should not be bound in the same way as before to all the general obligations common to religious, but that thereupon as a result of their advancement they should also enjoy some special privileges.[4]

[2] Fanfani, *De Iure Religiosorum ad Normam Codicis Iuris Canonici* (ed. altera, Taurini-Romae: Marietti, 1925), n. 465 (hereafter cited as *De Iure Religiosorum*); Oesterle, *Praelectiones Iuris Canonici* (Tomus I, Romae: Prostat in Collegio S. Anselmi, 1931), I, 353.

[3] Blat, *Ius De Religiosis,* nn. 596, 597; Schaefer, *De Religiosis,* nn. 492, 493.

[4] Berutti, *op. cit.*, p. 304: *Ratio Ordinis.*

CHAPTER IV

NECESSARY CONDITIONS FOR THE PROMOTION OF RELIGIOUS TO ECCLESIASTICAL DIGNITIES (Canon 626)

ARTICLE 1. THE NECESSARY PERMISSION OF THE HOLY SEE (CANON 626, §1)

Canon 626-§1. *Religiosus nequit, sine Sedis Apostolicae auctoritate, ad dignitates, officia aut beneficia promoveri, quae cum statu religioso componi non possint.*

A religious cannot without the authority of the Holy See be promoted to dignities, offices or benefices which are incompatible with the religious state of life.

The Code of Canon Law contains no explicit definition of the word *dignitas* to stabilize its significance. Canonists offer definitions which verge more towards the notion of dignities in cathedral chapters, or which are applicable only to the higher episcopal or cardinalitial ranks. Hence it is necessary to inquire into the usage of the word dignity in the Code in order to arrive at the constitutive elements of that term.[1]

I. Dignity in a very general sense:
- (a) The Code in some canons employs *dignitas* in the sense of moral worth, integrity, or uprightness as coupled with a position of eminence: canon 1789, 1°, and canon 2077.
- (b) In other canons the intent of dignity is the elevation to a higher level, ex. gr., the elevation to a sacramental rank or character, as in canons 1012, §2, and 1084.

II. Ecclesiastical dignity, or dignity in reference to the Church:
- A. Ecclesiastical dignity in general:

[1] Cf. Köstler, ***Wörterbuch zum Codex Iuris Canonici*** (München: Verlag Josef Kösel & Friedrich Pustet, 1927–1929), s. v. *dignitas*.

(a) Quite a few canons of the Code merely mention a dignity as such with no indication of its meaning.[2]

(b) Other canons in a general way list dignities with offices and benefices, mostly in the connection of privation of offices, benefices or dignities.[3]

B. Ecclesiastical dignity indicating a position or office attached:

(a) Some canons demonstrate that a dignity signifies at least a certain attached honorary position, preferment or ministry.[4]

(b) A dignity in a chapter of canons also falls into this category, since it intimates a post of honor in the chapter—canons 391 ss.

(c) Finally, there are canons in the Code with explicit reference as dignities in regard to judges, abbots, prelates, bishops, metropolitans or archbishops, and cardinals.[5]

The foregoing scheme presents a conspectus of the Code on the use of the word *dignitas*. Before the drawing of any conclusions, it is necessary to propose definitions of office and prelate, as both enter into the concept of an ecclesiastical dignity. Dignity in the very general sense of moral worth or integrity can be passed over, since ecclesiastical dignities alone are in question.

An ecclesiastical office in the wider sense of the term is any position or employment which is legitimately practiced for a spiritual end. But taken in the strict sense, an ecclesiastical office is a stable position established either by divine or ecclesiastical law, conferred according to the rules of the sacred canons, and implying some participation at least in ecclesiastical power, whether of orders or of jurisdiction. In law this term is used in its strict sense, unless the context should prove the contrary.[6]

When the participation in the power of the Church is jurisdictional—one of the alternate requirements for an ecclesiastical office

[2] Confer the following canons: 235; 622, §4; 729, 1°; 1224, 2°; 2352; and others.

[3] Confer canons: 2237, §1, 3°; 2265, §1, 2°; 2298, 5°; 2303, §1; 2354, §2; 2381; 2394; 2395; 2400; 2403; and others.

[4] Canons 58; 515; 2088, §1; 2218, §1; 2299, §2; 2351.

[5] Canons 232, §2, 1°; 269, §2; 272; 319, §1; 409, §1; 914; 1219, §2; 1299, §1; 1406, §1, 2°; 1925, §3; 2371; 2397.

[6] Canon 145, §§1 and 2.

in the strict sense—and when this jurisdiction is ordinary and possessed in the external forum, then the status of a prelacy is approached. The term prelate in its proper sense denotes in law clerics, secular or religious, who have ordinary jurisdiction in the external forum; however, the term is found also as an honorary title which does not necessarily imply the according of any jurisdiction to the clerics designated with that title.[7] Properly considered, then, only the possession of ordinary jurisdiction in the external forum, i.e., of a quasi-episcopal jurisdiction, is recognized by the law of the Code as the mark of a true prelate.[8] Therefore prelates in the proper sense are the Pope, all residential bishops, abbots and prelates *nullius*, administrators apostolic, vicars and prefects apostolic, vicars general, and superiors of exempt clerical institutes. As such, cardinals, patriarchs, primates, apostolic delegates and nuncios are not prelates in the strict sense, since in the external forum they have no ordinary jurisdiction which originally and inherently derives from their offices.[9] But if ordinary jurisdiction in the external forum has been bestowed on them, ex. gr., when they are at the same time residential bishops, or hold some other office implying jurisdiction in the external forum, on this score they rightly merit the title of prelates.[10]

Prelacies are divided into major and minor, in so far as the incumbents of the above mentioned offices possess or lack the episcopal character. Among the minor prelates are especially the members of the papal household, some of whom are prelates in the proper sense, while others are merely honorary prelates (Monsignors).[11]

---

[7] Canon 110.

[8] Ojetti, *Commentarium in Codicem Iuris Canonici* (Vol. III, Romae: Apud Aedes Universitatis Gregorianae, 1930), III, 25–27.

[9] Cf. canons 230, 267, and 271.

[10] Cardinals enjoy ordinary jurisdiction for the internal sacramental forum according to canon 873, §1. Cf. Hynes, *The Privileges of Cardinals*, The Catholic University of America Canon Law Studies, n. 217 (Washington, D. C.: The Catholic University of America Press, 1945), pp. 39, 40.

[11] Cf. Regatillo, *Institutiones Iuris Canonici* (2 vols., Santander: Sal Terrae, 1941-1942), I, nn. 218, 466, 472; Coronata, *Institutiones Iuris Canonici* (5 vols., Taurini: Marietti; Vol. I, ed. altera, 1939), I, n. 172; Beste, *Introductio in Codicem*, pp. 258-262, particularly on the different classes of Monsignors.

The various elements of the term *dignitas* having been discussed at some length, it can be concluded that there is essential to it the element of pre-eminence linked to some position or office. Thus the following notion of a dignity in the broad sense would be adequate: An ecclesiastical dignity imports pre-eminence of honor and precedence. It may attach to a position or office, in the wide meaning of office, with which any honorary preferment or precedence is associated.[12] That exactly is the juridic condition today of dignities in the chapters of canons, and of the honorary or titular prelates. In the earlier law dignities in chapters possessed, besides precedence, also some jurisdiction in the external forum (the Archdeacon, for instance). Thus a dignity was distinguished from the *personatus,* which status connoted a lack of jurisdiction, but vindicated a certain rank in precedence. In the law of the Code there is no distinction of this kind, for the dignity today in a chapter is the same in meaning as the personate in the pre-Code law.[13]

However, the principal subject matter of this dissertation concerns ecclesiastical dignities in a more precise connotation. From the initial remarks of this article on the use of the word *dignitas* in the Code, it is clear that ecclesiastical dignities proper are united with an ecclesiastical office strictly so called, and enter into the notion of prelacies in the proper sense. Of course, the idea of pre-eminence or precedence is intimately allied with the term of dignity. Hence an ecclesiastical dignity in the strict sense connotes the possession of an ecclesiastical office which endows its incumbent with precedence, rank and jurisdiction; in fact, it implies the possession of ordinary jurisdiction in the external forum and a corresponding degree of pre-eminence.[14] In other words, an ec-

[12] Voltas, "De vi can. 515 quoad prohibitionem honorum et exemptionum" —*Commentarium pro Religiosis* (later [1935]: *Commentarium pro Religiosis et Missionariis*), I (1920), 273-275, under *Consultationes,* n. 20, on p. 273 (hereafter this periodical will be identified through the use of the letters *CpR* and *CpRM* respectively).

[13] Chelodi, *De Personis,* n. 204; Prümmer, *Manuale,* Q. 139.

[14] The following authors cover the word of dignity in canon 626, §1, with similar definitions: Fanfani, *De Iure Religiosorum,* n. 465; Blat, *Ius De Religiosis,* n. 596; Schaefer, *De Religiosis,* n. 493; Augustine (1872-1943), *A Commentary on the New Code of Canon Law* (8 vols., St. Louis, Mo.:

clesiastical dignity adheres to every incumbent of an ecclesiastical office with which pre-eminence and jurisdiction is annexed in the external forum.

Besides ecclesiastical dignities and offices, canon 626, §1, makes mention of ecclesiastical benefices. An ecclesiastical benefice is a juridical entity, permanently constituted or erected by competent ecclesiastical authority, and consisting of a sacred office and the right to receive the revenues accruing from the endowment of that office.[15] That a benefice is intimately connected with an ecclesiastical office is quite evident, for those who serve the Church in some ecclesiastical office merit proper sustenance. For that reason the right to receive revenues from the office is joined to the sacred office, whether the revenues accrue in the form of a salary, or flow from the stable endowment of the office.[16] Therefore, when the spiritual element of a sacred office is combined with the temporal element of the obtaining of revenue from the office, an ecclesiastical office becomes a benefice. Benefices have various divisions. For instance, the episcopate and the cardinalate are consistorial benefices, as they are conferred in consistory. Usually offices which have episcopal power connected *ipso iure* are also consistorial benefices, even though the incumbent does not have the episcopal character, such as an abbacy or prelacy *nullius*. All others are known as non-consistorial benefices.[17] Chief attention naturally must be paid to ecclesiastical dignities in relation to the present canon under discussion, as this dissertation is restricted

B. Herder Book Co.; Vol. III, *De Personis, or Ecclesiastical Persons, Religious and Laymen,* 2. ed., 1919), p. 355, §1 (hereafter this volume is cited as *Religious and Laymen*); Papi (1861–1929), *Religious in Church Law* (New York: P. J. Kenedy & Sons, 1924), n. 28, 1.

[15] Canon 1409. In connection with this canon one must consider canon 1412, which lists certain offices and positions in the Church that bear some similarity to benefices, but in law do not come under the name of benefices.

[16] Chelodi, *De Personis,* n. 131.

[17] For the purpose of this dissertation there is no need to go into more detail about the divisions of benefices; they are listed in canon 1411. Cf. Prümmer, *Manuale,* Q. 423, n. 1; Cappello, *Summa Iuris Canonici in Usum Scholarum Concinnata* (Vol. II, ed. 4., Romae: Apud Aedes Universitatis Gregorianae, 1945), n. 535 (hereafter cited as *Summa Iuris*); Beste, *Introductio in Codicem,* p. 698.

to the consideration of the promotion of religious to the episcopal or cardinalitial dignities.

Canon 626, §1, states as a general rule that religious may not without the permission of the Holy See be promoted to dignities, offices or benefices which are incompatible with the religious state. What in the concrete the phrase *dignities, offices or benefices incompatible with the religious state* comprehends can hardly be set forth in a general principle.[18] Particularly it is not clear which dignities are to be considered as compatible with the religious state and which are not. Authors disagree in a nominal determination of them.[19]

Some hold that the papacy, the cardinalate, the episcopacy, as well as the offices of apostolic legate, of vicar and of prefect apostolic, and of the ecclesiastical superior of missions *sui iuris* are compatible with the religious state.[20] The main proof for the advocates of the compatibility of these dignities with the religious state is really the fact that the Holy See apportions these selfsame

---

[18] Beste, *op. cit.*, p. 424.

[19] A. D., "De Obligationibus et Privilegiis Religiosi ad Ecclesiasticam Dignitatem Promoti," *CpRM,* XIX (1938), 169-192; 261-268; on 172, n. 7 (hereafter referred to as "Religiosi ad Eccl. Dignitatem Promoti"); Oesterle, *Praelectiones Iuris Canonici,* I, 353.

[20] Coronata, referring to canon 1442 which provides that secular benefices are to be conferred on the secular clergy exclusively, states that only offices or benefices strictly secular are incompatible with the religious state; and that therefore the papacy, the episcopacy, and the offices of vicar or of prefect apostolic are compatible with the religious state, since they are not secular benefices.—*Institutiones Iuris Canonici,* I, n. 633. Wernz (1842–1914)-Vidal (1867–1938) propounded the same opinion.—*Ius Canonicum ad Codicis Normam Exactum* (7 vols. in 9, Romae: Apud Aedes Universitatis Gregorianae; Tomus III, *De Religiosis,* 1933), n. 413 (hereafter this volume is cited simply as *De Religiosis*). Vermeersch-Creusen testify that according to the present day discipline religious can be promoted to the papacy, the cardinalate, the episcopacy, and to the offices of vicar or of prefect apostolic equally as well as seculars.—*Epitome,* I, n. 786, 1. The same was held by Raus (1881–1943).—*Institutiones Canonicae* (Parisiis: Typis Emmanuelis Vitte, 1923), n. 202. Cf. the following: Augustine, *Religious and Laymen,* p. 355, §1; Regatillo, *Institutiones Iuris Canonici,* I, n. 749; Goyeneche, *De Religiosis—De Laicis* (Roma: Apud Herder S. A. L. E. R., Montecitorio, 1938), n. 88, b (hereafter cited as *De Religiosis*).

dignities indifferently to both the secular and the regular clergy. Then, too, a definite prohibition is lacking in law.

Others, to the contrary, claim that the cardinalate, the episcopate, and the offices of apostolic legate, of vicar or of prefect apostolic, and of the superior of ecclesiastical missions *sui iuris* are incompatible with the religious state.[21]

Still others, also denying the compatibility of dignities and offices with the religious profession of life, are content merely to point this out in a general way wthout committing themselves as to which dignities are meant. Instead they offer some rules which are useful in adjudicating dignities and offices as compatible or incompatible with the religious state; thus they aver, after taking into account the nature of dignities and offices, that some are rendered incompatible by the common law, while others are so affected by particular law or by custom. Besides, the incompatibility may also spring from the end or purpose intended by the religious institute, or from the special work or activity of the respective institute. And any dignity that would detract from the stability of religious life, or from the total observance of the vows, must necessarily be judged as incompatible with the religious state.[22]

When these rules are applied, the reasons advanced by those who contend for the incompatibility of dignities with the religious state become evident: All dignities which are to be conferred only on seculars, ex. gr., secular benefices according to canon 1442, are incompatible with the religious state. Also every dignity outside the religious community is not compatible with the religious state,

---

[21] Cocchi, *Commentarium in Codicem Iuris Canonici ad Usum Scholarum* (8 vols., Taurinorum Augustae: Marietti, Vol. IV, 3. ed., 1932), n. 122 (hereafter cited as *Commentarium in Codicem*); Schaefer, *De Religiosis*, n. 493; Prümmer, *Manuale*, Q. 249, n. 1; Sipos, *Enchiridion Iuris Canonici* (Pécs: Ex Typographia "Haladás R. T.," 1926), §73, n. 1, a; Chelodi, *De Personis*, n. 284; Toso, *Ad Codicem Juris Canonici Commentaria Minora* (Vol. V, Romae: Apud Ephemerides Jus Pontificum, 1933), p. 214, n. 1 (hereafter cited as *Commentaria Minora*).

[22] Cappello, *Summa Iuris*, II, n. 63, 1; Beste, *Introductio in Codicem*, p. 424; Oesterle, *Praelectiones Iuris Canonici*, I, p. 353; Pejška, *Jus Canonicum Religiosorum*, p. 179, n. 1, a; Eichmann (1870–1945), *Lehrbuch des Kirchenrechts auf Grund des Codex Juris Canonici* (2. ed., Paderborn: Ferdinand Schöningh, 1926), §97, n. 1 (hereafter cited as *Lehrbuch des Kirchenrechts*).

since such dignities in general prevent religious from following the religious discipline. For instance, religious in the ecclesiastical dignities of the cardinalate or the episcopate are compelled to live outside their religious houses for the greater part of the year, but canon 606, §2, forbids superiors to allow their subjects to dwell outside the houses of their Order or congregation for more than six months, except for study.[23]

Moreover, the promotion to dignities withdraws the religious from the observance of his vow of obedience, as he is exempted from his superiors' jurisdiction; and also the observance of poverty is somewhat mitigated, as will be seen. At times the particular law proper to some religious institute may effect this incompatibility in consequence of a prohibition, promise or vow against the seeking or acceptance of dignities outside the institute. All these reasons demonstrate that, as such, dignities derogate from the religious profession of life.[24]

It can be affirmed, then, that dignities as a rule are foreign to the religious state and destined for the secular clergy. The most cogent argument, it seems to the writer, comes from a consideration of both the nature of the religious life and the dignitary status.

St. Thomas had explained that the religious state is not opposed or repugnant to the episcopal status.[25] Though the two states are not mutually exclusive, nevertheless the dignitary status does accidentally take away something from the religious profession, since a religious in an ecclesiastical dignity, when drawn away from the religious state—a state of acquiring or striving for perfection—is transferred to a state of perfection—as St. Thomas describes the

---

[23] Canon 606—§2. "Superioribus fas non est, salvis praescriptis in can. 621-624, permittere ut subditi extra domum propriae religionis degant, nisi gravi et iusta de causa atque ad tempus quo fieri potest brevius secundum constitutiones; pro absentia vero quae sex menses excedat, nisi causa studiorum intercedat, semper Apostolicae Sedis venia requiritur."

[24] Woywod (1880-1941), *A Practical Commentary on the Code of Canon Law* (Revised by Callistus Smith, 8th Printing, 2 vols., New York: Joseph F. Wagner, Inc., 1944), I, n. 540 (hereafter cited as *A Practical Commentary*); Oesterle, *Praelectiones Iuris Canonici,* I, 353; Pejška, *Jus Canonicum Religiosorum,* p. 179, n. 1, a; Eichmann, *Lehrbuch des Kirchenrechts,* §97, n. 1; Toso, *Commentaria Minora,* V, p. 214, n. 1.

[25] *Summa Theologica,* IIa, IIae, q. 184, art. 7; *supra,* p. 26.

episcopal state. And yet a religious by his very profession has chosen freely and lawfully a state of humility alien to signal honors and dignities. And, no doubt, a dignitary religious cannot fully live up to the rules, traditions, and constitutions of his former way of community life.[26] Therefore, one can aptly speak of some kind of incapacity on the part of religious to be advanced to ecclesiastical dignities, which as a result must be viewed as being incompatible with the religious state.[27]

The foregoing discussion on the incompatibility of dignities with the religious state, it must be admitted, is only theoretical. In practice there is no difficulty, since the Supreme Pontiff himself directly creates cardinals. The same is true in the promotion to the episcopacy which usually comes directly from the Holy Father. In other words, a religious promoted to the cardinalate by the Pope needs no explicit permission from the Holy See, and the same applies to a religious raised to the episcopal dignity by the Pope, i.e., in the case when this is not done by an election, since all necessary permission and authority of the Holy See are contained implicitly in the act of creation or appointment respectively.[28]

The prohibition of canon 626, §1, viz., that religious cannot be promoted to dignities, offices or benefices which are incompatible with the religious state, lies in the words *nequit promoveri.* Of and by itself the term *nequit* does not reveal the exact juridic force

---

[26] A. D., "Religiosi ad Eccl. Dignitatem Promoti," *CpRM,* XIX (1938), 173, n. 7; Papi, *Religious in Church Law,* n. 28, 2.

[27] Maroto, "De Consultoribus Dioecesanis"—*Apollinaris* (Romae, 1928—), IV (1931), 252-253, on p. 253, n. 4, c: "Religiosi videntur esse inhabiles non solum ad ea munera quae exprimuntur in Can. 626, verum et ad alia quae secumferant dignitatem, iurisdictionem, imputationem iuridicam et similia, extra propriam religionem."

[28] A. D., "Religiosi ad Eccl. Dignitatem Promoti," *CpRM,* XIX (1938), 173, note 11; Prümmer, *Manuale,* Q. 249, n. 1; Cocchi, *Commentarium in Codicem,* IV, n. 122, 1; Oesterle, *Praelectiones Iuris Canonici,* I, p. 353; Jansen(+1941), *Ordensrecht* (2. ed., Paderborn: Ferdinand Schöningh, 1920), pp. 202-203, n. 1; Eichmann, *Lehrbuch des Kirchenrechts,* §97, n. 1; De Meester, *Juris Canonici et Juris Canonico Civilis Compendium* (nova ed., 3 vols. in 4, Brugis: Desclee, 1921-1928), II, n. 1044, 1 (hereafter cited as *Juris Canonici et Civilis Compendium*); Goyeneche, *De Religiosis,* n. 88, b, note 3; Creusen-Ellis-Garesché, *Religious Men and Women in the Code* (5. ed., Milwaukee: The Bruce Publishing Co., 1940), p. 244.

of the prohibition, i.e., whether a religious cannot be promoted validly or licitly to these dignities, offices or benefices without the authority of the Holy See.[29]

Authors make no allusion to this problem in connection with canon 626, §1, perhaps for the reason that no practical issue appears at stake. In regard to the promotion of religious to the episcopal or cardinalitial dignity there is no need of raising the question whether religious cannot be promoted validly or licitly without the authority of the Holy See, since in all cases the promotion comes directly from the Pope alone. Hence it is difficult to conceive how a promotion to the cardinalate or episcopate could indeed happen without the authority of the Holy See. However, the determination of the juridic force of the prohibition of canon 626, §1, is important and practical for the promotion of religious to other dignities, offices or benefices, when these are conferred by others than the Pope or the Holy See.

It is the opinion of the writer that religious cannot validly be promoted to ecclesiastical dignities, offices or benefices without the authority of the Apostolic See when the promotion is effected by others than the Supreme Pontiff or the Holy See. These are the reasons: Since a religious by his profession has assumed duties which make a prior claim upon him, and moreover has chosen a state in which dignities and honors are understood not only as precluded, but even as incompatible with the religious state, it appears that a religious labors under an incapacity with reference to these dignities, offices and benefices. Hence canon 626, §1, must be viewed in the light of an incapacitating law, which disqualifies the person of a religious in relation to such dignities, offices and benefices.[30] It is to be noted that only the Holy See, the supreme authority in the Church, can neutralize or offset that incapacity. Therefore, it must follow that a religious cannot validly be advanced to ecclesiastical dignities, offices or benefices without the authority of the Apostolic See.

---

[29] The same expression *nequit* occurs in other canons of the Code. Authors in given cases interpret it differently; some defend the view that *nequit* signifies a prohibition *sub illiceitate,* but others uphold the view that *nequit* intends a prohibition *sub nullitate.* For example, cf. canons 113; 1941, §3.

[30] Cf. canon 11.

ARTICLE 2. THE NECESSARY PERMISSION OF THE RELIGIOUS SUPERIOR IN CASE OF ELECTION (CANON 626, §2)

Canon 626—§2. *Legitime ab aliquo collegio electus, nequit electioni assentiri sine licentia Superioris.*

One [a religious] legally elected [to dignities, offices or benefices] by a body of voters cannot consent to the election without the permission of the superior.

Canon 626, §2, proclaims another general principle by which the capability of religious to attain dignities and offices outside the Order or congregation is reconciled with the common condition of the religious state.[31] This paragraph of the canon mentioned demands the permission of the religious superior when one of his subjects is elected to some dignity, office or benefice incompatible with his religious state. On the superior's permission hinges the consent of the religious to the election lawfully concluded. It is evident that as far as this dissertation is concerned, there can be no question about any election to the cardinalate; the Pope exclusively and directly creates cardinals. But in the elevation to the episcopal dignity there can be an election, though ordinarily also such an elevation is accomplished directly by the Pope.[32]

In the former law, after the eighth century specifically, cathedral chapters possessed the right of electing bishops. And not until the fourteenth century did the Roman Pontiffs reserve more and more the appointment of bishops to themselves. However, under the present law it still is possible that bishops should be elected by cathedral chapters. Some countries have, through concordats with the Holy See, obtained the approval of this method of designating new bishops, though in these instances the ultimate canonical institution (*institutio canonica*) of bishops in their offices rests exclusively with the Holy See.[33] Therefore, if and when an electoral

---

[31] Vermeersch-Creusen, *Epitome,* I, n. 786.

[32] Canon 232—§1. "Cardinales libere a Romano Pontifice ex toto terrarum orbe eliguntur . . ."

Canon 329—§2. "Eos [Episcopos] libere nominat Romanus Pontifex."

§3. "Si cui collegio concessum sit ius eligendi Episcopum, servetur praescriptum can. 321."

[33] Chelodi, *De Personis,* n. 188; Coronata, *Institutiones Iuris Canonici,* I,

college elects a religious to the episcopal dignity, the religious elected necessarily must have his superior's permission before signifying his consent to the election.

The election must be legitimate, i.e., one performed according to the norms in the common law on elections (canons 160–182), and according to the norm of canon 321, which latter canon is to the effect that the candidate who receives an absolute majority of votes is the one elected, unless particular law should require a greater number of votes than an absolute majority—for instance, two-thirds of all the votes.[34] The Code here speaks only of a legitimate election in the strict sense. Some authors indicate that the rule of canon 626, §2, can be extended at least analogically to cases of nomination or presentation. Obviously, the necessity of the superior's permission would be present in these cases, too.[35]

The necessity to procure the permission of the superior on the part of a religious elected prior to the manifestation of his own consent and acceptance of the election stems from the religious profession, and specifically from the vow of obedience by which a professed member in any religious institute has subjected himself and subordinated his will to the behests of his superiors. Hence permission would be required in elections to any dignity or office, compatible or incompatible with the religious state; of course, dignities and offices outside the Order or congregation are meant, since those within the institute itself would not demand a special permission of the superior.[36] By his profession, then, a religious gives himself over entirely to his Order or congregation; therefore he cannot enter into any contract, as he would be doing if he accepted the election to rule a vacant church as its bishop, without the permission of the proper superior.[37]

---

n. 393, 1° and 2°; Claeys Bouuaert-Simenon, *Manuale Juris Canonici*, I, n. 470.

[34] Coronata, *op. cit.*, I, n. 393, 2°, b; Blat, *Ius De Religiosis*, n. 599.

[35] Coronata, *op. cit.*, I, n. 633, 2°, note 2; Claeys Bouuaert-Simenon, *Manuale Juris Canonici*, I, n. 681, 2; Raus, *Institutiones Canonicae*, n. 202; Goyeneche, *De Religiosis*, n. 88, note 1.

[36] De Meester, *Juris Canonici et Civilis Compendium*, II, n. 1044, 2; Beste, *Introductio in Codicem*, p. 425; Cocchi, *Commentarium in Codicem*, IV, n. 122, 2; Wernz-Vidal, *De Religiosis*, n. 413, I; Blat, *Ius De Religiosis*, n. 599.

[37] Schaefer, *De Religiosis*, n. 493, 1, b; Prümmer, *Manuale*, Q. 249, n. 1; Sipos, *Enchiridion Iuris Canonici*, §73, n. 1, b.

Who is the superior competent to give this permission? Here the particular statutes of the individual Order or congregation must be consulted, but certainly the major superiors would be empowered in this regard: the Superior General, i.e., the highest superior in the religious institute whatever his title, and the Provincial Superiors, and most certainly the Pope, the supreme head of all religious.[38]

In the earlier law this petition for permission from the competent superior in the case of an election of a religious was designated by the term of non-solemn or simple postulation.[39] The Code makes no mention of postulation; it merely speaks in canon 626, §2, of a religious legitimately elected. Yet, some canonists uphold this terminology of the former law and seem to insist that one should not say that religious are elected, but rather that they are postulated by a simple or non-solemn postulation as distinguished from the solemn or postulation proper, which is employed as a subsidiary to election only when a true canonical impediment is present.[40]

It seems best to dismiss this unnecessary distinction today. The simple postulation of the pre-Code law, in fact, is no postulation in

---

[38] Canon 499—§1. "Religiosi omnes, tamquam supremo Superiori, subduntur Romano Pontifici cui obedire tenentur etiam vi voti obedientiae." Cf. Schaefer, *loc. cit.*; Goyeneche, *De Religiosis*, n. 88, note 1.

[39] Vermeersch-Creusen, *Epitome*, I, n. 786, 2; Wernz-Vidal, *De Religiosis*, n. 413, I, note 3; Coronata, *Institutiones Iuris Canonici*, I, n. 633, 2°; Sipos, *Enchiridion Iuris Canonici*, §73, n. 1, b; Biederlack (1845–1930)—Führich, *De Religiosis Codicis Iuris Canonici* (Oeniponte: Typis Feliciani Rauch, 1919), n. 159, 1 (hereafter cited *De Religiosis*); Ferreres (1861-1936), *Institutiones Canonicae iuxta Novissimum Codicem* (ed. altera, 2 vols., Barcinone: Eugenius Subirana, 1925), I, n. 911, II (hereafter cited as *Institutiones Canonicae*); Schaefer, *De Religiosis*, n. 493, 1, b, note 13.

[40] Toso declares that there is no necessity to mention postulation in canon 626, §2; the reason is the fact that a postulation must be directed not to the person postulated, but to the superior with the power of dispensing from the impediment (canon 181, §1), namely, the same superior whose permission is required by canon 626, §2.—*Commentaria Minora*, V, p. 215, n. 2. Pejška bases the necessity of postulation on the fact that dignities outside the religious institute coerce religious to live outside the religious community, which is against the religious profession.—*Jus Canonicum Religiosorum*, p. 179, n. 1, a. Schaefer simply states that juridically there is question here of postulation.—*De Religiosis*, n. 493, 1, b, note 11.

the strict sense of the term. It merely indicated that the person elected did not possess full liberty to consent to an election; hence the petition for permission was required in order to obtain from the superior the consent necessary that such a person, who was in no way hindered by a canonical impediment, be elected.[41] But the Code takes no cognizance of simple postulation.[42] As a matter of fact, the necessity of seeking the superior's permission on the part of a religious elected to the episcopacy is owing to his religious state, and that can hardly be deemed a canonical impediment in the sense of canon 179, §1.[43] Hence at the present time there is no foundation in law demanding that one speak of the postulation of religious to the episcopal dignity; when chosen by a body of electors, they are elected.

In the light of the former law, since simple postulation was a kind of postulation, it could take place immediately before or after the election of the religious; either the body of electors, though a collegiate act was not of necessity, could petition the superior for the necessary permission, or the religious person elected by the body could do so.[44] But more in keeping with the idea of postulation, the duty of obtaining permission did devolve on the electoral college.[45]

The Code does not touch upon this point at all, whether the electoral college is obliged, or whether the religious who is elected is under the obligation of asking the requisite permission from the superior. The better answer seems to be that the religious elected should be the one on whom the obligation rests; after all, it is the religious who labors under the necessity of having his superior's permission in order to consent to the election, and not the electors. It is true, if there were question of a postulation in the proper

---

[41] Chelodi, *De Personis,* n. 142; Raus, *Institutiones Canonicae,* n. 74, I; Beste, *Introductio in Codicem,* p. 209.

[42] Canon 179—§1. "Si electioni illius quem electores aptiorem putent ac praeferant, impedimentum obest, super quo dispensari possit ac soleat, suis ipsi suffragiis eum possint, nisi aliud iure caveatur, a competente Superiore postulare, etsi agatur de officio, pro quo electus confirmatione non egeat."

[43] Oesterle, *Praelectiones Iuris Canonici,* I, 354.

[44] Cf. Coronata, *Institutiones Iuris Canonici,* I, n. 633, 2°.

[45] Cf. Sipos, *Enchiridion Iuris Canonici,* §73, n. 1, b; Vermeersch-Creusen, *Epitome,* I, n. 786, 2.

sense, that then the electors as such would be obliged, but nothing is said of postulation in canon 626, §2.[46] For all practical purposes under the law of the Code it appears to be of no moment whether the permission is obtained immediately before or after the election, or by the body of electors or by the religious elected—as long as there has been compliance with the prescript of obtaining the competent superior's permission.[47]

The promotion of a religious to the episcopal dignity by way of an election has effect only through the acceptance of the election by the religious elected,[48] and by the subsequent confirmation of the Pope.[49] The consent of the one elected is of the very essence of a true election.[50]

If then a religious presumes to give his consent to the election on his own authority without the permission of his superior, would that consent be invalid, and as a result invalidate and void the election? In the Decretal Law both the consent and the election were null and void.[51] Several authors by relying upon the former law apply it as a norm to be followed in the present law, despite the fact that the wording of the canon, "nequit electioni assentiri," is not explicit, and so can be interpreted as standing either for the invalidity of the consent or simply for its unlawfulness.[52] How-

[46] Blat, *Ius De Religiosis,* n. 599; Sipos, *loc. cit.*; Vermeersch-Creusen, *loc. cit.*; Biederlack-Führich, *De Religiosis,* n. 159. Blat is opposed by Coronata who remarks that the Code does not put the burden on the one elected, for, he adds, even a third party can seek the permission from the superior. —*Institutiones Iuris Canonici,* I, n. 633, 2°, note 4.

[47] Chelodi, *De Personis,* n. 142.

[48] Canon 175. "Electio illico intimanda est electo, qui debet saltem intra octiduum utile a recepta intimatione manifestare utrum electioni consentiat, an eidem renuntiet; secus omne ius ex electione quaesitum amittat."

[49] Wernz-Vidal, *De Religiosis,* n. 413, I. The subsequent confirmation of the Pope is manifested in this that every candidate for the episcopate needs the canonical institution:

Canon 332—§1. "Cuilibet ad episcopatum promovendo, etiam electo, praesentato vel designato a civili quoque Gubernio, necessaria est canonica provisio seu institutio, qua Episcopus vacantis dioecesis constituitur, quaeque ab uno Romano Pontifice datur."

[50] Pejška, *Ius Canonicum Religiosorum,* p. 179, n. 1, b.

[51] C. 27, *de electione et electi potestate,* I, 6, in VI°; *supra,* p. 29. Cf. c. 2, *de electione,* I, 3, in Extravag. com.; *supra,* p. 30.

[52] Schaefer in the section of his book where he treats of elections (*De

ever, the penalty of invalidity enacted in the former law [53] as attaching to the consent given by a religious to an election of himself to some dignity or prelacy outside the Order or congregation, for instance, the episcopacy, without the prior permission of the proper superior can be said to come under the regulation of canon 6, 5°, with regard to the question of its continued application in the present.[54] Therefore, so it is argued, this penalty of the Decretal Law, not now renewed in the Code, should be considered as abrogated in consequence of the lack of its restatement in the Code.[55]

Naturally, it must be understood that by religious are meant men bound by the vows of religion, who are elected to dignities outside the Order or congregation. They must observe the rule of canon 626, §2, which is one of the necessary conditions for their promotion to ecclesiastical dignities. Now, if a religious has taken only temporary vows and the period of their obligation has lapsed, it is clear that no permission from the superior is required

---

Religiosis, n. 136, 1, c) has this to say: "Assensus in electionem a Religioso absque legitima licentia praestitus, electionem nullam redderet, quod eruitur ex verbis: Nequit assentiri etc. (cf. can. 626)." When later commenting on canon 626, §2 (*op. cit.,* n. 493, 1, b), he contradicts his former statement: "Licentia ad assentiendum electioni vel designationi non videtur requiri ad validitatem." The following authors, by relying on the former law, claim that the consent which a religious gives to an election without the permission of his superior is invalid: Berutti, *De Religiosis,* n. 138, B; Pejška, *Jus Canonicum Religiosorum,* p. 179, n. 1, b.

[53] The invalidity was regarded as a penalty against the presumption of a religious in giving his consent without the proper permission: "Si religiosus, cuius arbitrium non ex sua, quum velle vel nolle non habeat, sed ex illius, quem vice Dei supra caput suum posuit et cuius imperio se subiecit, voluntate dependet, electioni, de se ad praelationem aliquam extra suum monasterium vel suam ecclesiam celebratae, sui Superioris, qui dare ipsam valeat, non petita licentia et obtenta, praesumpserit consentire: consensus sic praestitus non teneat, et in poenam praesumptionis illius electio eadem ipso facto viribus vacuetur omnino."—C. 27, *de electione et electi potestate,* I, 6, in VI°.

[54] Canon 6. "Codex vigentem huc usque disciplinam plerumque retinet, licet opportunas immutationes afferat. Itaque:

5°. Quod ad poenas attinet, quarum in Codice nulla fit mentio, spirituales sint vel temporales, medicinales vel, ut vocant, vindicativae, latae vel ferendae sententiae, eae tanquam abrogatae habeantur."

[55] Prümmer, *Manuale,* Q. 249, n. 1; Schaefer, *De Religiosis,* n. 493, 1, b; Goyeneche, *De Religiosis,* n. 88, c.

for him. Likewise, it is quite evident that a religious with vows which bind him only while he remains associated with the religious institute has no need to seek the superior's permission if he be elected to a dignity when he is no longer associated with the institute.[56]

Again, if the Pope immediately confers the cardinalate or the episcopate on a religious before the consent of the superior is obtained in the case of an election, then in the very act of promotion itself there is implicitly contained the necessary permission. The Supreme Pontiff as the highest superior of all religious thus supplies for the permission of the religious superior. Therefore, recourse to the proper religious superior for his permission is no longer necessary in that instance.[57]

Today the appointment of bishops by way of election is rare. Admittedly canon 626, §2, is of little practical value in this country. The Holy See by freely appointing bishops is pre-supposed to give its consent, which disposes of the necessity of having the superior's permission on the part of the religious.[58]

ARTICLE 3. THE NECESSARY DISPENSATION OF THE HOLY SEE IN CASE OF A FOURTH VOW OF NOT ACCEPTING DIGNITIES (CANON 626, §3)

Canon 626—§3. *Si voto teneatur non acceptandi dignitates, specialis Romani Pontificis dispensatio est necessaria.*

If a religious is bound by a vow not to accept dignities, a special dispensation from the Roman Pontiff is necessary.

There are some religious who have bound themselves by an extraordinary vow, a fourth vow besides the ordinary three vows of religion. Thereby they have freely and deliberately promised to God not to accept any ecclesiastical dignities. On that account,

---

[56] Fanfani, *De Iure Religiosorum*, n. 466, A; Biederlack-Führich, *De Religiosis*, n. 159, 1.

[57] Cappello, *Summa Iuris*, II, n. 63, 1; Biederlack-Führich, *loc. cit.*; Eichmann, *Lehrbuch des Kirchenrechts*, §97, n. 2; Berutti, *De Religiosis*, n. 138, B.

[58] Toso, *Commentaria Minora*, V, p. 215, n. 2; Augustine, *Religious and Laymen*, p. 356, §2.

they need a special dispensation from the Roman Pontiff, who is the Vicar of Christ on earth, before they may consent to a promotion to ecclesiastical dignities.[59] The Discalced Carmelites and certain members of the Jesuits pronounce this vow.[60] The acceptance of simple ecclesiastical offices is not contemplated under the prohibitive legislation of canon 626, §3, which distinctly circumscribes the vow there in question as one of not accepting dignities. It is in this restrictive sense, i.e., as concerning the acceptance of ecclesiastical dignities alone, that this vow must be considered as pointing to the need of a special dispensation.[61] Hence in any religious Order or congregation in which this vow of not accepting ecclesiastical dignities is taken, the granted permission of the superior does not alone suffice, whether the promotion comes through an election or in some other way; in any event the special dispensation or a mandate of the Pope is required.[62]

What kind of vow is designated in the phrase " votum non acceptandi dignitates"? Is there question only of a public vow, only of a private vow, or possibly of both? The text of canon 626, §3, could indicate both the private and the public vow, since its general tenor, in speaking simply of a vow not to accept dignities, lends itself to this interpretation according to the old legal axiom: " Ubi lex non distinguit; neque nos distinguere debemus." [63]

However, the vow of not accepting dignities should be understood as pointing to a public vow, whether solemn or simple, according to the definitions of canon 1308, §§1 and 2.[64] Not many authors touch on this problem. Relatively few have given it any consideration.[65] Yet there are conclusive arguments at hand to

---

[59] Toso, *Commentaria Minora,* V, p. 215, n. 2; Blat, *Ius De Religiosis,* n. 599.

[60] Coronata, *Institutiones Iuris Canonici,* I, n. 633, 2°; Prümmer, *Manuale,* Q. 249, n. 1; Schaefer, *De Religiosis,* n. 493, 1, c; Augustine, *Religious and Laymen,* p. 356, §3; Papi, *Religious in Church Law,* n. 28, 4.

[61] Augustine, *loc. cit.*

[62] Wernz-Vidal, *De Religiosis,* n. 413, I; Vermeersch-Creusen, *Epitome,* I, n. 786, 3; Berutti, *De Religiosis,* n. 138, C.

[63] Augustine, *Religious and Laymen,* p. 356, §3, and note 8.

[64] Canon 1308—§1. " Votum est publicum, si nomine Ecclesiae a legitimo Superiore ecclesiastico acceptetur, secus privatum.

§2. Solemne, si ab Ecclesia uti tale fuerit agnitum; secus, simplex."

[65] Cf. Oesterle, " Annahme kirchlicher Würden durch Ordenspersonen "—

show that it is a public vow that is meant. These arguments may be drawn from the sources of the present law of canon 626, §3, and also from the Code itself.

Argument from the sources of the present law: Cardinal Gasparri (1852–1934) in the footnote to canon 626, §3, has made reference to two Constitutions as the sources of the present disposition of the Code: The Constitution "*Cum sicut accepimus*" of May 21, 1635, and the Constitution "*Honorum*" of February 24, 1643 —both proceeding from the same Pontiff, Urban VIII.[66] A closer examination and perusal of these two pertinent documents reveals the fact that the Pope did have in mind a public vow, i.e., a religious vow, whether solemn or simple.

In the opening words of the Constitution "*Cum sicut accepimus*" Pope Urban VIII spoke of the vow, promise or oath, solemn or simple, of not seeking or accepting dignities, as found in several Orders, congregations or institutes, also in the Society of Jesus.[67] Now, the notion of solemn or simple in the usually accepted sense pertained rather to a vow than to a promise or to an oath. And further, this vow, solemnly or simply taken, had to be a public vow, since the Pope made explicit reference to this vow as taken in certain Orders, congregations or institutes besides the other usual vows. Hence the vow of not accepting dignities had to be a religious or public vow.

That the vow of not accepting dignities referred to a public vow was even more apparent in the Constitution "*Honorum.*" In clear language Pope Urban VIII in the first paragraph mentioned

---

Theologisch-praktische Quartalschrift, LXXIV (1921), 415-418, on pp. 415, 416 (hereafter this periodical will be cited as *TpQ*). The following authors, like Oesterle, likewise postulate a public vow in this connection, but offer no arguments, to substantiate their view: Sipos, *Enchiridion Iuris Canonici*, §73, n. 1, c, note 2; Pejška, *Jus Canonicum Religiosorum*, pp. 179–180, n. 1, c. Cf. Schaefer, *De Religiosis*, n. 493, 1, c.

[66] *Supra*, p. 47.

[67] §1: "Cum sicut accepimus, diversorum Ordinum, Congregationum et Institutorum, ac etiam Societatis Jesu, personae regulares, ultra alia vota etiam votum, promissionem, sive iuramentum solemniter sive simpliciter emittant, aut praestent de non petenda nec procuranda minusve acceptanda aliqua dignitate, neque aliqua superioritaté extra eorum Religionem: . . ."—*Fontes*, n. 216.

expressly that some religious, either at the time of their profession or perhaps before or after the profession, had pronounced besides the three essential vows of religion an additional vow of not seeking or accepting ecclesiastical dignities, viz., a solemn vow, or, as it is called, a simple one.[68] Now, the fact that the Pope aligned the additional vow of not accepting dignities on a parity with the three essential vows of religion bears out the contention that the additional vow also was thought of in the nature of a public vow.[69]

Argument from the Code: Upon closer examination one can note that several canons which in the Code deal with vows likewise establish the fact that the vow of not accepting dignities, as mentioned in canon 626, §3, must be regarded exclusively as a public vow.

Canon 1309 lists two private vows which are reserved to the Holy See.[70] The vow not to accept dignities does not receive mention there. Besides, if the vow of not accepting dignities were a private vow made before profession, it would be suspended by the religious profession as long as the person remained in the religious institute, as canon 1315 provides.[71] And if the vow were pronounced after the profession, such a private vow would fall

[68] §1: "Quamvis igitur, ut accepimus, tam Fratres Discalceati S. Augustini, et B. M. de Monte Carmelo, etiam discalceati Ordinum, quam Clerici Regulares ministrantes infirmis respective nuncupati, et nonnulli aliorum Ordinum, seu Congregationum Regulares, etiam Societatis Iesu, et alii Regulares, etiam individuam expressionem requirentes, aut in ipsa professione una cum tribus essentialibus votis, paupertatis scilicet, castitatis et obedientiae, aut ante, vel post professionem praedictam, sive solemne, sive, ut dicunt, simplex votum, in manibus tamen Superioris emittant de non procurando, nec acceptando aliquam dignitatem, seu Praelationem, vel Praelaturam extra Religionem, nisi coacti, vel adstricti fuerint praecepto eius, qui sibi iure praecipere potest, et aliqui addant etiam illa verba, videlicet, sub poena peccati, iuxta formam suarum Constitutionum a Sede Apostolica confirmatarum, . . ."—*Fontes,* n. 227.

[69] Oesterle, "Annahme kirchlicher Würden durch Ordenspersonen," *TpQ,* LXXIV (1921), 416.

[70] Canon 1309. "Vota privata Sedi Apostolicae reservata sunt tantummodo votum perfectae ac perpetuae castitatis et votum ingrediendi in religionem votorum solemnium, quae emissa fuerint absolute et post completum decimum octavum aetatis annum."

[71] Canon 1315: "Vota ante professionem religiosam emissa suspenduntur, donec vovens in religione permanserit."

under the power of the superior according to canon 1312, §1.[72]

In marked contrast to these last canons is canon 626, §3, which necessitates a special dispensation by the Roman Pontiff for the vow of not accepting ecclesiastical dignities. Obviously, in view of these canons a private vow must be ruled out of the scope of canon 626, §3. Therefore the vow of not accepting dignities as envisioned by the Code in regard to religious promoted to ecclesiastical dignities outside the religious institute must be a public vow, be it solemn or be it simple.[73]

Another question is this: Who can dispense from the vow not to accept ecclesiastical dignities? Canon 626, §3, calls for the special dispensation of the Roman Pontiff. The purpose of this discussion is to determine the connotation of these words: *specialis Romani Pontificis dispensatio.*

In some cases the dispensation from the vow of not accepting ecclesiastical dignities can be granted by religious superiors according to their respective Constitutions.[74] Nevertheless, in connection with the subject of this dissertation, viz., the promotion of religious to the episcopal or cardinalitial dignities, the dispensation can only come from the Pope himself. Pope Urban VIII in his Constitution "*Honorum,*" a source of the provision contained in canon 626, §3, had most definitely stated that no religious superior, not even the supreme superior, nor the chapter of the Order, nor the apostolic nuncio, nor the cardinal protector, or any other cardinal or legate of the Holy See, had the right to dispense from that vow. The dispensation remained reserved to the Pope alone. As can readily be seen, the Pontiff was very strict on this point. He seemed to indicate that this vow was reserved to the Roman Pontiff personally inasmuch as the dispensation flowed entirely from the full power of dispensing as invested solely in the Supreme Pontiff as the Vicar of Christ here on earth.[75]

---

[72] Canon 1312—§1. "Qui potestatem dominativam in voluntatem voventis legitime exercet, potest eius vota valide et, ex iusta causa, etiam licite irrita reddere, ita ut nullo in casu obligatio postea reviviscat." Cf. Augustine, *Religious and Laymen,* p. 356, §3, note 8.

[73] Oesterle, "Annahme kirchlicher Würden durch Ordenspersonen," *TpQ,* LXXIV (1921), 417.

[74] Schaefer, *De Religiosis,* n. 493, 1, c.

[75] *Fontes,* n. 227, §2; *supra,* p. 47.

The words, then, "specialis Romani Pontificis dispensatio" of canon 626, §3, must be explained in the sense of a vow whose dispensation is reserved to the person of the Pope.[76] Biederlack-Führich confuse the issue by their contention that the dispensation from the vow of not accepting dignities outside the religious institute must be obtained from the Apostolic See, since to it this vow is reserved.[77] If this were so, then it would follow that in accord with canon 7 of the Code the Sacred Congregation of Religious also would be competent to dispense from this vow.[78]

But canon 626, §3, does not mention the Apostolic See; it expressly requires the special dispensation of the Roman Pontiff. The question here resolves itself to this: Are the Apostolic See and the Roman Pontiff the same? They could be, no doubt; but canon 7 does not admit this if the context reveals the contrary. Now, is that not the case in canon 626, §3? Why the explicit mention of the Roman Pontiff—when in the canons on censures, even those most specially reserved, the term Apostolic See is constantly used[79]—if not to show that the person of the Holy Father is intended? Therefore, the position of Biederlack-Führich that the Apostolic See has the faculty to dispense from the vow not to accept dignities outside the religious institute is untenable. The significance of the words "specialis Romani Pontificis dispensatio" in canon 626, §3, must be that this vow is reserved for its dispensation to the very person of the Holy Father himself.[80]

[76] Pejška, *Jus Canonicum Religiosorum*, pp. 179–180, n. 1, c; Sipos, *Enchiridion Iuris Canonici*, §73, n. 1, c, note 3; A. D., "Religiosi ad Eccl. Dignitatem Promoti," *CpRM*, XIX (1938), 172, n. 6.

[77] *De Religiosis*, n. 158.

[78] Canon 7. "Nomine Sedis Apostolicae vel Sanctae Sedis in hoc Codice veniunt non solum Romanus Pontifex, sed etiam, nisi ex rei natura vel sermonis contextu aliud appareat, Congregationes, Tribunalia, Officia, per quae idem Romanus Pontifex negotia Ecclesiae universae expedire solet."

[79] Cf. the following canons: 2314; 2320; 2332; 2333; 2334; 2338; 2341; 2342; 2343; 2363; 2367; 2369; 2392; 2405; and others.

[80] Oesterle, "Annahme kirchlicher Würden durch Ordenspersonen," *TpQ*, LXXIV (1921), 417–418; Sipos, *Enchiridion Iuris Canonici*, §73, n. 1, c, note 3; Pejška, *Jus Canonicum Religiosorum*, pp. 179–180, n. 1, c; Berutti, *De Religiosis*, n. 138, C.

It may be remarked here that since the vow of not accepting dignities of canon 626, §3, is reserved for its dispensation to the person of the Pope,

Again, let it be noted that religious promoted to the episcopal or cardinalitial dignities may at once give their consent, for the Pope by his own direct action creates the cardinals, and as a rule himself nominates the bishops. Thereby the Roman Pontiff, the supreme head of all religious, grants the necessary dispensation from the vow of not accepting dignities outside the religious Order or congregation.[81] In fact, it is the Pope alone who can command the acceptance of a dignity by a religious under the obligation of such a vow.[82]

---

this dispensation may possibly be considered as a *causa maior*. Canon 220 merely states in general that affairs of greater importance which are reserved exclusively to the Supreme Pontiff either by their very nature or by positive legislation are called *causae maiores*. Certainly the promotion to ecclesiastical dignities, in relation to which the question of the dispensation from the vow of not accepting dignities on the part of religious comes to the fore, is an affair of serious moment. And since this vow is dispensed by means of the personal intervention of the Roman Pontiff alone according to the ruling of canon 626, §3, it is evident that the necessary conditions for a *causa maior* are fulfilled. Authors do not include this dispensation in their lists of *causae maiores*, but they do admit that no exhaustive enumeration can be given, since any affair which the Pope remands to his own consideration, or in which he personally intervenes, may be named a *causa maior*. Cf. Chelodi, *De Personis*, n. 152, note 8; Beste, *Introductio in Codicem*, p. 230.

81 Pejška, *op. cit.*, p. 180, n. 1, c; Schaefer, *De Religiosis*, n. 493, 1, c; Beste, *op. cit.*, p. 425; Fanfani, *De Iure Religiosorum*, n. 466, C; Regatillo, *Institutiones Iuris Canonici*, I, n. 749.

82 Berutti, *loc. cit.*

CHAPTER V

JURIDIC STATE OF RELIGIOUS PROMOTED TO THE CARDINALATE OR EPISCOPATE (CANONS 627 and 628)

After having set forth the general rules to be observed as necessary conditions prior to the promotion of religious to ecclesiastical dignities (canon 626), the Code turns to the special norms concerning the rights and obligations of religious after their promotion to the cardinalate or episcopate in relation to their own religious institute (canons 627 and 628).[1] It may be proper to recall again that the rights and obligations here considered refer to these dignitary religious as religious. Of course, by virtue of the dignity attained they partake of all the privileges and are bound by the obligations inherent in these same dignities.[2] The latter are not within the scope of the present canons; the former are. Thus the rights and obligations of religious in the cardinalate or the episcopate are viewed in the light of the dignitary status in connection with the religious state. Hence the heading of this chapter: Juridic State of Religious Promoted to the Cardinalate or Episcopate.

ARTICLE 1. THE EFFECTS OF THE PROMOTION IN GENERAL (CANON 627, §1)

Canon 627—§1. *Religiosus, renuntiatus Cardinalis aut Episcopus sive residentialis sive titularis, manet religiosus, particeps privilegiorum suae religionis, votis ceterisque suae professionis obligationibus adstrictus, exceptis iis quas cum sua dignitate ipse prudenter iudicet componi non posse, salvo praescripto can. 628.*

---

[1] Schaefer, *De Religiosis,* n. 494; Cocchi, *Commentarium in Codicem,* IV, n. 123.

[2] Berutti, *De Religiosis,* n. 139, II; A. D., "Religiosi ad Eccl. Dignitatem Promoti," *CpRM,* XIX (1938), p. 191, n. 29.

A religious who is proclaimed a cardinal or a bishop, either residential or titular, remains a religious: he continues to enjoy the privileges of his religious institute; he is bound by the vows and other obligations of his profession, except with respect to those things which, according to his own prudent judgment, are not compatible with his dignity, without prejudice to the rule stated in canon 628.

Canon 627, §1, is specifically limited to the consideration of religious in the cardinalitial or episcopal dignities. The inter-relations of the dignitary status and the religious state are recognized; from them the Code derives special norms, in this canon and the next, to regulate these same relations. The guiding and fundamental principle is this: A cardinal or bishop religious remains a religious. Therefrom flow the other norms enumerated:

(a) The dignitary religious partakes of all the privileges of his Order or congregation;
(b) the obligations of the three religious vows persist in the dignitary status;
(c) the other obligations of his religious profession also remain in force.

However, paragraph one of canon 627 permits an exception to the last mentioned group, namely, in regard to the obligations of his profession aside from his essential religious vows. With respect to them the bishop or cardinal religious is allowed to pass prudent judgment whether or not these obligations are compatible with the episcopal or cardinalitial dignity. If they are judged compatible, he remains bound to their observance; on the contrary, if they are incompatible with the dignity attained, the religious is not bound to their observance. Thus it can be readily inferred that a religious raised to the episcopate or cardinalate perseveres juridically in the same position as before his promotion.[3]

After this summary view of the scope of canon 627, §1, a closer and more detailed scrutiny of the legislation involved is in order. At the outset it may be noted here that the attestation to the requisite qualifications of the religious candidate for the episcopacy burdens the major superiors of the institute. Canon 331 recounts

[3] Toso, *Commentaria Minora,* V, p. 216, n. 1.

the necessary qualities on the part of a candidate for the episcopacy, and takes notice also of the case in which a religious is a candidate, particularly as regards the certification to his learning from the part of his religious superiors.[4] Therefore, a religious candidate for the episcopacy would not need a degree either in Sacred Theology or Canon Law, for the proper testimony in attestation of his competent learning would suffice.[5]

Canon 627, §1, employs the term *renuntiatus,* i.e., a religious proclaimed a cardinal or a bishop either in a Consistory or through an authentic decree announcing the creation or promotion respectively.[6] The implication appears to be that the effects of this canon and the next are in force from the moment of the proclamation of the promotion to the cardinalate or the episcopate, residential or titular. Thus it does not seem probable that the effects of canon 627 or 628 stay in abeyance till the installation ceremonies or the consecration have taken place; at least, such an interval or lapse of time as pointing to a state of abeyance can hardly be construed from the term *renuntiatus.*

Ellis indicates that the effects of canon 628, 1°, follow upon the act of taking possession of the dignity by the religious. If his words *upon taking possession of his dignity* are to mean the canonical possession taken by bishops according to the norm of canon 334, or any installation ceremonies and the like for other dignities, then the writer disagrees for the reasons already given. Moreover, the canonical possession taken by bishops is necessary for their entering upon the government of the diocese, but the effects of canon 628 do not concern government in any way; therefore, there seems to be no need for such a canonical taking of possession if the effects mentioned in canon 628 are to be realized.

Rather, it appears from the introductory words of the canon,

---

[4] Canon 331—§1. "Ut quis idoneus habeatur, debet esse:

5°. Laurea doctoris vel saltem licentia in sacra theologia aut in iure canonico potitus in athenaeo aliquo vel in Instituto studiorum a Sancta Sede probatis, vel saltem earundem disciplinarum vere peritus; quod si ad religionem aliquam pertineat, a suis Superioribus maioribus vel similem titulum vel saltem verae peritiae testimonium habeat." Cf. *supra,* pp. 39, 40.

[5] Pejška, *Jus Canonicum Religiosorum,* p. 180, n. 2.

[6] Schaefer, *De Religiosis,* n. 494, note 17; Blat, *Ius De Religiosis,* n. 601.

namely, " a religious raised to the episcopal dignity or to any other dignity," that the moment when he is raised to the dignity, i.e., the promotion itself, determines the time after which the effects ensue. Ellis renders the introductory words of canon 628 in the same way, for his words are: *A religious raised to the episcopal dignity or to some other* . . . Perhaps, then, the words of Ellis, " upon taking possession of his dignity," must be understood in the sense of the former introductory words, thus implying as the point at which the effects are produced the time that the religious are raised to the dignities, or the act of promotion itself. At any rate, his words are not altogether clear.[7]

Expressly mentioned in the canon are the two dignities of the cardinalate and the episcopate. Cardinals of the Holy Roman Church are members of the college of clerics instituted by ecclesiastical law as the senate of the Church and as the Roman Pontiff's chief advisors and counsellors to assist him in ruling the Church. When the Roman See is vacant, it is their exclusive prerogative to elect the new Pope. Individually or as a college, cardinals possess the highest dignity in the Church after the Supreme Pontiff.[8]

Bishops, the successors of the Apostles in regard to their office, are prelates invested with the fulness of the priesthood, and are by divine institution placed over individual churches which they govern with ordinary power, but under the authority of the Roman Pontiff.[9] This definition connotes the hierarchy of jurisdiction in the Church, and does not include those who are bishops through the act of Orders or consecration alone. Therefore the distinction between residential and titular bishops is valid; the former are bishops who actually rule and exercise the power of jurisdiction over a determinate clergy and people of a certain territory; the

[7] Bouscaren-Ellis, *Canon Law, A Text and Commentary* (Milwaukee: The Bruce Publishing Co., 1946), p. 298, Art. 1.

[8] Canon 230. " S. R. E. Cardinales Senatum Romani Pontificis constituunt eidemque in regenda Ecclesia praecipui consiliarii et adiutores assistunt." Cf. Coronata, *Institutiones Iuris Canonici*, I, n. 321, 2°; Hynes, *The Privileges of Cardinals*, p. 1.

[9] Canon 329—§1. "Episcopi sunt Apostolorum successores atque ex divina institutione peculiaribus ecclesiis praeficiuntur quas cum potestate ordinaria regunt sub auctoritate Romani Pontificis." Cf. Woywod, *A Practical Commentary*, I, n. 241; Beste, *Introductio in Codicem*, p. 262.

latter have the power of Orders or consecration alone, since they are bishops by consecration, and do not thereby acquire any power of jurisdiction.[10] But both are included among the dignities contemplated in canon 627, §1.

Among titular bishops must be enumerated auxiliary or coadjutor bishops, with or without the right of succession. Also vicars apostolic belong to this class, if they are bishops, and generally they do obtain the episcopal character.[11] As to the question whether vicars and prefects apostolic, abbots and prelates *nullius*, when they are not endowed with the episcopal character, should be included under canon 627, §1, with relation to its juridic effects, one must respond in the negative. The principal reason is that these lack the episcopal character, and so cannot be included under the terms of either residential or titular bishops. Truly, in the nature and powers of their offices they are equivalent to residential bishops as long as they continue in office.[12] But the fact that canon 627, §1, expressly speaks of religious proclaimed as bishops, whether residential or titular, seems to preclude the consideration of a mere juridic condition which is based on the dignity of an office; the insistence is rather on the dignity of the person in virtue of the episcopal character.[13]

The next inquiry touches on the juridic state of a religious after his proclamation as a cardinal or as a bishop, either residential or titular, as explained above. The exposition of canon 627, §1, treats of the dignitary religious in relation to the bond joining him to his

[10] Chelodi, *De Personis*, n. 187; Vermeersch-Creusen, *Epitome*, I, n. 455; Beste, *op. cit.*, p. 263.

[11] Coronata, *Institutiones Iuris Canonici*, I, n. 372, 1°; Chelodi, *op. cit.*, n. 183; Vermeersch-Creusen, *op. cit.*, I, n. 402, 2.

[12] Cf. canons 293-311, concerning vicars and prefects apostolic, and canons 319-328, for abbots and prelates *nullius*.

[13] Cf. Toso, *Commentaria Minora*, V, p. 216, n. 1. Some authors claim that the effects of canon 627, §1, can be extended to vicars and prefects apostolic, as also to abbots and prelates *nullius*, because of a declaration of Pope Benedict XV (1914-1922) in an audience on December 2, 1920, on the testimony of Vermeersch-Creusen.—*Epitome*, I, n. 787, 1. However, Vermeersch-Creusen witness that the Pope asserted that canon 627, §2, applied also to prefects apostolic during the term of their office.—Regatillo, *Institutiones Iuris Canonici*, I, n. 749; Cocchi, *Commentarium in Codicem*, IV, n. 123, 1, e.

Order or congregation, which endures after his promotion.[14] For in fact the Code establishes this as a fundamental principle: A religious in the cardinalitial or episcopal dignity remains a religious.

It is clear that it must be thus when one considers that a religious by taking the three vows of religion has become incorporated in a particular religious institute. His profession implicitly connotes his incorporation, since by means of his profession the religious has in all truth offered his person to the religious institute which in turn has accepted this offer (*traditio*). Thus the incorporation is accomplished, and thus the bond arises that makes the religious a member of the religious institute.

The religious state imports a stable manner of community life.[15] And this community life entails both the incorporation and the factual common life, i.e., a common dwelling under the same roof in subjection to the same rules, constitutions and superiors, and a life that looks to a common participation in the food, the clothing and whatever other means are necessary in the pursuing of the aim that motivates the existence of the religious institute. The incorporation in all events is the essential thing; without it a person could not be properly called a religious.

However, the common life of the religious in the same house together with the other attendant elements of the life in common are not essential. They may be lacking, as is the case with cardinals and bishops religious; and yet as incorporated members they remain true religious, for the bond which has resulted from their incorporation in the religious institute endures.[16] As an external sign of this lasting bond between the religious institute and the cardinal or the bishop religious, the obligation of wearing the tonsure and habit proper to the institute, if such exist as distinctive

[14] Schaefer, *De Religiosis*, n. 494, 2; Claeys Bouuaert-Simenon, *Manuale Iuris Canonici*, I, n. 682, I.

[15] Canon 487. "Status religiosus seu stabilis in communi vivendi modus, quo fideles, praeter communia praecepta, evangelica quoque consilia servanda per vota obedientiae, castitatis et paupertatis suscipiunt, ab omnibus in honore habendus est."

[16] Larraona, "Commentarium Codicis," *CpR*, II (1921), 134-139, on pp. 138-139, n. 5, b; Schaefer, *op. cit.*, n. 35.

signs of the Order or congregation, is imposed on the dignitary religious.[17]

Since the cardinals and bishops religious remain true religious, the rest of the norms of canon 627, §1, follow logically. Accordingly, these cardinals and bishops religious continue to enjoy the privileges of their particular institutes, i.e., the spiritual favors, suffrages, indulgences, or special indults granted to the Order or the congregation.[18]

Again, religious in the cardinalitial or episcopal dignities, since they remain religious, are bound to their three vows of poverty, chastity and obedience as any other member of their religious institute.[19] However, because of their dignitary status some mitigation is allowed with respect to the observance of poverty in accord with the rules of canon 628;[20] the vow of chastity remains as before and in fact acquires a greater intensity through the episcopal consecration;[21] the vow of obedience similarly remains in force, though accidentally the dignitary religious is withdrawn from obedience to his religious superiors—according to canon 627, §2.[22]

A cardinal or bishop religious remains bound not only to the essential vows of religion, but also to special vows which may have been added to them in his Order or congregation,[23] as well as any other obligations of his profession. For instance, the Minims have the vow of fasting during Lent.[24] Therefore, members of this

---

[17] Beste, *Introductio in Codicem*, p. 425; Wernz-Vidal, *De Religiosis*, n. 413, II; Fanfani, *De Iure Religiosorum*, n. 467, 3°. The writer has deferred a detailed commentary on the obligation of wearing the religious garb to a later chapter. Cf. *infra*, Chapter VI.

[18] Augustine, *Religious and Laymen*, p. 357; Fanfani, *op. cit.*, n. 467, 2°.

[19] A. D., "Religiosi ad Eccl. Dignitatem Promoti," *CpRM*, XIX (1938), p. 174, n. 9.

[20] Confer Article 3 of this chapter, pp. 100 ff.

[21] Schaefer, *De Religiosis*, n. 494; A. D., "art. cit.," *CpRM*, XIX (1938), p. 181, n. 19.

[22] See the next article, Article 2 of this Chapter; A. D., "art. cit.," *CpRM*, XIX (1938), p. 178, n. 16.

[23] Schaefer, *De Religiosis*, n. 494, note 18.

[24] Cf. Ferraris, *Prompta Bibliotheca*, III, s. v. *Episcopus*, Art. VII, n. 3; Biederlack-Führich, *De Religiosis*, n. 159, 2. This Order, the so called *Fratres Minimi*, was founded by St. Francis of Paula (+1507).—Cf. Heimbucher, *Die Orden und Kongregationen der katholischen Kirche*, II, 48 ff.

Order in the cardinalitial or episcopal dignity are still obliged to keep that vow. The canon includes such an accessory vow as obligatory after promotion, for it expresses in general that a religious in those dignities is under obligation to observe the vows and other obligations of his profession.[25] However, such accessory vows would not be obligatory if in the discretion of the dignitary religious they proved incompatible with the dignitary status, as will be seen in the next paragraphs.

What is comprehended in the words "ceterisque suae professionis obligationibus" of canon 627, §1? Outside the vows, i.e., the essential vows of religion, there are left the rule, the constitutions, and the traditions of the individual institute which prescribe and regulate the way of life, devotions and prayers, silences, fasts and abstinences, penances, etc., as proper to the particular institute. All the matters here enumerated comprise the other obligations of the religious profession, summarily referred to as the rule, the constitutions and the traditions of the Order or the congregation.

To them all a cardinal or bishop religious is bound as such, for he remains a religious. But here the law of the Code permits exceptions, either permanently or for particular cases, in so far as the dignitary religious may himself pass prudent judgment whether or not the precriptions of his rule or constitutions are compatible with the dignity attained. Thus, he must observe the rule and the constitutions as before his promotion when they command things that do not conflict with his new dignity; on the other hand, if the special vows, the way of life, special prayers and devotions, silences, fasts or abstinences, penances and the like as prescribed by the rule or the constitutions are incompatible with his dignity inasmuch as they are repugnant to the cardinalitial or episcopal status, or for the reason that they impede the fulfillment of the

[25] Cf. A. D., "art. cit.," *CpRM*, XIX (1938), p. 180, n. 18. St. Alphonsus (1696–1787) admitted that a bishop religious remained bound to the essential vows of his Order or congregation, since these are personal. But he favored the opinion that dignitary religious were freed from other non-essential vows which were only accessory to the religious profession.—*Theologia Moralis* (ed. nova, cura et studio P. Leonardi Gaudé, 4 vols.; Vol. II, Romae, 1907), Lib. IV, dub. I, q. 2, and q. 3. Cf. also Piat (1815–1904), *Praelectiones Juris Regularis* (3. ed., 2 vols., Tornaci, 1906), I, Q. 266, ad II.

duties and obligations in the dignitary status, the dignitary religious may for any just cause consider himself excused both licitly and validly. In such circumstances he is exempted from the observance of his rule or constitutions along with any of its prescripts.[26]

Moreover, the religious created a cardinal or consecrated a bishop attains the rank of a prelate, and so no longer can be a subject of his religious superiors; his subjection henceforth is due to the Pope alone (canon 627, §2). Accordingly, since he is a prelate, the dignitary religious can dispense himself from the observance of the rule and the constitutions in a similar fashion as his religious superiors can dispense themselves and their subjects from certain commands of the rule or the constitutions. However, it must be understood that dignitary religious are not confined by the limits of the dispensing power of superiors provided for in the rule or the constitutions.

Further, since the dignitary religious is responsible to the Pope alone in these matters, it would be too grave a burden to require him to have recourse to the Pope in each and every single case.[27] Therefore, the cardinal or bishop religious possesses the faculty to judge personally whether or not the observances of his rule or constitutions can be harmonized with the dignitary status.[28]

A correct answer, then, to the query whether religious when promoted to the cardinalitial or episcopal dignity are bound to the observances of the rule, the constitutions and the traditions proper to their institutes must distinguish the following hypotheses: If the observances are compatible with the cardinalitial or episcopal dignity, the religious is bound as before his promotion; if the observances are incompatible or repugnant to the dignitary status, the religious is freed from their obligation.[29] The prudent judgment about the compatibility or incompatibility is left to the cardinal or bishop religious. But the compatibility or incompatibility must be

[26] Augustine, *Religious and Laymen,* p. 357; Berutti, *De Religiosis,* n. 139, II; Schaefer, *De Religiosis,* n. 494.

[27] Coronata, *Institutiones Iuris Canonici,* I, n. 634, 1°; Schaefer, *loc. cit.*

[28] On the contrary, this faculty could not be claimed by a bishop secular who had resigned with the permission and authority of the Holy See and then entered the religious state.—A. D., "Religiosi ad Eccl. Dignitatem Promoti," *CpRM,* XIX (1938), p. 173, note 12, bis.

[29] A. D., "art. cit.," *CpRM,* XIX (1938), p. 174, n. 9.

measured in reference to the cardinalitial or episcopal dignities alone, since these two dignities form the ambit of the measure permitted by canon 627, §1.[30]

Today there can be no doubt that dignitary religious are bound to the observance of their rule and constitutions. That obligation has been clearly established since the time of the memorable Constitution "*Custodes*" of Pope Benedict XIII.[31] The older authors discussed in what measure the obligation of this observance existed. They pointed to varying degrees relative to the obligation attendant upon the observance of the rule and the constitutions:[32]

The Roman theologian who appended additional notes to the articles in the work of Ferraris held that a religious dignitary was obliged under pain of mortal sin to keep the rule and the constitutions of the Order or the congregation in which he had been professed when these were befitting and in accord with his dignity.[33] St. Alphonsus (1696–1787) considered as more probable the opinion that a bishop religious was not bound to the observance of his rule or constitutions under pain of sin (*sub culpa*); the obligation arose rather from a natural propriety due to the rule or constitutions (*ex honestatis debito*), which could not oblige the religious even *sub levi*.[34]

But the Code seems to sanction the opinion which affirms that a bishop religious is bound to the observance of his rule and constitutions *sub levi* or *sub gravi* dependent on the obligation which he had assumed by his religious profession before his promotion, in all matters that are compatible with his dignitary status, i.e., as long as these do not impede or oppose the fulfillment of the duties inherent in his new state. At least the decision of the Sacred Congregation of Bishops and Regulars to this effect is cited in the

---

[30] Fanfani, *De Iure Religiosorum*, n. 467, 3°.

[31] Piat, *Praelectiones Juris Regularis*, I, Q. 212, n. 1. Cf. *supra*, pp. 40, 41.

[32] Cf. A. D., "art. cit.," *CpRM*, XIX (1938), 191-192, n. 30; 188-189, n. 26.

[33] Ferraris, *Prompta Bibliotheca*, III, s. v. *Episcopus*, notae in Art. VII, n. 3.

[34] *Theologia Moralis*, Lib. IV, dub. I, q. 3; also Suarez, *De religiosis*, Tractatus Octavus, Lib. III, cap. XVII, n. 7 ss.—*Opera Omnia*, XVI, 413 ss.; Piat, *op. cit.*, I, Q. 212, n. 2. Cf. Coronata, *Institutiones Iuris Canonici*, I, n. 634, note 10.

footnotes of Cardinal Gasparri to canon 627, §1, as one of the sources of the present discipline on this point.[35] This response, it is true, referred to bishops regular, for the case concerned a Franciscan friar, but it can be extended to bishops religious of simple vows as well, since the same reasons for the obligation to observe the rule and constitutions are present in their case. Likewise cardinals religious are included for the same reason.[36]

The general principle, then, is this: Cardinals or bishops religious are obliged, *sub levi* or *sub gravi* in accord with the obligation assumed at their religious profession, to the observance of the rule and the constitutions proper to their institute when and if the prescripts of the rule and the constitutions are compatible with the dignitary state.

There could arise a situation in which such a prescript of the rule, compatible as such with the dignitary status, threatens a censure or some penalty against transgressors. Would that penalty be incurred by a religious in the cardinalitial or episcopal dignity? The answer is and must be in the negative, since such a penalty is inflicted by the religious Order or congregation against its own subjects. But the Order or congregation has no authority any longer over one of its members who is now a cardinal or a bishop; canon 627, §2, has lifted him from the jurisdiction of the Order or congregation; being a prelate in his own right, he is no longer a subject of the religious superior. Even apart from this consideration canon 2227, §2, exempts cardinals entirely from the penal law, and bishops from all *latae sententiae* penalties of suspension and interdict, as long as they are not expressly mentioned as subject to the enacted penalty. With that rule obtaining in the common law, there seems all the more reason for their exemption from the penal sanctions enacted in the rule and constitutions of a religious institute.[37]

---

[35] S. C. Ep. et Reg., *Alexien.*, 6 maii 1864; *supra*, pp. 41, 42. The elaborate *votum* of one of the consultors on this case confirms this doctrine.—*ASS*, I (1865–1866), 449-466.

[36] Piat, *Praelectiones Juris Regularis*, I, Q. 212, n. 3, and notes 1 and 2; A. D., "Religiosi ad Eccl. Dignitatem Promoti," *CpRM*, XIX (1938), p. 192, n. 30, 3.

[37] Schaefer, *De Religiosis*, n. 494, note 18; A. D., "art. cit.," *CpRM*, XIX (1938), p. 190, n. 27, a. Cf. Piat, *op. cit.*, I, Q. 266, ad II.

A cardinal or bishop religious, either residential or titular, must follow the Roman rite in the celebration of Mass, though in his own institute the use of a special rite obtains. For example, Carthusians and Dominicans when advanced to the cardinalate or the episcopate must cease celebrating Mass in the rite special to their Orders.[38] And since the adherence to the Roman rite in the celebration of Mass can be enumerated as one of the effects of canon 627, §1, it follows that these religious are obliged to adhere to the Roman rite from the time of their preconization, i.e., from the time of their promotion in Consistory.[39]

Cardinals and bishops religious also from the moment of their promotion must change to the Roman breviary.[40] Religious as residential bishops are bound to follow the calendar (*ordo*) of their diocese in the recitation of the breviary and in the celebration of feasts.[41] As a residential bishop the religious must follow the Roman breviary according to the *ordo* of the diocese whose government he will assume. On the other hand, cardinals and titular bishops religious, it would appear, must follow the general Roman *ordo,* unless they obtain some office with the obligation of residence in a certain diocese or territory. In the latter case probably they could follow the *ordo* of that respective territory from the time of their promotion. However, such a cardinal or bishop religious would be obliged to add to his Office any special prayers ordered by the rule and constitutions of his religious institute, unless a sufficiently grave and proportionate cause excused him according to his prudent judgment. The Cistercians, for example, are under the obligation to join the Office of the Blessed Virgin to the recitation of the divine Office.[42]

In the former law it had been ruled that religious when pro-

---

[38] A. D., "art. cit.," *CpRM,* XIX (1938), p. 191, n. 29; Prümmer, *Manuale,* Q. 249, n. 4; Coronata, *Institutiones Iuris Canonici,* I, n. 634, 1°; Cappello, *Summa Iuris,* II, n. 63, 2.

[39] Cf. *supra,* pp. 86, 87.

[40] Sipos, *Enchiridion Iuris Canonici,* §73, n. 2, f.

[41] This had been clearly established in the former law by decree of the Sacred Congregation of Rites on June 11, 1605.—*Decreta Authentica,* n. 181; cf. *supra,* p. 50. Cf. also Coronata, *loc. cit.*; Blat, *Ius De Religiosis,* n. 601.

[42] Cf. Augustine, *Religious and Laymen,* p. 357; A. D., "art. cit.," *CpRM,* XIX (1938), p. 191, n. 29.

moted to the cardinalitial or episcopal dignities could carry with them from their institutes all written matter of their own (*manuscripta*), the necessary personal clothing, and their breviary.[43] For things beyond the items thus specified they needed the legitimate permission of the religious superior, for instance, if books were to be taken along.[44] Modern authors agree that the same restriction applies today.[45] Coronata proffers the reasonable assertion that in the matter of books the necessary permission may be presumed about those which had been given to the religious for his use, and which may be necessary to him in his new dignity, especially if they are annotated with his own personal notes.[46]

Another juridic effect of the promotion of religious to the episcopacy is seen in canon 1224, 2°. Canons 1223–1229 deal with the choice of the church or of the cemetery of burial, or of both. All the faithful may freely choose a church and a cemetery for their burial, unless the law explicitly prohibits the choice.[47] Canon 1224 sets forth who are prohibited from invoking a free choice relative to the church and the cemetery of their burial. The second section expressly deprives professed religious of the right to elect a church and a cemetery for their burial, i.e., religious with vows, temporary or perpetual, simple or solemn, in any religious institute, and no matter what their rank or dignity—unless they are bishops. Therefore, bishops religious, residential or titular—for the canon makes no distinction—enjoy the right to choose a church for their funeral, and a cemetery for their burial.[48] Obviously, cardinals religious who are not bishops do not have the

---

[43] Of course, if their monastic or religious breviary differs from the Roman breviary, there would be no need for bishops or cardinals religious to take that special religious breviary with them; from the time of their promotion, as explained before, they are obliged to follow the Roman breviary.

[44] *Supra*, pp. 45, 46.

[45] Prümmer, *Manuale*, Q. 249, n. 2; Cocchi, *Commentarium in Codicem*, IV, n. 123, 1, e; Coronata, *Institutiones Iuris Canonici*, I, n. 634, 1°; Schaefer, *De Religiosis*, n. 494, c; Oesterle, *Praelectiones Iuris Canonici*, I, pp. 354, 355.

[46] *Loc. cit.*

[47] Canon 1223.

[48] Cf. Woywod, *A Practical Commentary*, II, n. 1250; Eichmann, *Lehrbuch des Kirchenrechts*, §97, n. 3.

faculty of this free choice, since canon 1224, 2°, excludes from the privilege all religious of any rank or dignity with the sole exception of bishops religious.[49]

It stands to reason, of course, that a religious by his promotion to the cardinalate or the episcopate loses the offices which he may have held in the religious institute.[50] Canon 156, §§1 and 2, regarding the incompatibility of several offices, assuredly would come into operation here, since the duties of an office in the religious institute could hardly be combined with the duties of the cardinalate or the episcopate.[51] The higher status must supersede the lower, particularly since the fulfillment of the cardinalitial or episcopal duties lies outside the religious Order or congregation.[52]

Article 2. The Effects of the Promotion Regarding Obedience (Canon 627, §2)

Canon 627—§2. *Eximitur tamen a potestate Superiorum et, vi voti obedientiae, uni Romano Pontifici manet obnoxius.*

However, he [a religious proclaimed a cardinal or a bishop, either residential or titular] is exempt from the authority of his superiors, and by virtue of the vow of obedience remains subject to the Roman Pontiff alone.

A religious promoted to the cardinalitial or episcopal dignity remains bound to the essential vows of religion, for he remains a religious (canon 627, §1). One of these vows is the vow of obedience, whose obligation persists for a religious in his dignitary status.[53] However, canon 627, §2, exempts a cardinal or a bishop religious from the obedience previously due to his own religious superiors in fulfillment of that vow. This does not destroy the

[49] However, some authors extend this privilege of choosing a church and a cemetery of burial to cardinals: Cappello, *Summa Iuris*, II, n. 476, 2, 2°; Regatillo, *Institutiones Iuris Canonici*, II, n. 66.

[50] Pejška, *Ius Canonicum Religiosorum*, p. 180, n. 2, b.

[51] Canon 156—§1 "Nemini conferantur duo officia incompatibilia.
§2. Sunt incompatibilia officia quae una simul ab eodem adimpleri nequeunt."

[52] Cf. canon 188, 3°.

[53] Fanfani, *De Iure Religiosorum*, n. 468, A.

obligation of the vow, for the duty of obedience as arising from the vow is thenceforth to be referred to the Roman Pontiff as due to him.[54] Hence, while the religious remains in the episcopal or cardinalitial status, he is freed from the obligations of this vow with respect to the religious superiors.

He is in no way subject to them, but this is only circumstantially so. When such a dignitary religious returns again to the institute (canon 629, §1), he is bound automatically by his vow of obedience in regard to his religious superiors, similarly as he was bound before his departure on the occasion of his promotion to the dignity.[55] The creation of a religious as a cardinal, or his appointment as a bishop, effects his transition from the position of a mere subject to that of a prelate, in consequence of which he cannot any longer be obliged to obey his former superiors. And yet the vow remains in force virtually, so that his obedience is due in virtue of the vow to any superiors above him in dignity (the Pope), and eventually to the religious superiors when he again is placed under their authority on his return to the religious institute.[56]

In reality, the effects of the vow of obedience are suspended in relation to the religious superiors as long as the religious occupies the dignitary station. The vow of obedience is not nullified; it must exist also in the dignitary status, for canon 627, §1, declares that when a religious is elevated to the episcopal or cardinalitial rank he still continues as a religious, and one of the vows essential to his status as a religious is his vow of obedience. Now, since the religious dignitary is withdrawn from the obedience *vi voti* to the religious superiors so that in this relationship the vow no longer binds him, there must be someone who in a similar relationship supplants the religious superiors during the time while the religious is a bishop or a cardinal outside the Order or congregation. Otherwise how could such a religious be called a religious in the proper sense? Therefore, though exempt from the authority of the religious superiors, the cardinal or the bishop religious is sub-

---

[54] This is in accord with the norm of canon 499, §1. Cf. Blat, *Ius De Religiosis*, n. 601; Eichmann, *Lehrbuch des Kirchenrechts*, §97, n. 3, a.

[55] A. D., "Religiosi ad Eccl. Dignitatem Promoti," *CpRM*, XIX (1938), 178, nn. 16, 17.

[56] Blat, *loc. cit.*

ject in matters of the vow of obedience to the authority of the Pope alone.[57]

Since the vow of obedience endures in the dignitary status, it is apparent that a cardinal or a bishop religious substantially remains a religious. The fact that he is withdrawn from the authority of the superiors in religion is an exception granted out of deference to the rank obtained, as well as a potential guarantee for the proper fulfillment of the duties of the cardinalate and the episcopate without interference. The exception pertains also to the obedience due to the Order or congregation as such. Though canon 627, §2, states that a religious in the cardinalate or the episcopate is exempt from the authority of the religious superiors, the intent must be the exemption from the authority of the Order or the congregation as well, since that is obviously included in the former exemption.[58]

Accordingly, neither the superiors nor the chapter of the religious institute can exercise any power over the cardinal or the bishop religious. It makes no difference whether this power is jurisdictional (exempt religious Orders) or merely dominative (religious congregations). In either case the religious when raised to the episcopal or the cardinalitial dignity is entirely exempt so far as his Order or congregation is concerned. Thus, the power to command in virtue of the vow of obedience lies with the Pope, to whom alone the dignitary religious has become subject in his duty of obedience from the very time of his original profession.[59]

Practically, then, the exemption from the vow of obedience for the cardinal or the bishop religious is tantamount to a severance or a separation from his religious institute. But this severance

---

[57] Berutti, *De Religiosis,* n. 139, III.

[58] Toso, *Commentaria Minora,* V, p. 216, nn. 1, 2.

[59] Toso, *op. cit.,* p. 216, n. 2; Chelodi, *De Personis,* n. 284, a; Berutti, *De Religiosis,* n. 139, III; Prummer, *Manuale,* Q. 249, n. 3.

Whether the same applies to vicars and prefects apostolic appointed from religious institutes, when they are not bishops, at best seems doubtful.—Cf. Toso, *op. cit.,* p. 216, n. 1; Vermeersch-Creusen, *Epitome,* I, n. 787, 1; Schaefer, *De Religiosis,* n. 494, and note 21; Berutti, *op. cit.,* n. 139, III, *Scholion;* Goyeneche, *De Religiosis,* n. 88, III; Fanfani, *De Iure Religiosorum,* n. 468, B; Papi, *Religious in Church Law,* n. 28, 6.

or separation should in turn be considered in the light of an event whereby the religious through his promotion to these dignities becomes removed from subjection to the Order or the congregation with a view to the utility of the Church at large.[60]

Article 3. The Effects of the Promotion Regarding Property (Canon 628)

Canon 628 contemplates the vow of poverty in its obligations for religious in the dignitary status. It turns to a consideration of the temporal goods of a dignitary religious in their relation to one of his essential vows, the vow of poverty.[61]

Whereas canon 627 is in its scope specifically limited to the consideration of religious in the cardinalitial or the episcopal dignities, canon 628 extends its consideration to any dignity to which religious are promoted outside their religious institutes and expounds their juridic condition in regard to the vow of poverty after their promotion.[62]

In general it can be said that the vow of poverty remains substantially in existence as before the promotion of the religious to a dignity, but that it is altered somewhat in accidentals, inasmuch as the law allows some modifications in the effects of the vow.[63] Therefore the law of the Code in canon 628 grants a special position to the vow of poverty with the proper distinctions for the respective cases of dignitary religious professed with solemn or with simple vows.[64]

A. Religious of Solemn Profession (Canon 628, 1°)

Canon 628. *Religiosus ad dignitatem episcopalem vel aliam extra propriam religionem evectus:*

---

[60] Toso, *op. cit.*, p. 216, n. 2.

[61] Blat, *Ius De Religiosis*, n. 602; Schaefer, *De Religiosis*, n. 494.

[62] Toso, *Commentaria Minora*, V, p. 217, n. 1. Coronata admits that canon 628 and the next canon refer to any dignity to which religious are advanced, and that canon 627 considers cardinals and bishops religious alone. He nevertheless claims that canon 627 seems to be applicable also to religious in other dignities as well.—*Institutiones Iuris Canonici*, I, n. 634, 2°, a, note 7.

[63] A. D., "Religiosi ad Eccl. Dignitatem Promoti," *CpRM*, XIX (1938), p. 182, n. 20; Eichmann, *Lehrbuch des Kirchenrechts*, §97, n. 3, b.

[64] Goyeneche, *De Religiosis*, n. 89.

1°. Si per professionem dominium bonorum amiserit, bonorum quae ipsi obveniunt, habet usum, usumfructum et administrationem; proprietatem vero Episcopus residentialis, Vicarius Apostolicus, Praefectus Apostolicus, acquirit dioecesi, vicariatui, praefecturae; ceteri, Ordini vel Sanctae Sedi, ad normam can. 582, salvo praescripto can. 239, §1, n. 19.

A religious who has been raised to the episcopal or any other dignity outside his religious institute:

1. If by his profession he has lost the ownership of property, has the use, usufruct, and administration of all the goods which now accrue to him; but the proprietorship of the goods the residential bishop, the vicar apostolic, and the prefect apostolic acquires for the diocese, the vicariate and the prefecture respectively; others acquire the proprietorship either for the religious Order or for the Holy See, according to the provision made by canon 582, without prejudice to the prescript of canon 239, §1, n. 19.

As it has been noted above, canon 628 has in view not only religious who have been elevated to the episcopate, but also those who have attained any other dignity outside the religious institute, for instance, that of a legateship.[65] Therefore the scope of canon 628 is all-inclusive as regards dignities. Moreover, the canon deals with all dignitary religious with respect to their vow of poverty, for they still are bound by this vow (canon 627, §1). It touches on the vow of poverty in reference to the ownership, the use and usufruct, and the administration of temporal goods during the actual exercise of the dignity.

Canon 628, 1°, in particular is concerned with religious of solemn profession in the dignitary state.[66] This section of the canon does not mention explicitly religious who are professed with solemn vows, for it begins with the words, " if the religious has lost the right of ownership." The signification is of course the same. Only a solemn profession abolishes the capacity to own property, for the religious has renounced this right at the time of his solemn profession, and for the reason that any acts executed contrary to

[65] Schaefer, *De Religiosis*, n. 494, note 22; Blat, *Ius De Religiosis*, n. 603.

[66] Augustine, *Religious and Laymen*, p. 358, n. 1.

the solemn vow of poverty are invalid.[67] Men who make solemn profession in any religious Order are called *regulars.*[68] Hereafter that term shall be so employed.

Canon 628, 1°, contains the following legislation for regulars who have been promoted to the episcopal or any other dignity outside their religious institutes. That legislation effects a twofold derogation from the common law on religious: [69]

1. Dignitaries regular have the faculty to administer all temporal goods that accrue to them after their promotion, and enjoy also the right of their use and usufruct.

Ordinarily, before the profession of simple vows novices must, for the whole time that they will be bound by their vows, cede the administration of all temporal goods to a person of their choice, and also dispose of the use and usufruct of these goods at their pleasure. This is set forth in canon 569, §1, which speaks of the profession of simple vows alone.[70] However, this can also apply to regulars, since a profession of simple vows for the period of three years must precede the solemn profession.[71]

---

[67] Canon 579. "Simplex professio, temporaria sit vel perpetua, actus votis contrarios reddit illicitos, sed non invalidos, nisi aliud expresse cautum fuerit; professio autem solemnis, si sint irritabiles, etiam invalidos."

Canon 581—§1. "Professus a votis simplicibus antea nequit, sed intra sexaginta dies ante professionem solemnem, salvis peculiaribus indultis a Sancta Sede concessis, debet omnibus bonis quae actu habet, cui maluerit, sub conditione secuturae professionis, renuntiare." Cf. Toso, *Commentaria Minora*, V, p. 217, n. 1; Schaefer, *De Religiosis,* n. 274, 2, b; Woywod, *A Practical Commentary,* I, n. 541; Eichmann, *Lehrbuch des Kirchenrechts,* §97, n. 3, b.

[68] Canon 488. "In canonibus qui sequuntur, veniunt nomine:

2°. *Ordinis,* religio in qua vota solemnia nuncupantur . . .

7°. *Religiosorum,* qui vota nuncuparunt in aliqua religione; . . . *regularium,* qui in Ordine; . . ."

[69] Berutti, *De Religiosis,* n. 140, A.

[70] Canon 569—§1. "Ante professionem votorum simplicium sive temporariorum sive perpetuorum novitius debet, ad totum tempus quo simplicibus votis adstringetur, bonorum suorum administrationem cedere cui maluerit et, nisi constitutiones aliud ferant, de eorundem usu et usufructu libere disponere."

[71] Canon 574—§1. "In quolibet Ordine tam virorum quam mulierum et in qualibet Congregatione quae vota perpetua habeat, novitius post expletum

Within two months before the solemn profession the religious must, under the condition of the profession which is to follow, renounce the right of ownership in favor of someone he selects (canon 581, §1); from the moment of solemn profession all the goods which fall to the regular revert to the Order or to the Holy See, as the case may be,[72] which besides the ownership gains also the right of administration, as well as the enjoyment of the use and usufruct. Thus it is evident that the faculty to administer the temporal goods that fall to dignitaries regular after their promotion to a dignity and the right to enjoy the use and usufruct of these goods are concessions that derogate from the common law of religious.[73]

Accordingly, regulars in the dignitary status possess the right of personally administering all property that accrues to them after their promotion and also the right to its use and revenues. This includes not only regulars who are in the dignities explicitly enumerated in the canon, i.e., residential bishops, and vicars and prefects apostolic, but also others, who are certainly comprehended by the term *ceteri*. Thus, titular bishops, even though they do not rule an abbacy or a prelacy *nullius*, or a vicariate or a prefecture apostolic, as well as regulars elevated by the Pope to some dignitary office outside the religious institute when they are not endowed with the episcopal character—all these can lawfully and freely administer the temporal goods coming to them in the dignitary status, and enjoy also their use and usufruct.[74]

In regard to the administration of property the dignitary regu-

---

novitiatum, in ipsa novitiatus domo debet votis perpetuis, sive solemnibus sive simplicibus, praemittere, sàlvo praescripto can. 634, votorum simplicium professionem ad triennium valituram, . . ."

[72] Canon 582. "Post solemnem professionem, salvis pariter peculiaribus Apostolicae Sedis indultis, omnia bona quae quovis modo obveniunt regulari:

1°. In Ordine capaci possidendi, cedunt Ordini vel provinciae vel domui secundum constitutiones;

2°. In Ordine incapaci, acquiruntur Sanctae Sedi in proprietatem."

Cf. Woywod, *A Practical Commentary*, I, n. 475; Blat, *Ius De Religiosis*, n. 603.

[73] Berutti, *De Religiosis*, n. 140, A, a.

[74] Berutti, *op. cit.*, n. 140, A, b; Coronata, *Institutiones Iuris Canonici*, I, n. 634, 2°, a.

lar at his own discretion can perform the necessary acts of administration by himself or through the agency of another.[75] Moreover, it must be inferred that the use and the usufruct flowing from these temporal goods can be available to the dignitary regular only when such property falls to the dignitary religious personally, for canon 628, 3°, excludes all goods that are received for purposes of religion or charity.[76]

Though what has been thus far stated demonstrates that some of the juridic effects of the vow of poverty are suspended when the regular attains the dignitary state outside his Order, it must be remembered that the vow as such does not cease in its obligatory force. The vow is operative at least in regard to the moral effects, for the dignitary regular remains a religious bound by his vows (canon 627, §1). On this account the spirit of poverty must govern his use of the temporal goods which by privilege are allotted to his benefit and convenience in the dignitary status. Accordingly, superfluous expenditures incurred by him for useless travel or needless recreation, for any form of luxury in dress or food, offend against his vow of poverty, for which he is accountable to God.[77]

2. The proprietorship or ownership of goods acquired by a residential bishop, a vicar apostolic, or a prefect apostolic belongs to the diocese, the vicariate, or the prefecture respectively.

According to the common law on religious (canon 582) all the property which falls in whatever way to a solemnly professed religious after his solemn profession belongs to the Order, or the province or the house, as established by the rule or the constitutions, if the Order is capable of ownership; but if the Order is incapable of ownership, the Holy See becomes the owner of such property. Now, regulars who are residential bishops, or vicars or prefects apostolic, acquire the ownership not for the Order, the province

[75] Blat, *Ius De Religiosis,* n. 603, a.

[76] Toso, *Commentaria Minora,* V, p. 217, n. 1; cf. section C of the present article, pp. 117 ff.

[77] Prümmer, *Manuale,* Q. 249, n. 3, a; A. D., "Religiosi ad Eccl. Dignitatem Promoti," *CpRM,* XIX (1938), p. 188, n. 25.

or the house as prior to their promotion, but instead for the diocese, the vicariate or the prefecture.[78]

Though canon 628, 1°, mentions only residential bishops, and vicars or prefects apostolic, yet abbots and prelates *nullius* must also be accounted with them. The reason that a certain territory is governed by the abbot or the prelate *nullius* in an equivalent manner as the territories of the prelates mentioned offers the basis for this conclusion, since in law an abbacy and a prelacy *nullius* are classed under the term of diocese, and the abbot and the prelate are acknowledged as contemplated in the law through the use of the term bishop.[79] Therefore, the property belongs to the diocese, to the vicariate or the prefecture apostolic, and to the abbacy or prelacy *nullius,* when the regular who acquires it is a residential bishop, a vicar or a prefect apostolic, and an abbot or a prelate *nullius* respectively.[80]

For regulars in other dignities, i.e., when they are none of those already mentioned in the canon, there is no derogation from the common law of religious. They follow the normal rule as enunciated in canon 582, and thus acquire the ownership for the religious Order, the province or the house, as determined by their rule, if the Order is capable of possessing property, or for the Holy See, if the Order is incapable of ownership. For instance, the Friars Minor, the Capuchins, and the Carmelites are forbidden

[78] The latter as juridic persons are capable of acquiring and owning temporal goods.—Schaefer, *De Religiosis,* n. 494, a, note 25; Eichmann, *Lehrbuch des Kirchenrechts,* §97, n. 3, b, and note 1.

[79] Canon 215—§2. "In iure nomine dioecesis venit quoque abbatia vel praelaturae *nullius*; et nomine Episcopi, Abbas vel Praelatus *nullius,* nisi ex natura rei vel sermonis aliud constet." Cf. Berutti, *De Religiosis,* n. 140, A, b; Blat, *Ius De Religiosis,* n. 603, b. Toso, however, by grouping abbots and prelates *nullius* under the word *ceteri* of canon 628, 1°, apparently denies this contention.—*Commentaria Minora,* V, p. 217, n. 1. Berutti, on the other hand, reasoning from the parity between the offices of vicars and prefects apostolic and of ecclesiastical superiors of independent missions, assimilates the latter to the former in this connection.—*Op. cit.,* n. 140, A, b, note 1. Schaefer in a note to the word *ceteri* of this section of canon 628 merely mentions Berutti's opinion.—*Op. cit.,* n. 494, a, note 26.

[80] Berutti, *op. cit.,* n. 140, A, b.

by their rules to enjoy ownership even in common, and not only as individual members within their Orders.[81]

The other dignities, specified by the word *ceteri* of canon 628, 1°, comprise cardinals who are not at the same time residential bishops, all titular bishops, nuncios, internuncios, and other legates.[82] Regulars, then, during the term of their possession of these dignities gain the ownership of all goods falling to them personally, not indeed for themselves, but for their Order or for the Holy See, in accordance with the rule that obtained before their departure from the institute.[83] However, they gain the faculty to administer all temporal goods that accrue to them after their promotion, and also the right to enjoy their use and usufruct. The differentiation between the first group of regulars who are residential bishops, or vicars and prefects apostolic, of abbots and prelates *nullius*, and the second group in the category of the *ceteri* of canon 628, 1°, must be ascribed to this: The distinction is made in regard to the subject who acquires the ownership, and not in regard to the subject who has the free administration, use and usufruct of the temporal goods.[84]

The closing words of canon 628, 1°, "salvo praescripto can. 239, §1, n. 19," compel the recognition of a privilege granted to cardinals. All cardinals from the time of their promotion in Consistory have the privilege of disposing of the revenues of their benefices by means of a last will and testament, with the excep-

---

[81] Augustine, *Religious and Laymen,* p. 283; Vermeersch-Creusen, *Epitome,* I, n. 736; Prümmer, *Manuale,* Q. 249, n. 3, b.

[82] Augustine, *op. cit.,* p. 359; Schaefer, *De Religiosis,* n. 494, a, note 26; Prümmer, *loc. cit.*; Claeys Bouuaert-Simenon, *Manuale Juris Canonici,* I, n. 682, II, 1; Wernz-Vidal, *De Religiosis,* n. 413, III; Toso, *Commentaria Minora,* V, p. 217, n. 1; Blat, *Ius De Religiosis,* n. 603, b; Eichmann, *Lehrbuch des Kirchenrechts,* §97, n. 3, b; Pejška, *Jus Canonicum Religiosorum,* p. 180, n. 2, c.

[83] In pre-Code law it had been argued that a titular bishop, not having any church for which he could acquire the ownership of temporal goods, was bound instead to devote such goods entirely to pious works.—Cf. A. D., "Religiosi ad Eccl. Dignitatem Promoti," *CpRM,* XIX (1938), 182–183, nn. 21, 22.

[84] Berutti, *De Religiosis,* n. 140, A, b; Prümmer, *Manuale,* Q. 249, n. 3, b; Coronata, *Institutiones Iuris Canonici,* I, n. 634, 2°, a.

tions mentioned in canon 1298.[85] Any regular, therefore, who is created a cardinal, whether he be a residential bishop at the same time, or not even a bishop, from the moment of his promotion in the consistory has the right to dispose freely of the revenues derived from his benefices, even by means of a last will, to the exclusion however of the sacred furnishings whose use has been permanently devoted to divine worship.[86]

Hence, cardinals regular can freely dispose also by will of the revenues deriving from their benefices, but of these alone, since a like freedom is not accorded with reference to the sacred furnishings. If the cardinal regular is a residential bishop, the beneficiary revenues would certainly comprise the funds which serve for the upkeep of his table. Other revenues falling due to him personally through the performance of some other office or duty, such as that of the Prefect of a Congregation, etc., would be included under the beneficiary revenues.[87]

Goyeneche on this point is more generous, since he extends the concept of beneficiary revenues to other temporal goods not strictly of the benefice, such as donations, legacies, etc.[88] However, Fanfani affirms, and rightly in the opinion of the writer, that cardinals regular cannot dispose freely by means of a last will of all the temporal goods that accrue to them, since canon 239, §1, 19°, expressly limits that privilege of the cardinals with relation to strictly beneficiary revenues. Therefore, according to canon 628, 1°, the temporal goods which do not derive from the benefice must pass over to the diocese, or to the vicariate or prefecture apostolic; or if the cardinals regular are not residential bishops, or vicars and prefects apostolic, then the goods belong to the Order or to the Holy See.[89] The cardinal regular has no power to dispose of

[85] Canon 239—§1. "Praeter alia privilegia quae in hoc Codice suis in titulis enumerantur, Cardinales omnes a sua promotione in Consistorio facultate gaudent:

19°. De reditibus beneficiariis libere disponendi etiam per testamentum, salvo praescripto can. 1298." Cf. Hynes, *The Privileges of Cardinals*, p. 143 ss.

[86] Cf. Berutti, *loc. cit.*; Fanfani, *De Iure Religiosorum*, n. 469, 3°.

[87] Schaefer, *De Religiosis*, n. 494, a; Goyeneche, *De Religiosis*, n. 89.

[88] *Loc. cit.*

[89] Fanfani, *op. cit.*, n. 469: *Dubium*.

temporal goods or revenues which are not proceeds of the benefice.

There are special regulations regarding the sacred furnishings of cardinals, which regulations hold also for cardinals regular. Thus the sacred furnishings and all other appurtenances permanently devoted to divine worship which were possessed by a deceased cardinal who had his domicile in the City of Rome become the property of the papal sacristy, unless the cardinal had donated or bequeathed his appurtenances to some church, public oratory, pious place, or to an ecclesiastical or religious person during his lifetime; the sole exceptions with reference to these sacred furnishings are the rings and the pectoral crosses, also when they contain sacred relics. The cardinal, if he uses the faculty to donate or will the sacred furnishings, should leave at least a part of them to the churches in which he exercised the claim of title or administration, or also the right of commendam.[90]

If, however, the deceased cardinal regular was a residential bishop, then the sacred furnishings accrue to his cathedral church, with the exception again of his rings and pectoral crosses, including those which contain relics (except for the provision of canon 1288), and of all the sacred furnishings of any kind regarding which it is established that they were acquired by the deceased bishop with other than the funds of the cathedral church, and that they have not been turned over to the proprietorship of the cathedral church.[91]

Finally, regulars who are cardinals or residential bishops, or abbots or prelates *nullius*, as well as regulars in other dignities outside the religious Order, have the obligation to take care that through a last will, or by means of some other document drawn up in a form recognized by civil law, the provisions of canons 628, 1°, 1298, §1, and 1299, §1, may have effect also in civil courts.[92]

As has been seen, the rings and pectoral crosses, also those which contain sacred relics, are excepted from the rule of seizure by the pontifical sacristy (canon 1298, §1); exception is likewise

---

[90] Canon 1298, §§1 and 2.

[91] Canon 1299, §1. Cf. Berutti, *De Religiosis*, n. 140, A, b; Vermeersch-Creusen, *Epitome*, I, n. 787, 2, b; Regatillo, *Institutiones Iuris Canonici*, I, n. 749; Hynes, *The Privileges of Cardinals*, p. 146.

[92] Canon 1301, §1. Cf. Berutti, *loc. cit.*

made for them in canon 1299, §1. Canon 1288 prescribes that any relics of the Holy Cross which the bishop may carry in his pectoral cross become the property of the cathedral church at his death, and are later to be transmitted to the successor. If the government of several dioceses had been entrusted to the deceased bishop, the cathedral church is determined according to the latter part of canon 1288.[93] The rings and pectoral crosses, then, are to be given to the successor by the diocese if the cardinal regular was a residential bishop, or if the dignitary regular was a residential bishop, or a vicar or a prefect apostolic. If, on the other hand he was merely a titular bishop, the rings and the pectoral crosses belong to the Order or to the Holy See, as the case may be.[94]

What is to be understood by these sacred furnishings which have been permanently devoted to use in divine worship? They are the following: Mitres, copes, tunics, other vestments; chalices, patens, gold and silver vases, and other utensils, especially those blessed or consecrated for use in the private chapels of cardinals, no matter by what name they are called. Also included in the term *sacra supellex* are the sandals, altar cloths, albs and cinctures, pyxes, ostensoria, holy water fonts, aspergils, receptacles for the holy oils, pastoral staffs, faldstools, etc.[95] All these items here enumerated are not at the free disposal of the cardinal regular, and hence must be bestowed according to the prescriptions of canons 1298 and 1299.

Regulars in the dignitary status cannot make a will, since they do not obtain the dominion or ownership of temporalities acquired after their promotion. It is true that the right to dispose freely even by means of a will is vindicated for cardinals regular, but only with respect to strictly beneficiary revenues. Outside of the revenues of the benefice, with reference to which cardinals are espe-

---

[93] Canon 1288. "Sanctissimae Crucis reliquiae, quas in cruce pectorali Episcopus forte defert, ecclesiae cathedrali, ipso defuncto, cedunt, Episcopo successori transmittendae; et si defunctus pluribus praefuerit dioecesibus, ecclesiae cathedrali dioecesis, in cuius territorio supremum diem obiit aut, si extra dioecesim mortuus est, ex qua ultimo discessit." Cf. Berutti, *op. cit.*, n. 140, A, b, note 4.

[94] A. D., "Religiosi ad Eccl. Dignitatem Promoti," *CpRM*, XIX (1938), 186, n. 23.

[95] Cf. A. D., "art. cit.," *CpRM*, XIX (1938), 185, n. 23.

cially privileged, cardinals regular are incapacitated from making a will as are other dignitaries regular. Therefore the diocese, the vicariate or the prefecture apostolic, and the abbacy or prelacy *nullius* has the right to succeed to and to lay claim to all the temporal goods which have accrued to regulars after they have become residential bishops, vicars or prefects apostolic, abbots or prelates *nullius*. Similarly, the Order or the Holy See may claim all the property of regulars who were cardinals, not residential bishops at the same time, or titular bishops, nuncios, and other legates, after their demise. These dignitaries regular have only the administration, the use and usufruct of the temporal goods that fall to them after their promotion, as has been seen. The administration and the enjoyment of the use and usufruct ceases at their death, and therefore they cannot dispose of temporal goods by will; the goods were never their own, and thus must revert to the respective owners.[96]

Canon 537 does not permit donations from the goods of a house, a province or a religious institute except as an alms or for some other just cause, and with the permission of the superior. Usually the constitutions of religious institutes have detailed regulations on this matter.[97] This prohibition affects the single religious of the Order or congregation, the superiors and the chapter.[98] But this canon does not directly bear upon regulars who have been elevated to an ecclesiastical dignity outside the Order. Though they remain religious, nevertheless they are not in the institute as subjects. As a result they cannot in any way touch the goods of the province, of the house, or of the institute.[99]

Yet it may be asked: Are regulars who are in possession of an ecclesiastical dignity empowered to give donations? It appears that they are not, for a donation imports the transfer of goods to another without implying any benefit to the donor.[100] For such a

---

[96] Coronata, *Institutiones Iuris Canonici*, I, n. 634, 2°, a; Augustine, *Religious and Laymen*, p. 359; Blat, *Ius De Religiosis*, n. 603, b.

[97] Canon 537. "Largitiones ex bonis domus, provinciae, religionis non permittuntur, nisi ratione eleemosynae vel alia iusta de causa, de venia Superioris et ad normam constitutionum."

[98] Cf. Coronata, *op. cit.*, I, n. 560, 3°.

[99] Cf. Schaefer, *De Religiosis*, n. 211.

[100] Cf. Woywod, *A Practical Commentary*, I, n. 424.

transfer the donor must possess free and absolute ownership, which is lacking for dignitaries regular according to the provisions of canon 628, 1°, as discussed above. However, it may be said that they have the right to give donations from the temporal goods which accrue to them personally, and which are subject to their administration and enjoyment, as alms or for any other worthy and reasonable causes. Such donations would perhaps be in the interests of good administration; at least they could be reckoned as part of the proper use of the temporal goods, especially when there is question of the giving of alms, or when other just causes such as the considerations of equitable remuneration, of piety and of Christian charity warrant such a procedure.[101] Naturally, the spirit of poverty must guide the dignitary regular; in the use of goods he is bound by the vow.

Since religious in the dignitary status remain bound by their vows, attention must be directed to the effects of the solemn vows as obliging the dignitary regular. Undoubtedly canon 628, 1°, introduces some modifications of the solemn vow of poverty as affecting regulars in the dignitary state. But since the solemn vow is in force, it follows that the dignitary regular must observe the regulations of canon 628, 1°, in virtue of this vow. Thus, contrary acts would be rendered invalid in consequence of the solemn profession.[102]

Particularly is this true in regard to contracts if the dignitary regular would presume to make a contract in his own name and with the intentions of ownership. It would be null and void in the ecclesiastical forum. Complications may arise in the civil forum here in our country, inasmuch as the civil law as such does not recognize the rules of the Code as to the invalidating effects of the solemn vow of poverty.[103] In such a case natural justice demands

[101] As an argument *a pari:* Canon 1535. "Praelati et rectores de bonis mobilibus suarum ecclesiarum donationes, praeterquam parvas et modicas secundum legitimam loci consuetudinem, facere ne praesumant, nisi iusta interveniente causa remunerationis aut pietatis aut christianae caritatis; secus donatio a successoribus revocari poterit."

[102] Canon 579. Cf. A. D., "Religiosi ad Eccl. Dignitatem Promoti," *CpRM,* XIX (1938), 183, n. 22.

[103] A parallel canon is canon 536, §3. "Si contraxerit religiosus sine ulla Superiorum licentia, ipsemet respondere debet, non autem religio vel provincia, vel domus." Cf. Woywod, *A Practical Commentary,* I, n. 422.

that, if possible, the regular return what he received as a result of the illegally executed deal or contract. Both parties, therefore, are placed in the same condition as before the invalid contract. However, from canon 536 it is clear that contracts entered into by regulars are valid if this is done through an implied or express agency.

A regular, then, in the dignitary status differs from simple regulars in only two points. Dignitaries regular are the administrators of all temporal goods that accrue to them after their promotion, and also the dispensers of their usufruct, which is not the case for ordinary religious after their solemn profession. Dignitaries regular have moreover the use and usufruct of all property coming to them personally during their incumbency in the dignitary state outside the Order, and this for their own benefit in all reasonable matters according to the spirit of poverty. This prerogative likewise is withheld from the ordinary regulars.[104] Both the dignitary regular and the ordinary regular have lost the dominion over temporal goods by their solemn profession. The difference which exists is to be found in the fact that regulars who are residential bishops, or vicars and prefects apostolic, or abbots and prelates *nullius*, acquire the ownership for the respective territories which they govern, rather than for their Order or the Holy See.

B. RELIGIOUS OF SIMPLE PROFESSION (CANON 628, 2°)

Canon 628. *Religiosus ad dignitatem episcopalem vel aliam extra propriam religionem evectus:*

2°. Si per professionem dominium bonorum non amiserit, bonorum quae habebat, recuperat usum, usumfructum et administrationem; quae postea ipsi obveniant, sibi plene acquirit.

A religious who has been raised to the episcopal or any other dignity outside his religious institute:

2. If by his profession he has not lost the ownership of property, regains the use, usufruct and administration of whatever property he owned; what falls to him after his promotion, he acquires for himself absolutely.

---

104 A. D., "Religiosi ad Eccl. Dignitatem Promoti," *CpRM*, XIX (1938), 184, n. 22.

The second section of canon 628 in its opening words indicates that religious of simple profession are there considered, for religious with simple vows do not lose the right of owning property; they retain the radical dominion of temporal goods and the capacity to acquire additional property even after their profession.[105] As a rule this occurs in religious congregations, which term designates an institute whose members make their profession with simple vows.[106] However, it could happen that the same is verified in some Order in which possibly through a special indult individual regulars are allowed to keep the ownership of temporal goods; individual religious also may obtain such an indult.[107] These latter cases exist rather by way of exception, but must be understood to be included in the prescripts of canon 628, 2°, which concern dignitaries religious with simple vows, temporary or perpetual.[108]

Canon 628, 2°, deals with religious of simple profession, temporary or perpetual, who have been advanced to the episcopal or any other dignity outside their congregation. As in the foregoing section, here a twofold derogation from the common law on religious is found.[109]

1. Dignitaries religious of simple vows have the right to the use, usufruct, and the administration not only of the temporal goods that accrue to them after their promotion, but also of the goods in their dominion, whose administration had been ceded to another, and regarding whose use and usufruct a free disposition had been made before profession (canon 569, §§1 and 2).

The promotion to the dignitary status automatically re-establishes

---

[105] Canon 580—§1. "Quilibet professus a votis simplicibus, sive perpetuis sive temporariis, nisi aliud in constitutionibus cautum sit, conservat proprietatem bonorum suorum et capacitatem alia bona acquirendi, salvis quae in can. 569 praescripta sunt." Cf. Woywod, *A Practical Commentrary*,. I, n. 541.

[106] Canon 488. "In canonibus qui sequuntur, veniunt nomine:
2°. . . . *Congregationis religiosae* vel *Congregationis* simpliciter, religio in qua vota dumtaxat simplicia sive perpetua sive temporaria emittuntur."

[107] Schaefer, *De Religiosis*, n. 194, b, note 27; Coronata, *Institutiones Iuris Canonici*, I, n. 634, 2°, b.

[108] Toso, *Commentaria Minora*, V, p. 217, n. 2.

[109] Berutti, *De Religiosis*, n. 140, B.

the rights of administration, use and usufruct for the religious personally.[110] Though a religious as a member of a congregation still holds the radical ownership of property and can acquire additional items of property in his own name, he is not permitted to involve himself in temporal affairs, such as administration and the enjoyment of the use and usufruct of his temporal goods would imply. Hence, the rule of canon 569, §1, which requires the cession of the administration for the whole period of the obligation of the simple vows, and the disposal of the use and usufruct of these temporal goods to another person at the free choice of the religious.

Canon 569, §2, covers other eventualities. If, when such a cession was not made, property should subsequently fall into the possession of the religious with simple vows, or if after the cession the religious became owner of other property under any title, he must then, even though there has preceded the profession with simple vows, provide according to the first paragraph of this canon for the newly obtained property.[111] However, when a religious of simple vows attains the episcopal or cardinalitial dignity, or any other dignity outside the congregation, he regains the administration, use and usufruct of his own property. Canon 628, 2°, accords this to him automatically upon his promotion, since his new status withdraws him from association with the institute as one of its subjects.[112] Therefore such dignitary religious have full title and control of the property which they possessed before profession.[113]

2. Religious of simple profession in the dignitary state acquire with full right whatever they receive personally.

This prescript is a derogation from the rule of canon 580, §2:[114] Whatever the religious, while in the congregation, acquires by per-

[110] Berutti, *op. cit.,* n. 140, B, a; Schaefer, *De Religiosis,* n. 494, b, note 29; Toso, *loc. cit.*; Blat, *Ius De Religiosis,* n. 603, a.

[111] Canon 569—§2. "Ea cessio ac dispositio, si praetermissa fuerit ob defectum bonorum et haec postea supervenerint, aut si facta fuerit et postea alia bona quovis titulo obvenerint, fiat aut iteretur secundum normas §1 statutas, non obstante simplici professione emissa."

[112] Cf. Eichmann, *Lehrbuch des Kirchenrechts,* §97, n. 3, b.

[113] Woywod, *A Practical Commentary,* I, n. 541.

[114] Berutti, *De Religiosis,* n. 140, B, b.

sonal labor or in relation to his institute belongs to the institute.[115] In the dignitary status, however, everything that the religious gains personally or as a remuneration for his own labors belongs to him; thereby he has full title and control of all temporal goods which he gains after his promotion.[116]

Accordingly, since the religious dignitary has not only the administration, but also the dominion over all temporal goods, it follows that he can dispose of his property by means of a will.[117] Excluded from the free disposal by means of a will are indeed any temporal goods that fall to him for other purposes (canon 628, 3°). As long as these goods are his own, or have been given him personally,[118] or in recompense for his own labors after his promotion, they are his own property, to be disposed of at his pleasure.

The surplus revenues of a benefice are also excepted from the free disposal by a dignitary religious of simple vows; he is bound to spend the superfluous income for the benefit of the poor or for charitable causes, unless he is a cardinal.[119]

Canons 239, §1, 19° and 1298–1301, as explained above for cardinals regular, apply in the same manner to cardinals religious with simple vows. The latter canons (1298–1301) concerning sacred furnishings likewise refer to religious of simple profession if they are residential bishops, vicars or prefects apostolic, or prelates *nullius*.[120] Since a cardinal religious of simple vows is not restricted in the disposal of his beneficiary revenues even by means of a last will, it seems clear that he has the faculty to do the same in all other goods that come to him personally; they are his own.[121]

---

[115] Canon 580—§2. "Quidquid autem professus a votis simplicibus industria sua vel intuitu religionis acquirit, religioni acquirit."

[116] Schaefer, *De Religiosis*, n. 494, b, notes 30, 31; Blat, *Ius De Religiosis*, n. 603, b.

[117] Schaefer, *op. cit.*, n. 494, c.

[118] Toso, *Commentaria Minora*, V, p. 217, n. 2.

[119] Canon 1473. "Etsi beneficiarius alia bona non beneficialia habeat, libere uti frui potest fructibus beneficialibus qui ad eius honestam sustentationem sint necessarii; obligatione autem tenetur impendendi superfluos pro pauperibus aut piis causis, salvo praescripto can. 239, §1, n. 19."

[120] *Supra*, pp. 106-109. Cf. Berutti, *De Religiosis*, n. 140, B, b; Schaefer, *De Religiosis*, n. 494, b, note 30; Goyeneche, *De Religiosis*, n. 89.

[121] Cf. Fanfani, *De Iure Religiosorum*, n. 469: *Dubium*.

Another logical inference from the fact that a dignitary religious with simple vows has full title and unlimited control of all the temporal goods which he possessed and owned before his profession, as also those which he gains after his promotion to a dignity, is this: He can sell, donate, or alienate them in any licit way, or enter into lawful contractual agreements regarding them. The ownership as well as the administration and use rests with him; therefore he may transfer his goods to another without the need of a previous permission from anyone.[122]

Acts contrary to the simple vows, i.e., acts prohibited for the reason that they are opposed to the observance of the vows, have no nullifying sanction attached; canon 579 merely states that simple profession renders acts contrary to the vows illicit, but not invalid.[123] Now, despite the relaxations granted by canon 628, 2°, in the matters pertaining to the vow of poverty, the dignitary religious of simple profession is still obliged and bound by the vow of poverty (canon 627, §1). Therefore, if he performs acts contrary to what is allowed him in his dignitary status, then the effect of unlawfulness touches upon those acts.[124]

In short, it is quite evident that the chief juridic effects of the vow of poverty cease for religious of simple profession in the dignitary state. They possess full and unlimited dominion over their temporal goods and are absolved from the precepts of seeking permission from superiors and of fulfilling other requirements with respect to the vow of poverty as determined in the rule or the constitutions. In this objective view of poverty the religious dignitary does not differ from secular dignitaries. But in the subjective view, i.e., in the personal use of the temporal goods, the religious dignitary is bound by his vow of poverty. Hence in the use of his temporal goods he must exclude luxuries and superfluous expenses which would be sins against the vow. In other words, before God and in conscience the moral effects of the vow

---

122 Cappello, *Summa Iuris,* II, n. 63, 3, 2°; Coronata, *Institutiones Iuris Canonici,* I, n. 634, 2°, b.

Cf. canon 536.

123 Cf. Augustine, *Religious and Laymen,* pp. 272, 273.

124 Cf. A. D., "Religiosi ad Eccl. Dignitatem Promoti," *CpRM,* XIX (1938), 187, n. 25.

of poverty remain for the religious with simple vows who has been advanced to the episcopal, the cardinalitial, or any other dignity outside the congregation.[125]

C. BOTH CLASSES OF RELIGIOUS (CANON 628, 3°)

Canon 628. *Religiosus ad dignitatem episcopalem vel aliam extra propriam religionem evectus*:

3°. *In utroque autem casu de bonis, quae ipsi obveniunt non intuitu personae, debet disponere secundum offerentium voluntatem.*

A religious who has been raised to the episcopal or any other dignity outside his religious institute:

3. In both cases [under n. 1 and n. 2] must, in accordance with the will of the donors, dispose of those goods which fall to him in some other way than in consideration of his own person.

Canon 628, 3°, refers to the two foregoing sections of the same canon. Accordingly, both religious with solemn profession and religious with simple profession of vows who have been promoted to a dignity are obligated by the rule here expressed.[126] The rule demands that they use all donations and dispose of all goods according to the intention of the donors when these proffered goods have not been intended for the person of these religious, or when they have been offered without being marked as a recompense for their labors.[127]

The reason why the religious dignitary cannot dispose of these goods arbitrarily is this: The goods or donations thus received by the dignitary for religious or charitable purposes according to the will of the donors fall to him as an administrator of Church property. In fact, by accepting them he enters into a quasi-con-

[125] A. D., "art. cit.," *CpRM, loc. cit.*; Pejška, *Jus Canonicum Religiosorum*, p. 180, n. 2, c; Augustine, *op. cit.*, p. 359; Jansen, *Ordensrecht*, p. 204, n. 2; Prümmer, *Manuale*, Q. 249, n. 3, a and c; Schaefer, *De Religiosis*, n. 494, b.

[126] Augustine, *Religious and Laymen*, p. 359, n. 3; Schaefer, *De Religiosis*, n. 494, c.

[127] Schaefer, *op. cit.*, n. 494, c, note 32; Toso, *Commentaria Minora*, V, p. 217, nn. 1, 2.

tract with the donors to the effect that their intentions will be fulfilled faithfully.[128] Therefore, as administrator he must abide by the wishes of the donors. The safeguarding of the defined purposes for which the donations were given could even necessitate the making of a will to that effect on the part of the dignitary religious.[129]

In a similar manner the goods or revenues which are strictly beneficiary must be expended according to the norm of canon 1473: All beneficiaries may use the revenues and the goods belonging to the benefice for their proper maintenance, but they are obliged to devote the superfluous beneficial income for the benefit of the poor or for charitable causes, with the sole exception of cardinals. On this account some authors classify the provision of this canon under canon 628, 3°.[130]

---

[128] Prümmer, *Manuale,* Q. 249, n. 3, c; Woywod, *A Practical Commentary,* I, n. 541; Schaefer, *op. cit.,* n. 494, c; Blat, *Ius De Religiosis,* n. 603.

[129] Berutti, *De Religiosis,* n. 140, C.

[130] Fanfani, *De Iure Religiosorum,* n. 469, 3°; Regatillo, *Institutiones Iuris Canonici,* I, n. 749.

CHAPTER VI

OBLIGATION OF RETAINING THE PROPER RELIGIOUS HABIT

The Code has no explicit legislation on the obligation of dignitaries religious to wear the religious habit. However, implicitly this is included under canon 627, §1: Religious who are proclaimed cardinals or appointed bishops, residential or titular, remain religious, bound to their vows and the other obligations of their state, particularly the rule and the constitutions. Certainly, one of the prescriptions of the rule and the constitutions is the wearing of the religious garb, and in some cases the wearing of a special tonsure, as a distinctive mark proper to the particular institute. Furthermore, that bond which arose between the religious and the institute at his profession is not disrupted by the promotion to the episcopal or cardinalitial dignity.[1]

As an external sign of this permanent union the religious is charged to continue the wearing of the religious garb and tonsure, which obligation he assumed at his entrance into the religious state, even though he is now in the dignitary state, in all cases wherein the wearing of such a special habit or tonsure is of obligation in his own Order or congregation.[2] This is true especially of cardinals and bishops religious, since canon 627, §1, from which the obligation of the dignitary religious to wear the religious habit during his incumbency in the dignitary status is deduced, speaks exclusively of them.[3]

In pre-Code law express legislation demanded that bishops or cardinals regular wear their woolen religious habit with its proper color, and the tonsure proper to the Order.[4]

---

[1] *Supra,* pp. 88-90.

[2] Fanfani, *De Iure Religiosorum,* n. 467; Beste, *Introductio in Codicem,* p. 425; Wernz-Vidal, *De Religiosis,* n. 413, II.

[3] Coronata extends the legislation of canon 627, §1, to religious in other dignities.—*Institutiones Iuris Canonici,* I, n. 634, 2°, a, note 7.

[4] Benedictus XIII, Const. "*Custodes,*" 7 mart. 1726—*Fontes,* n. 291; c. 15, X, *de vita et honestate clericorum,* III, 1.—*Supra,* pp. 48-49, 16.

Pope Benedict XV (1914–1922) confirmed the old law in his Motu Proprio "*Episcopis*," of April 25, 1920, whereby he permitted bishops regular from monastic or Mendicant Orders to wear the rochet. Practically bishops regular are vested the same as bishops secular, with the exception of the color and quality of their religious habit. Therefore, by the retention of the latter restriction Pope Benedict fully adopted the former legislation which had decreed this as the customary rule for bishops regular.[5]

Quite a number of the modern authors point back to the former law as the basis for the present-day discipline concerning the obligation of wearing the religious habit on the part of bishops and cardinals religious.[6]

In addition, it must be recalled that all patriarchs, archbishops and bishops had been granted the use of the violet zucchetto and biretta, instead of the black.[7] Religious, of course, when they hold these dignities are afforded the same privileges.[8]

---

[5] Motu Proprio "*Episcopis*," 25 apri. 1920: "Episcopis e regularibus Ordinibus, monachorum scilicet et mendicantium, consuevit Apostolica Sedes postulantibus concedere *rocheti* gestandi facultatem. Nobis autem, occasione sacrorum solemnium, quae appetunt, ob duplicem Canonizationem, placet, uniformitatis quoque gratia, omnes Venerabiles Fratres huius facultatis compotes facere. Quare motu proprio in perpetuum statuimus, ut omnes Episcopi regulares iam nunc rocheto utantur, atque eodem prorsus modo induti incedant ac saeculares Episcopi, salvo nimirum usitato vestimentorum colore et qualitate. Itaque, praeter casus in quibus, iuxta Caeremoniale Episcoporum et Decreta, mozzeta tantum super rocheto, aut mozzeta cum mantelleto gestari debet aut potest, alias, uti omnes Episcopi, semper in hac alma Urbe mantelletum tantum super rocheto gerant: non obstantibus Constitutionibus Apostolicis, ceterisque quamvis speciali mentione dignis, in contrarium facientibus quibuslibet."—*Acta Apostolicae Sedis, Commentarium Officiale* (Romae, 1909–1929; Civitate Vaticana, 1929—), XII (1920), 149 (hereafter cited *AAS*).

[6] Berutti, *De Religiosis,* n. 139, II; Blat, *Ius De Religiosis,* n. 601; Pejška, *Jus Canonicum Religiosorum,* p. 181, n. 2, e; Oesterle, *Praelectiones Iuris Canonici,* I, p. 354; Schaefer, *De Religiosis,* n. 495, note 38; Fanfani, *De Iure Religiosorum,* n. 467; Beste, *Introductio in Codicem,* p. 425; Wernz-Vidal, *De Religiosis,* n. 413, II.

[7] Pius IX, litt. ap., "*Ecclesiarum,*" 17 iunii 1867—*Fontes,* n. 545; Leo XIII, litt. ap., "*Praeclaro,*" 3 febr. 1888—*Fontes,* n. 597. *Supra,* pp. 49-50.

[8] Sipos, *Enchiridion Iuris Canonici,* §73, n. 2, f; Pejška, *loc. cit.*; Schaefer, *loc. cit.*; Vermeersch-Creusen, *Epitome,* I, n. 787, 1; Prümmer, *Manuale,* Q. 249, n. 4; Beste, *loc. cit.*; Wernz-Vidal, *loc. cit.*

Besides establishing the general norm that bishops regular from monastic or Mendicant Orders must keep the woolen habit with its own color, Pope Benedict XV permitted them the use of the rochet instead of the surplice.[9] But thereby not every distinction between the dress of bishops regular and other bishops vanished, for the Pope explicitly desired that the usual norm about the color and quality of dress be preserved by regulars.[10] The Motu Proprio refers explicitly to regulars of monastic or Mendicant Orders who have become bishops; to them as to other bishops is granted the right of using the rochet.[11] All other bishops religious, whether or not they were regulars, had the use of the rochet as allowed them by the *Ceremoniale Episcoporum* (Lib. I, c. III, n. 4); therefore the need of the specific mention of bishops regular from the ranks of a monastic or Mendicant Order is apparent.[12] In regard to the use of the rochet all bishops regular obviously are now on equal standing with bishops secular. This the Pope specifically indicated, for the permission was given for the sake of uniformity in dress among bishops.[13] For the future, then, bishops without distinction, religious or secular, regulars or non-regulars, can wear the rochet.[14]

The concession of Pope Benedict XV derogated from the prior regulation according to which the use of the rochet had been interdicted for bishops regular of monastic or Mendicant Orders:

Ceremoniale Episcoporum (Lib. I, c. I, n. 4; c. III, n. 4);
Pontificale Romanum (*Rubrica*, Pars Prima, *De Confirmandis*);
Missale Romanum (*Ritus servandus in celebratione Missae*, tit. I, n. 2);

---

[9] Cf. Schaefer, *De Religiosis*, n. 495, note 39.

[10] Pauwels, "Motu Proprio '*Episcopis*': Annotationes," *Periodica de Religiosis et Missionariis* (Brugis, 1905–1919; from 1920: *Periodica de Re Canonica et Morali utilia praesertim Religiosis et Missionariis*, Brugis, 1920–1927; from 1927: *Periodica de Re Morali, Canonica, Liturgica*, Brugis: 1927–1936, et Romae: 1937—), X (1922), 142–143, on p. 143 (hereafter cited simply as *Periodica*).

[11] Garcia, "Annotationes," *CpR*, II (1921), 102–104, on p. 103, n. III; Oesterle, *Praelectiones Iuris Canonici*, I, 354.

[12] Garcia, *loc. cit.*; Schaefer, *De Religiosis*, n. 495.

[13] Garcia, *ibid.*, p. 102, nn. I and II.

[14] Garcia, *ibid.*, p. 103, n. V; Schaefer, *loc. cit.*

Rituale Romanum (Tit. II, c. 6, n. 3);
Collectio C. S. Rituum (Decr. 1131, §9).

Hence, the Motu Proprio "*Episcopis*" of April 25, 1920, as the last phrase confirms, must be understood as amending the rules on the use of the rochet which had appeared before that time.[15]

The dispositions of the various legal enactments discussed above concerning the retention of the religious habit center mostly about regulars who have been elevated to the dignitary status of a bishop or a cardinal. Nevertheless, the identical reasons indicating that religious in the episcopal or the cardinalitial state remain religious, as well as those revealing the existence of the bond uniting the dignitaries religious to their own institutes—from which the obligation of wearing the religious habit is deduced in the present law—are as true of religious with simple vows as of regulars. On that account it seems admissible to insist that religious of simple vows are obliged in the same manner as regulars to retain the color and quality of their religious garb in the episcopal or also in the cardinalitial dignity, if their institute requires the wearing of a distinctive habit.

Provided, then, that the Order or the congregation have a special habit as its characteristic mark, or perhaps a special tonsure, members of these Orders or congregations when promoted to the episcopacy or the cardinalate are under obligation *sub gravi* to retain both.[16] With respect to the habit, the proper color, or one similar to it, and also the woolen quality must be retained. In form and cut the habit may be patterned on that used by secular prelates in these same dignities, but religious must abstain from the use of silken material.[17] Canons or clerics regular, and religious

[15] Garcia, *ibid.*, p. 103, n. II; Schaefer, *loc. cit.*; Pauwels, "Motu Proprio '*Episcopis*': Annotationes," *Periodica,* X (1922), 142, 143.

[16] Cf. A. D., "Religiosi ad Eccl. Dignitatem Promoti," *CpRM,* XIX (1938), 190, n. 27, c.

[17] Oesterle, *Praelectiones Iuris Canonici,* I, 354; Augustine, *Religious and Laymen,* p. 358; Sipos, *Enchiridion Iuris Canonici,* §73, n. 2, f; Prümmer, *Manuale,* Q. 249, n. 4; Schaefer, *De Religiosis,* n. 495; Coronata, *Institutiones Iuris Canonici,* I, n. 634, 1°; Cappello, *Summa Iuris,* II, n. 63, 2; Beste, *Introductio in Codicem,* p. 425.

who are especially privileged, dress like bishops or cardinals secular, with the sole exception of silken robes.[18]

As noted above, bishops religious have the right of wearing the violet biretta and zucchetto, and the rochet. Cardinals in virtue of canon 234 have the use of the red biretta, and abbots and prelates *nullius* in virtue of canon 325 have the use of the pontifical insignia and the violet zucchetto.[19] Certainly cardinals religious, besides the red biretta, obtain also the other insignia proper to the cardinalate, namely, the cardinal's hat, and the red skull-cap. In the rest of their apparel, of course, they retain the color of their religious habit.[20]

Canon 627, §1, then, in its statement that a religious who is proclaimed a cardinal or a bishop, whether residential or titular, remains a religious and remains bound also to his vows and the other obligations of his profession is even outwardly sustained, since the dignitary religious must wear his distinctive religious habit, at least in regard to its color and quality. Thereby also the law in canon 596, which requires that religious wear the habit proper to their institute at all times except for legitimate exemptions is maintained, as far as possible, in the case of cardinals or bishops religious.[21]

---

[18] Vermeersch-Creusen, *Epitome,* I, n. 787, 1, Beste, *loc. cit.*; Oesterle, *loc. cit.*; A. D., "art. cit.," *CpRM,* XIX (1938), 190, n. 28; Augustine, *loc. cit.* The Holy See may of course concede, and in fact has conceded, special permission to religious to wear the usual episcopal dress.—Augustine, *op. cit.,* p. 358, note 11.

[19] Canon 234. "Promotus absens a Curia debet in recipiendo bireto rubro iurare se intra 'annum, nisi legitimo detineatur impedimento, Summum Pontificem aditurum."

Canon 325. "Abbas vel Praelatus *nullius,* licet charactere episcopali careat, utitur tamen in proprio territorio insignibus pontificalibus cum throno ac baldachino et iure ibidem officia divina pontificali ritu celebrandi; crucem autem pectoralem, annulum cum gemma, ac pileolum violaceum potest etiam extra territorium deferre." Cf. Schaefer, *loc. cit.*; Hynes, *The Privileges of Cardinals,* p. 24.

[20] Cf. Nainfa, *Costume of Prelates of the Catholic Church* (New and revised edition, Baltimore: John Murphy Co., 1926), p. 20.

[21] Canon 596. "Religiosi omnes proprium suae religionis habitum deferant tum intra tum extra domum, nisi gravis causa excuset, iudicio Superioris maioris aut, urgente necessitate, etiam localis." Garcia, "Annotationes," *CpR,* II (1921), 103, n. VI; Schaefer, *De Religiosis,* n. 495, note 40.

Particularly by retaining the color proper to their religious habit these dignitaries religious evidence the especial insignia of their Order or congregation, acknowledge the lasting union existent between them and profess the religious obligations deriving therefrom. By retaining the quality of the habit instead of adopting the silken robes of the dignitary status they make public avowal of religious poverty as obligatory even in the dignitary state.[22]

It is quite apparent that the use of the violet skull-cap (zucchetto) and biretta are privileges granted to all bishops, religious or secular. Bishops religious promoted from monastic or Mendicant Orders have obtained besides the use of the rochet. In regard to bishops religious these privileges derogate from the obligation of retaining the religious habit in the dignitary status. All this prompts a question: Are religious in the episcopal dignity under obligation to make use of these privileges?

Canon 69 states that no one is obliged to make use of a privilege which has been granted him for his own private benefit, unless the obligation to exercise it comes from some other source.[23] The Code thus distinguishes between privileges which are granted to someone for private use merely and privileges which are granted because of some common cause on the part of the community or of a certain class to which someone belongs.[24]

Only the former place no obligation on the privileged person to make use of the privilege. However, the privileges of using the rochet, the violet zucchetto and biretta do not seem to be privileges accorded to bishops religious for their own private benefit. On the contrary they are granted to them in view of their dignity. They are a part of the dignitary office, for they form the external signs and marks which proclaim the dignitary rank of the episcopate.

---

[22] Garcia, *loc. cit.* Cf. Prümmer, *Manuale,* Q. 249, n. 4, note 1; Coronata, *Institutiones Iuris Canonici,* I, n. 634, 1°, note 4; Schaefer, *De Religiosis,* n. 495, note 42. Nainfa offers a description of the different costumes of prelates elevated from religious Orders, and the various parts of the dress as allowed regulars.—*Op. cit.,* pp. 18–20, 32, 43, 49, 53, 59, 77, 83, 96, 97, 119, 120, 124, 129, 186, 187.

[23] Canon 69. "Nemo cogitur uti privilegio in sui dumtaxat favorem concesso, nisi alio ex capite exsurgat obligatio."

[24] Vermeersch-Creusen, *Epitome,* I, n. 184, 1.

It is true that they are personal privileges, but they must be classed in the category of *commonly personal privileges,* i. e., granted to a physical person in view of his pertinence to a certain state, or his possession of a certain dignity.[25] Hence they are not individually personal in the sense that they are for the mere private benefit of bishops, whether religious or secular. Rather, they are personal in the sense that their use is legitimate wherever such bishops happen to be. Accordingly there seems to exist an obligation on the part of bishops religious to make use of these privileges of dress on this score: Pope Benedict XV expressly granted to bishops regular who were elevated from monastic or Mendicant Orders the privilege of wearing the rochet for the sake of obtaining uniformity in dress among bishops.[26] If bishops regular had thereafter not been obliged to make use of the rochet, then the evident purpose intended by the Pope could have remained unfulfilled. The same reason of uniformity in dress among bishops could be advanced with reference to the other privileges of dress, since they were granted to all bishops without distinction.

For these reasons the writer is inclined to state that religious in the episcopal or in any other dignity could not simply continue wearing the full garb of their religious institute. They seem to be obliged to make use of the privileges of dress which modify their religious habit, but which make it conform to the dress of other prelates in the same dignity. Thus they show their esteem for the insignia proper to the dignity as such, and hence they do not simply manifest the use of an option which connotes a recognition of the personal favor granted to them.

---

[25] Cf. Roelker, *Principles of Privilege*, pp. 31–32.

[26] *Supra*, p. 120.

CHAPTER VII

ABDICATION FROM THE DIGNITY OR OFFICE
(Canon 629)

Canon 629 treats in general of the juridic condition of religious who have given up for any reasons whatsoever an ecclesiastical dignity or office which they had held outside the religious institute. In its two paragraphs the canon imposes the obligation of returning to the religious institute, but it grants the privilege of a free selection of a religious house of the institute for residence to former cardinals religious and to bishops religious. However, when the selection has been made, these dignitaries religious are deprived of all right of active and passive participation in elections in the Order or the congregation.[1]

Article 1. The Obligation of Returning to the Proper Religious Institute (Canon 629, §1)

Canon 629—§1. *Dimisso cardinalatu vel episcopatu vel expleto munere extra religionem sibi a Sede Apostolica commisso, religiosus ad religionem redire tenetur.*

When a religious abdicates from the cardinalate or the episcopate, or has discharged the mission committed to him by the Holy See, he is bound to return to his religious institute.

Canon 629, §1, it is clear, concerns those religious who have given up the dignity of the cardinalate or the episcopal office, or have completed the tasks of the mission assigned to them by the Holy See, which they had outside the Order or congregation. They are charged with the obligation of returning to their own religious institute, since upon the dismissal of the dignity or of the office, or upon the discharge of the duties of the office, there remains nothing that would externally detain them from the return to the religious

[1] Toso, *Commentaria Minora,* V, p. 218, n. 1.

life which they had professed. Bishops, of course, retain their dignity in virtue of the indelible episcopal character, but they also are constrained to return to their institute, since they are now separated from the episcopal office with its attendant duties.[2]

There is no doubt that upon the intimation of their accepted resignation or of their effected dismissal bishops lose their dignitary office, but retain the episcopal dignity in virtue of the indelible episcopal character which they received at their consecration. However, cardinals are not marked with an indelible character in consequence of their creation in the cardinalitial dignity. Unlike bishops, cardinals when they give up their dignity for any reason seem to retain no vestige of their former dignity.

The cardinalitial dignity is founded on the intimate relationship with the Pope, whose counsellors and chief advisors cardinals are. For that reason cardinals are considered to constitute one body with the Pope, of which body the Pope is the head and the cardinals the members.[3] Once that intimate relationship in its nature of a union with the Pope is disrupted, it follows that the dignity itself is gone. The cardinalitial dignity may be lost in the same ways as any other ecclesiastical office.[4] Hence the cardinalitial dignity can be lost not only through death, but also in consequence of a renunciation,[5] a privation, a deposition, and a degradation.[6]

Canon 629, §1, states the condition requiring the return of the religious to his obedience in general, *dimisso cardinalatu vel episcopatu,* thus indicating that any form of dismissal of the cardi-

---

[2] Toso, *loc. cit.*

[3] Hynes, *The Privileges of Cardinals,* p. 5.

[4] The cardinalate is an ecclesiastical office in the strict sense of that term according to canon 145.—Cf. Hynes, *op. cit.,* p. 40.

Canon 183—§1. "Amittitur officium ecclesiasticum renuntiatione, privatione, amotione, translatione, lapsu temporis praefiniti."

[5] The renunciation or resignation must be accepted by the Pope.—Cf. canon 187.

[6] Cf. the following: Wernz-Vidal, *Ius Canonicum ad Codicis Normam Exactum* (Tomus II, *De Personis,* ed. 3., Romae: Aqud Aedes Universitatis Gregorianae, 1943), n. 479 (hereafter this volume is cited as *De Personis*); Coronata, *Institutiones Iuris Canonici,* I, n. 326; Beste, *Introductio in Codicem,* p. 236; Maroto, *Institutiones Iuris Canonici* (Tomus II, Roma-Matriti, 1919), n. 823; Sipos, *Enchiridion Iuris Canonici,* §39, n. 10; Oesterle, *Praelectiones Iuris Canonici,* I, 125.

nalate or of the episcopal office fulfills it. Hence, in the case of both offices, the canon comprehends resignation, renunciation, privation, deposition, degradation. But its sense, in the opinion of the writer, is applicable differently to the two offices involved. It seems to mean that the former cardinals religious thereby have, indeed, lost their dignity, since nothing of their office of being the principal counsellors and advisors of the Pope, and nothing of the dignity constituted by that intimate union with the Pope, is retained thereafter. On the other hand, bishops religious, residential or titular, after their abdication in any of the mentioned ways still retain the episcopal dignity as a result of the episcopal character which is indelible and can never be lost.

There are authors who in commenting on the legislation of canon 629 simply state as a fact that cardinals religious equally with bishops religious retain their dignity after their abdication.[7] This can readily be admitted for bishops religious, since they do retain the episcopal character, but not for cardinals religious or for dignitary religious in any other ecclesiastical offices. They possess no character which like that of the bishops is retained, and therefore the dignity itself appears to be relinquished with the abdication of their offices.[8] Probably cardinals religious could be permitted by the Pope after their resignation to keep the name of cardinal and the privileges of the cardinalate, but this would be conditioned on a special act of the Supreme Pontiff, and not at all deducible from the nature of the cardinalate.

Besides renunciation, privation, deposition and degradation, canon 629, §1, mentions also as a condition requiring the return of

---

[7] Sipos is thus in contradiction to his statement in a former section of his work (§39, n. 10) that cardinals lose the dignity when they resign or are deprived of the cardinalate.—*Enchiridion Iuris Canonici,* §73, n. 2, g; cf. also the following: Claeys Bouuaert-Simenon, *Manuale Juris Canonici,* I, n. 682, III; Prümmer, *Manuale,* Q. 249, n. 5; Cocchi, *Commentarium in Codicem,* IV, n. 125, c; Pejška, *Jus Canonicum Religiosorum,* p. 181, n. 3.

[8] Toso distinguishes between bishops and other dignitaries, for he admits that the episcopal dignity remains because of the episcopal character. He states: "Scilicet, munere vel dignitate deposita, nihil ex eis superest, nisi agatur de Episcopo, cuius dignitas, ob indelebilitatem characteris, integra manet, quamvis a munere episcopali separata."—*Commentaria Minora,* V, p. 218, n. 1.

the religious, *expleto munere,* with reference to other dignitary offices or missions. Thus, on the completion of his mission, the dignitary religious goes out of office and gives up his dignitary position inasmuch as his special tasks and duties as a legate of the Supreme Pontiff, or as an envoy of the Holy See, or as an administrator or prefect apostolic, have been discharged.[9] In all these instances the religious is bound to return to his proper institute.

In the earlier law the obligation of dignitary religious to return to the religious life was not quite as clear as it is today.[10] Thus, it was thought that if a religious resigned the episcopacy or was deposed from that office, he was not obliged to return to his institute, inasmuch as he retained his pre-eminence in virtue of the episcopal character; in fact, that by his episcopal appointment he had been freed from the observance of the rule of his religious organization; and that therefore there was no reason which could urge his return to the religious life. It was held, however, that if a religious resigned the cardinalate, provided that he was not a bishop, he was under obligation to return, since he retained nothing of his former dignity.[11] Pope Benedict XIII (1724-1730) in his Constitution "*Custodes*" (March 7, 1726) imposed a strict obligation even on bishops regular to return to the cloister.[12] Now the Code in canon 629, §1, places the obligation on all religious of solemn or simple vows, who have been bishops or cardinals, or have had some other dignity or office outside the religious institute.[13] This obligation could be deduced from the fact that religious, while in the dignitary status of the episcopate or the cardinalate, were bound to the ob-

---

[9] Blat, *Ius De Religiosis,* n. 605; Claeys Bouuaert-Simenon, *Manuale Juris Canonici,* I, n. 682, II; Schaefer, *De Religiosis,* n. 496, note 43; Augustine, *Religious and Laymen,* p. 360; Eichmann, *Lehrbuch des Kirchenrechts,* §97, n. 4; Goyeneche, *De Religiosis,* n. 90.

[10] A. D., "Religiosi ad Eccl. Dignitatem Promoti," *CpRM,* XIX (1938), 263, n. 35.

[11] St. Alphonsus, *Theologia Moralis,* Lib. IV, dub. I, q. 2; Ferraris, *Prompta Bibliotheca,* III, s.v. *Episcopus,* Art. VII, n. 20.

[12] *Fontes,* n. 291; *supra,* p. 52; Oesterle, *Praelectiones Iuris Canonici,* I, 355.

[13] Oesterle, *loc. cit.*; Berutti, *De Religiosis,* n. 141, II; A. D., "Religiosi ad Eccl. Dignitatem Promoti," *CpRM,* XIX (1938), 263, n. 34.

servance of their rule and constitutions in so far as their prescripts are compatible with the dignity possessed. Certainly, the return to the religious life at the expiration of the duties of the dignitary state had to be accounted as a prescript that was compatible with the dignity.[14]

The obligation as now set forth in canon 629, §1, is but a logical consequence of canon 627, §1: If a religious who has been promoted to the episcopal or cardinalitial dignity remains a religious and continues to be bound by his vows and the other obligations of his religious profession, it follows that such a religious, once he has abdicated his dignity or has completed the mission entrusted to him, must return to his religious institute.[15] Thus it is evident that dignitaries religious must again resort to the common life in their religious communities, the obligation to observe which resulted from the religious profession; they no longer hold any office outide the Order or the congregation to hinder their return to the religious life.[16] An apostolic indult, of course, could exempt these religious from this obligation.[17]

The return to religious life must be active, not merely passive, i.e., a complete restoration of the obligations inherent in the religious state of life.[18] Pope Benedict XIII in the Constitution "*Custodes,*" a source of the present legislation, clearly indicated this duty: The Pope approved, confirmed, and included in this Constitution the decrees of his predecessors, Pope Alexander VII (Const. "*Quia Ecclesia,*" 26 iul. 1662) and Pope Clement XI (S. C. de Prop. Fide, 17 iun. 1715),[19] whereby regulars who were bishops or vicars apostolic were obliged to return to their cloisters if they were not actually in residence in their dioceses. The obligation to take up their religious life with their confrères in religion existed whether this lack of residence in their proper sees was due to their own fault or even to some legitimate impediment.[20]

---

[14] Cf. Piat, *Praelectiones Juris Regularis,* I, Q. 213.

[15] Blat, *Ius De Religiosis,* n. 605; Schaefer, *De Religiosis,* n. 496; Eichmann, *Lehrbuch des Kirchenrechts,* §97, n. 4.

[16] Berutti, *De Religiosis,* n. 141, II.

[17] Schaefer, *loc. cit.*; *supra,* p. 52.

[18] A. D., "art. cit.," *CpRM,* XIX (1938), 264, n. 37.

[19] *Supra,* pp. 51, 52.

[20] Const. "*Custodes,*" 7 mart. 1726, §7: ". . . . quibus decretis Regulares

Therefore it is patent that the legislator's mind in canon 629, §1, contemplates a full and active resumption of all the duties, obligations and observances of the religious life.[21]

After the return, then, to their proper institutes such religious who have abdicated the cardinalate or the episcopal office, or who have discharged the mission committed to them by the Holy See, are placed in the same juridical condition as the rest of their brothers in religion, since the former must resume *ipso iure* an active observance of their religious life.[22] Hence, the freedom in a lesser or greater degree from the religious observances of the rule or the constitutions on the part of these bishops and cardinals religious who have returned to the religious way of life, as defended by some commentators on their behalf, seems to be contrary to the intention of canon 629, §1.[23] At least in the direct light of the law such liberty is not apparent.

Accordingly, it follows that the former cardinals or bishops religious upon their return to the religious life in their institutes are bound to the same observance of the vow of obedience with respect to their religious superiors as rested upon them before their departure. During the actual stay outside the Order or congregation in the dignitary status, cardinals and bishops religious are circumstantially withdrawn from the authority of their religious superiors and of the Order or congregation; they are subject in obedience *vi voti* to the Pope alone. But the vow of obedience in

---

. . . iubentur ad pristina suorum Ordinum claustra reverti, cum reliquis Confratribus suis sub eodem insituto religiosam vitam ibidem acturi."—*Fontes*, n. 291.

[21] Toso, *Commentaria Minora*, V, p. 218, n. 1.

[22] Toso, *loc. cit.*; A. D., "art. cit.," *CpRM*, XIX (1938), 267, nn. 38, 39.

[23] Berutti simply states that in no way are the prescriptions of canon 627 taken away when the dignitary religious returns to his institute; therefore cardinals or bishops religious are not bound to religious observances which are not compatible with their dignity.—*De Religiosis*, n. 141, II.

Other commentators employ more cautious terminology, such as: They appear not to be obliged to a strict observance; most probably they are not obliged, or some liberty is to be granted out of deference to the episcopal or cardinalitial dignity which they always retain.—Coronata, *Institutiones Iuris Canonici*, I, n. 634, 3°; Sipos, *Enchiridion Iuris Canonici*, §73, n. 2, g; Claeys Bouuaert-Simenon, *Manuale Juris Canonici*, I, n. 682, III; Prümmer, *Manuale*, Q. 249, n. 5; Cocchi, *Commentarium in Codicem*, IV, n. 125, c.

regard to the religious superiors remains as such and automatically revives, since by their return they are subject again to the religious authority.[24] Their position is similar to that of religious superiors whose superiorship has ceased.[25]

Berutti makes the gratuitous assertion that even after the return of such bishops or cardinals religious to their religious communities the effects of canon 627 are still in force, while Coronata maintains that a bishop or cardinal religious does not seem to be bound to the obedience to his religious superiors.[26] But this cannot be admitted. For how can such a religious dignitary be deemed to be leading the religious way of life in his community if he is not obliged to the observance of one of the essential vows of the religious state itself? Besides, the contention of Berutti appears to be at variance with the explanation that he proffers for canon 627, §2, about the accidental retraction of the vow of obedience for religious while they are outside the institute in the exercise of the offices inherent in the cardinalitial or episcopal dignity.[27]

The modifications of the vow of poverty during the tenure of the dignitary office outside the Order or congregation (canon 628) cease when these bishops, residential or titular, or the religious who had been vicars or prefects apostolic, abbots or prelates *nullius,* cardinals, or legates, have abdicated or gone out of office inasmuch as their mission is fulfilled:

1. The religious who were cardinals can no longer make a will (canon 239, §1, 19°), since they have relinquished their dignity with the right to the beneficiary revenues.
2. A cession and disposition of the use and usufruct of the tem-

[24] Cf. canon 627, §2.—*Supra,* article 2 of Chapter V, pp. 97 ff.

[25] Cf. A. D., "Religiosi ad Eccl. Dignitatem Promoti," *CpRM,* XIX (1938), 265, n. 38, a.

[26] Berutti, *De Religiosis,* n. 141, II; Coronata, *Institutiones Iuris Canonici,* I, n. 634, 3°.

[27] Berutti, in fact, cites a part of the passage of St. Thomas (*Summa Theologica,* IIa, IIae, q. 88, art. 11, *ad quartum*), in which the Angelic Doctor explained that a bishop religious was only circumstantially withdrawn from the obedience due to his religious superiors, inasmuch as he was no longer a subject of theirs. However, at his return to religious life he again became bound by the vow of obedience to his superiors as before.—*Op. cit.,* n. 139, III.

poral goods acquired by dignitary religious of simple vows may be necessary; this requisite follows the norms of canons 569, §2, and 580, §3.

3. Whatever such religious acquire after their return to their proper communities is again acquired for the Order or the congregation, or for the Holy See, as the case may be (canons 580, §2, and 582).[28]

Coronata avers that the free administration of temporal goods remains in the hands of religious who are bishops or had been cardinals even after their return to the religious institute, since canon 628 is absolute in its text, at least as regards these bishops and cardinals religious. Hence the administration is theirs after their return to the religious community as well as during the actual exercise of their dignitary offices outside the Order or congregation.[29] However, such free administration would detract from the religious way of life which the cardinal or bishop religious must resume at the expiration of his office, and would also be in opposition to the rule of canon 569, §1.[30]

Though the cardinal or bishop religious as such was bound by the obligations of his profession, i.e., the prescriptions of his rule and constitutions while he was an incumbent in the dignitary status outside the institute,[31] he had the faculty to pass prudent judgment himself whether or not these prescripts of the rule and constitutions were compatible with his dignity. If they were not, he was excused from their observance (canon 627, §1). Upon his return to his religious institute he no longer possesses that faculty, and is obliged to observe all the prescripts of the rule and constitutions. In this respect such a religious in no way differs from his brothers in religion, for by his return he takes upon himself all the obligations in accord with that rule and way of life he has professed.[32]

The foregoing discussion demonstrates what are the full implica-

---

[28] A. D., *ibid.*, 265, n. 38, b.

[29] *Institutiones Iuris Canonici*, I, n. 634, 3° and note 1.

[30] Cf. *supra*, p. 102.

[31] Cf. *supra*, p. 85.

[32] A. D., "Religiosi ad Eccl. Dignitatem Promoti," *CpRM*, XIX (1938), 266, n. 38, c; Berutti maintains the opposite because of his claim that canon 627 is still effective.—*De Religiosis*, n. 141, II.

tions of the return of dignitaries religious to their religious institutes. *Ipso iure* the return entails the undertaking of the religious life in all its aspects, i.e., with all the attendant duties and obligations. And yet, in practice, due honor and esteem is owed to the person of the religious who has abdicated from the episcopacy or from the cardinalate. At times their dignitary position is recognized in the constitutions; if there is not such provision in the constitutions, it must be left to the prudence and discretion of the superiors to show the proper deference.

In this sense, certainly, but not *ex lege,* it seems very probable that superiors may grant some liberty and freedom from the strict observance of the religious discipline in minor or very minute details, ex. gr., in matters whose retained observance is not befitting to their dignity, or to their former high ecclesiastical rank and condition, such as rules of precedence in the community, or minor tasks apportioned among the members in accordance with the rule, etc.[33]

In addition, since religious bishops who have abdicated retain their dignity, they have the right to the special dress and insignia proper to the dignity, together with its privileges, in so far as these latter are not ruled out by the abdication.[34] The same, it seems, cannot be affirmed of cardinals religious who have abdicated and thereby lost the dignity, unless the Pope possibly has allowed them to keep the title of cardinal with its privileges (canon 239, §1).[35]

Bishops religious after their abdication may perform pontifical functions with miter and crozier, provided that they have obtained the permission of the local ordinary and of their own religious superiors.[36] Such religious who have returned to their communities after they have been dismissed from the office of a residential

[33] Toso, *Commentaria Minora,* V, p. 218, n. 1; Pejška, *Jus Canonicum Religiosorum,* p. 181, n. 3, and n. 3, b; Prümmer, *Manuale,* Q. 249, n. 5; Claeys Bouuaert-Simenon, *Manuale Juris Canonici,* I, n. 682, III.

[34] Cf. canon 349, §1.

[35] Pejška simply grants the right to the special dress and insignia of the dignity along with its privileges to cardinals religious who have abdicated, since he puts cardinals and bishops religious on a parity with respect to the retention of their dignity.—*Op. cit.,* p. 181, n. 3, c.

[36] Cf. canon 337, §1.

episcopate are to be considered thereafter as titular bishops; in that case as well as in the case in which they were always merely titular bishops, they may be called to attend general councils (canon 223, §2), plenary councils (canon 282, §2), or provincial councils (canon 286, §2).[37] Moreover, bishops religious continue to enjoy the right of choosing a church for their funeral and a cemetery for their burial.[38]

Lastly, it is to be noted that Pope Benedict XIII invoked the penalty of an *ipso facto* incurred suspension *a pontificalibus* against bishops regular who did not return to their cloister after the abdication of the episcopal office; if they remained contumacious, i.e., by not returning to the cloister for the period of a year, they incurred the penalty of suspension *a divinis*.[39] These penal sanctions are not renewed by the Code; hence, in virtue of canon 6, 5°, they must be considered as abrogated.[40]

Since dignitary religious remain religious, and thus are under obligation to return to their religious institute at the expiration of the duties incident to their dignity, they fall under the law which in canon 2385 enacts the censure of excommunication against apostate religious, i.e., the *ipso facto* incurred excommunication reserved to the proper major superior, or, if the religious institute is non-exempt, to the ordinary of the place where the apostate religious stays.[41] Apostate religious are also bound by the obligations of canon 645.[42]

It is definite and clear that the *ipso facto* incurred excommunication enacted in canon 2385 against apostate religious would be

---

[37] Pejška, *op. cit.*, p. 181, n. 3, c and d.

[38] *Supra*, p. 96; Pejška, *op. cit.*, p. 181, n. 3, e.

[39] *Supra*, p. 52. Wernz-Vidal, *De Religiosis*, n. 413, IV, note 9.

[40] Berutti, *De Religiosis*, n. 141, II; A. D., "Religiosi ad Eccl. Dignitatem Promoti," *CpRM*, XIX (1938), 267, n. 40.

[41] Canon 644—§1. "Apostata a religione dicitur professus a votis perpetuis sive solemnibus sive simplicibus qui e domo religiosa illegitime egreditur cum animo non redeundi, vel qui, etsi legitime egressus, non redit eo animo ut religiosae obedientiae sese subtrahat.

§2. Malitiosus animus, de quo in §1, iure praesumitur, si religiosus intra mensem nec reversus fuerit nec Superiori animum redeundi manifestaverit."

[42] Canon 645—§1. "Apostata et fugitivus ab obligatione regulae et votorum minime solvuntur et debent sine mora ad religionem redire." Cf. A. D., "art. cit.," *loc. cit.*

incurred by all dignitaries religious, including bishops, if they did not return to their religious communities upon their abdication. Bishops are not exempted from this penalty of excommunication as established in the common law (canon 2227, §2). However, it is not so clear whether cardinals religious would be liable to the same censure, since canon 2227, §2, rules that cardinals are not subject to the penal law, unless they are expressly mentioned. It may be argued that cardinals religious at their abdication lose the dignity itself, and thus revert to the juridic condition of ordinary religious, for by their return to their own institutes they would be obliged to undertake the full religious discipline and mode of life with all its duties and obligations, as they had lived it before their promotion to the dignity. In view of this one can affirm that such religious who effectively have given up the cardinalate cannot any longer be accounted as cardinals; hence they, like the ordinary religious, can incur the penalty of excommunication enacted against apostate religious.[48]

On the other hand, it may be objected that the dignity is retained by the religious even after he has relinquished the cardinalate. Since canon 2227, §2, speaks in a general way of cardinals, there may seem to be no basis, in that event, to exclude him. But one may counter: How can it be said that such a religious retains his former cardinalitial dignity? The cardinalate is not accompanied with an indelible character as is the episcopate, in virtue of which such a religious would retain his erstwhile dignity. Rather, once he has dismissed the cardinalate, his cardinalitial dignity, too, is lost with the cardinalitial office. Only cardinals in office are in possession of the cardinalitial dignity, and hence they alone have a proper claim to the exemption from penalties as the law of the Code grants it to cardinals. For these reasons it appears more probable that these former cardinals religious after their abdication from the cardinalate can incur the excommunication and the other penalties which are levied against apostate religious by the common law.

[48] A. D., "Religiosi ad Eccl. Dignitatem Promoti," *CpRM,* XIX (1938), 268, n. 40.

Article 2. The Privilege of Selecting a Religious House and the Deprivation of Active and Passive Voice in Elections (Canon 629, §2)

Canon 629—§2. *Potest tamen Cardinalis et Episcopus religiosus quamlibet suae religionis domum eligere in qua degat; sed caret voce activa et passiva.*

A cardinal or bishop religious upon relinquishing his dignitary status or office can [in returning to his community] choose any house of his institute for his residence, but he has neither an active nor a passive voice in elections.

Pope Benedict XIII in his Constitution "*Custodes*" of March 7, 1726, had conceded to bishops regular the privilege of free election of a monastery in the province for their residence upon their return to the Order.[44] The Code in canon 629, §2, extends that privilege to both cardinals and bishops religious, whether or not they be regulars, when they have abdicated and are on the point of returning to the religious life in their respective Orders or congregations.

In the present the choice is not restricted to the province as it was in the afore-mentioned Constitution, for under the Code there is given a wider range, inasmuch as these religious may choose any religious house of the institute for their home.[45] Religious who had held the dignity of cardinal, or religious who are bishops, even though they have abdicated from the office, enjoy this free election.[46] The wording of canon 629, §2, is general. On that account it may reasonably be maintained that they may employ the faculty of selecting any house of the institute for their residence for the rest of their lives and as often as they wish.[47] At least the canon does not restrict the use of the privilege as to place or assign it any definite time limit.

[44] *Supra,* p. 53. Oesterle, *Praelectiones Iuris Canonici,* I, 355.

[45] Schaefer, *De Religiosis,* n. 496.

[46] Toso, *Commentaria Minora,* V, p. 218, n. 2; Raus, *Institutiones Canonicae,* n. 202, I.

[47] Schaefer, *loc. cit.*; Goyeneche, *De Religiosis,* n. 90, a; A. D., "Religiosi ad Eccl. Dignitatem Promoti," *CpRM,* XIX (1938), 268, n. 41; Berutti, *De Religiosis,* n. 141, II.

A religious who had been created a cardinal or consecrated as a bishop on returning to his institute, lacks active and passive participation in elections. Again this deprivation affects exclusively dignitaries religious who had been made cardinals or bishops.[48] This lack of active and passive participation in elections really amounts to an incapacity;[49] in fact, it is an incapacity from which a dispensation is rarely given. Therefore also a postulation could not be admitted.[50] The incapacity for both the active and passive participation in elections extends in its application to the whole Order or congregation, and not merely to the house which such a religious has selected for his residence, for the canon is general in its terminology.[51]

The deprivation of the active and passive participation in elections must not be deemed a penalty. The reason for the lack of a voice in the deliberations of the religious institute seems rather to be this: A bishop religious, even after his abdication from the episcopal office and upon his resumption of the religious life, retains his dignity and with it a weight of authority and influence which may imperil the liberty of the religious family in its deliberations of importance. The same, of course, is true of a former cardinal who has returned to the religious life, for it is only natural that some deference and authority is accorded to him because of his former eminence and exalted rank in the cardinalitial dignity.

In regard to electoral rights, then, these religious should not be reinstated to the capacity which they had before their promotion.[52] Accordingly, in order to preclude any curtailing of the liberty necessary in the elections of the religious institute, the law of the Code wisely denies to cardinals and bishops religious upon their return to the religious life the prerogative of any active and passive voice in elections, i.e., they cannot partake in the elections of

---

[48] Goyeneche, *op. cit.*, n. 90, b.

[49] Schaefer, *De Religiosis*, n. 115, 1, d, note 131.

[50] Cf. canon 179, §1; A. D., "Religiosi ad Eccl. Dignitatem Promoti," *CpRM*, XIX (1938), 262, n. 32; Schaefer, *op. cit.*, n. 496.

[51] A. D., "art. cit.," *loc. cit.*; Augustine, *Religious and Laymen*, p. 360; Vermeersch-Creusen, *Epitome*, I, n. 787, 3.

[52] Pejška, *Jus Canonicum Religiosorum*, p. 181, n. 3, a; Cappello, *Summa Iuris*, II, n. 63, 4; Coronata, *Institutiones Iuris Canonici*, I, n. 634, 3°; Toso, *Commentaria Minora*, V, p. 218, n. 2.

the religious house, province, or institute in any way, neither by casting votes for others, nor by being eligible themselves to offices or superiorships.[53]

As has been seen, this deprival of the active and passive participations in elections is an absolute prohibition, so much so that it results in an incapacity for these religious to enjoy active or passive participation. On that account it seems that they also could not vote as proxies, even though when acting as proxies they would be voting not in their personal name, but in the name of another. The fact that they are actually employing the vote would run counter to the absolute denial, in canon 629, §2, of their right to participate in elections.[54]

A similar argument holds against the use of the vote by such religious when by unanimous consent of the electoral body the election is entrusted to one or more special representatives, for in such a case they would receive for that one election the right of electing, and by that power perform the election in the name of all.[55] Again, how could cardinals or bishops religious after their return to the religious life be empowered to vote even as representatives of the electoral body when the law itself in canon 629, §2, has made them incapable of participating in elections?

The law of the Code in canon 629, §2, as is evident, deals with cardinals and bishops religious after their abdication; accordingly, the deprivation of active and passive participation in elections has reference to them only from that time onward.[56] As such this legislation of the canon cannot be extended to religious while they are exercising their dignitary offices.[57] Actually, then, the Code does not touch upon the question whether cardinals religious who have not resigned, and bishops religious who are ruling their dioceses, retain the active and passive right to participate in elections in their institutes during that period.[58] Commentators, therefore,

---

[53] Beste, *Introductio in Codicem*, p. 425; Blat, *Ius De Religiosis*, n. 605; Schaefer, *loc. cit.*; Berutti, *De Religiosis*, n. 141, II.

[54] Canon 163 rules out the right to vote either by letter or by proxy in elections, unless particular law honors such a method.

[55] Cf. canon 172, §1.

[56] Coronata, *op. cit.*, I, n. 634, 1°, note 6.

[57] Chelodi, *De Personis*, n. 284, a, note 1.

[58] Oesterle, *Praelectiones Iuris Canonici*, I, 356; A. D., "Religiosi ad

discuss this question, for it is a controverted point whether religious who are cardinals or bishops can enjoy any active or passive participation in the elections of their institute while they are outside the religious institute in the exercise of their dignity.[59]

However, with more exactness it must be stated that this discussion can concern only the question whether these dignitaries religious have the right to a vote in their institute during their incumbency in the office of the episcopate, or in the dignity of the cardinalate. Pope Paul IV (1555–1559) had declared that archibishops and bishops religious were perpetually incapable of being elected to any dignity, office or superiorship in their respective Orders or congregations after their consecration, even though they had been legitimately freed from the charge of the diocese in their care and had returned to their religious institute.[60] This absolute denial of eligibility for elections in their institute was motivated by the fact that at the time of Pope Paul IV there was special need to restrain the ambitions of some bishops religious who endeavored to resign in order to attain a dignity or high office in their own religious institute.[61]

Some of the modern authors apply the law of the absolute deprivation enacted by Pope Paul IV also to cardinals religious, and maintain that eligibility for election in their institute must be absolutely disclaimed for both cardinals and bishops religious during the exercise of their dignity outside the institute.[62] Moreover, the arguments for the contention that a religious promoted to the cardinalate or episcopate loses the offices which he may have held in the institute seem to apply here as well, though conversely.[63]

Eccl. Dignitatem Promoti," *CpRM,* XIX (1938), 262, n. 33; Schaefer, *De Religiosis,* n. 496; Vermeersch-Creusen, *Epitome,* I, n. 787, 3.

[59] Cappello, *Summa Iuris,* II, n. 63, 2; Woywod, *A Practical Commentary,* I, n. 542.

[60] Const. "*In sacra,*" 19 iul. 1559, §2—*Fontes,* n. 95. Cf. *supra,* p. 53.

[61] Vermeersch-Creusen, *Epitome,* I, n. 787, 3.

[62] A. D., "Religiosi ad Eccl. Dignitatem Promoti," *CpRM,* XIX (1938), 262, n. 33; Oesterle, *Praelectiones Iuris Canonici,* I, 356; Berutti, *De Religiosis,* n. 141, I; Schaefer, *De Religiosis,* n. 496; Eichmann, *Lehrbuch des Kirchenrechts,* §97, n. 4. Some justification can be adduced from the fact that the Constitution "*In sacra*" by Paul IV is cited in the footnotes of Cardinal Gasparri to canon 629, §2.

[63] *Supra,* p. 97.

Assuredly, the duties and offices of cardinals or bishops outside the religious institute could hardly be joined with other offices within the religious institute without opposition to the legislation of canon 156, which is to the effect that no one shall be given two incompatible offices, i.e., offices which cannot be administered simultaneously by the same person.

Therefore, the point at issue is this: Do religious who are cardinals or bishops possess a vote in their Orders or congregations while they are outside the institute in the actual exercise of the duties of their dignity? There are several opinions:

1. Cardinals and bishops religious possess a vote in their Orders or congregations during the time that they are outside the religious institute in the actual exercise of the duties attendant upon their dignity.

The reasons for this opinion are these: Such cardinals and bishops religious (also vicars and prefects apostolic) remain religious, as is indicated by canon 627, §1; and since there is no express prohibition in canon 629, §2, against their voting while they are incumbents in the dignities of the cardinalate or the episcopate outside their institutes, they must be held to have this right. Their promotion does not take away their right to vote in the institute. Hence, the lack of a definite law would indicate that the right to vote in their Orders or congregations belongs to cardinals and bishops religious. This right must be employed prudently, so that the weight of authority attaching to their pre-eminent position may not oppress their religious confrères, or infringe upon the liberty of action of the religious institute itself in elections.[64]

2. Cardinals and bishops religious do not enjoy a vote in their Orders or congregations while they are outside the religious institute in the actual exercise of the duties of their dignity.

This negative opinion relies on the arguments drawn from the consideration of the nature of the juridic condition of religious who are cardinals or bishops. Such religious, it is true, remain religious (canon 627, §1). Nevertheless, they have been with-

[64] Chelodi, *De Personis*, n. 284, a, note 1. The following propose reasons for this opinion, though they personally hold the negative view: Schaefer, *De Religiosis*, n. 496; Woywod, *A Practical Commentary*, I, n. 542.

drawn from the obedience due to their religious superiors or institutes (canon 627, §2), and in the exercise of their duties as dignitaries are compelled to give up the common life in the religious community. Hence, they are no longer subjects of any particular, definite community, though the bond uniting them to the religious institute persists. Accordingly, it seems illogical to suppose that cardinals and bishops religious have the power of voting while they are outside the religious institute, possibly uninformed and not fully cognizant of the matters and affairs of their Orders and congregations, when the Code itself deprives those who return to the community of both the active and passive participation in elections. The religious who has been promoted to the episcopal, or even to the cardinalitial dignity, gains no right from that promotion to have a vote in the Chapters of the religious organization. Therefore, it seems alien to the legislator's mind that cardinals or bishops religious who carry such great authority in the dignitary status outside the Order or congregation should have the right to participate in the elections of their institute, with possible jeopardy to the liberty of the other religious who are members of the institute.[65]

3. Cardinals and bishops religious do not have the right to vote in their Orders or congregations while they are outside the religious institute in the exercise of the duties incident to their dignity, unless the constitutions or legitimate custom concede this right to them, or unless the dignitary religious at the same time holds some office in the institute with which the right to vote is associated.

This opinion embraces the negative view related above, but not to the extent of an absolute denial of the right to vote. Since there is no express positive law that prohibits the exercise of the vote by cardinals or bishops religious while in the dignitary state, the con-

---

[65] Wernz-Vidal, *De Religiosis,* n. 413, IV, note 10; Woywod, *loc. cit.*; Oesterle, *Praelectiones Iuris Canonici,* I, 356; Regatillo, *Institutiones Iuris Canonici,* I, n. 749; Eichmann, *Lehrbuch des Kirchenrechts,* §97, n. 4. The following concur in this negative opinion, but with some qualifications: Vermeersch-Creusen, *Epitome,* I, n. 787, 3; Goyeneche, "Consultationes," *CpR,* II (1921), 148–154, on p. 153; A. D., "Religiosi ad Eccl. Dignitatem Promoti," *CpRM,* XIX (1938), 262, n. 33.

stitutions or laudably established custom may allow the right of vote to these dignitaries religious. There are some congregations that permit bishops religious and vicars apostolic to intervene with a deliberative vote in the Chapters of the institute.

Indeed, it may appear inconsistent that cardinals and bishops religious upon abdicating and returning to their communities should suffer a diminution of their rights in losing the right of active and passive participation in elections, when they enjoyed that right while in the exercise of their dignity.[66] However, it seems to the writer that this apparent inconsistency vanishes when it is recalled that the lack of the right of active and passive participation in elections on the part of a cardinal or bishop religious who has returned to the community is a necessary precautionary measure to preclude the possibility of endangering the liberty of his brothers in religion. Most certainly, if the cardinal or bishop religious is granted the right of voting in his Order or congregation while in the exercise of his dignity, prudence in its use must guard against the same danger. Besides, the fact that the cardinal or bishop religious in the exercise of his dignity is outside the Order or congregation, and encumbered with the duties and tasks of his office, would lessen the perils to the liberty of the other religious in elections, whereas, when he has returned to the religious life in the community the danger is so much more imminent that positive legislation seems needed as an effective safeguard against its eventuation.

The right to vote in their Order or congregation could also be supplied to cardinals and bishops religious while they are outside the religious institute when at the same time they hold some position or office in the institute, with which position or office the right to vote is connected. As such, offices in the institute must be considered as incompatible with the cardinalitial and episcopal dignity.[67] However, there may be extraordinary cases in which an office in the religious institute may be combined with the episcopal charge, ex. gr., in mission countries especially, where bishops relig-

[66] Coronata, *Institutiones Iuris Canonici,* I, n. 634, 1°, and note 6; Vermeersch-Creusen, *loc. cit.*; Cappello, *Summa Iuris,* II, n. 63, 2; Schaefer, *De Religiosis,* n. 496; A. D., "art. cit.," *loc. cit.*

[67] Incompatible in the sense of canon 156. Cf. *supra,* p. 97.

ious or vicars apostolic are simultaneously the provincial superiors of the institute. As provincials, then, they have the right to vote in the religious Chapters. The same would be true of any other office in the institute to which the right of voting is in accordance with the norms of their constitutions duly annexed, since there is no law in the Code that forbids them the exercise of their vote in the Order or congregation while outside the religious institute they continue in the possession of the dignity to which they were promoted.[68]

With reference to the arguments here adduced, the writer feels that the arguments for the last discussed opinion (n. 3) are the more conclusive. It is the one supported by the greater number of canonists, a fact which lends it at least a greater external authority. Therefore, it should be held that cardinals and bishops religious do not have a vote in their institutes while they are outside them in the actual exercise of their dignitary offices, unless the constitutions of the institute or laudably established custom grant them the right to vote, or unless the cardinals or bishops religious hold some office in the institute in virtue of which the right to vote is acknowledged to them.

The conclusion from the legislation of canon 629 is evident. Dignitaries religious, other than bishops or cardinals, who have abdicated or who have discharged the special mission entrusted to them by the Holy See, do not differ from their brothers in religion after their return to their respective Orders or congregations.[69] Under the common law they are placed in the same juridic condition that obtained for them before their promotion to the dignities outside the religious institute.

[68] Goyeneche, *De Religiosis*, n. 90, b, and "Consultationes," *CpR*, II (1921), 153; A. D., "Religiosi ad Eccl. Dignitatem Promoti," *CpRM*, XIX (1938), 262, n. 33; Schaefer, *De Religiosis*, n. 496; Beste, *Introductio in Codicem*, p. 425.

[69] Toso, *Commentaria Minora*, V, p. 218, n. 2.

CONCLUSIONS

The following are offered as conclusions resulting from this study:

1. An ecclesiastical dignity properly so called signifies an ecclesiastical office which implies the possession of jurisdiction in the external forum and a corresponding degree of pre-eminence which imports precedence and rank. All ecclesiastical dignities as such are incompatible with the religious state, and hence the authority of the Holy See is required in the promotion of religious to dignities. However, in the promotion to the cardinalitial or the episcopal dignity no special permission of the Holy See is necessary for the religious. (Pp. 61-65, 66-69.)

2. The juridic force of the prohibition: *nequit promoveri,* of canon 626, §1, must be understood in the sense that religious cannot be promoted validly to ecclesiastical dignities outside the religious institute without the authority of the Holy See when the promotion is effected by others than the Pope or the Holy See. (Pp. 69-70.)

3. In case of the election or also of the nomination or the presentation, of a religious to the episcopal dignity, the religious thus elected, nominated or presented, necessarily must procure his superior's permission prior to consenting to the election. The determination of the superior competent to give this permission depends upon the particular statutes of each individual Order or congregation. Normally, the major superiors are empowered in this regard, and, of course, the Pope. For all practical purposes it is not important whether the elected religious or the body of electors procures the said permission, as long as it is obtained. As such it seems that the religious who has been elected is the one who is obliged to procure the permission. (Pp. 71-73, 74-75.)

4. The pre-Code terminology and practice of non-solemn postulation, which denoted the direction of a petition to the competent superior for his permission that a religious subject might consent

to an election of himself to the episcopate, has no foundation in the present law of the Code. (Pp. 73-74.)

5. If a religious presumes to give his consent to an election of himself to the episcopate without the prior permission of his superior, that consent is not invalid, but merely illicit in character. (Pp. 75-76.)

6. The vow, noted in canon 626, §3, not to accept dignities must be understood as a public vow, solemn or simple. And the special dispensation of the Roman Pontiff as required in this same canon must be explained in the sense that the dispensation from that vow is reserved to the person of the Pope, and hence may be considered a *causa maior.* But religious when promoted to the episcopal or cardinalitial dignities need not seek this special dispensation; it is implicitly contained in the creation or appointment by the Pope. (Pp. 78-83.)

7. The juridic effects enunciated in canon 627, §1, are to be referred to cardinals and bishops religious exclusively. Vicars or prefects apostolic, and abbots or prelates *nullius,* when they are not bishops, are not to be brought under the scope of canon 627, §1. Cardinals and bishops religious possess the faculty of judging whether or not the obligations of the religious profession are compatible with their dignity from the moment of their proclamation as cardinals or bishops. (Pp. 86-88.)

8. Cardinals and bishops religious are obliged—*sub levi* or *sub gravi* in accord with the obligations assumed at the time of their religious profession—to the observance of the rule and the constitutions proper to their institute when and if the prescripts of that rule and those constitutions are compatible with the dignitary state. However, cardinals and bishops religious do not incur any penalty threatened in any such prescript of the rule or the constitutions. (Pp. 92-94.)

9. Cardinals and bishops religious follow the Roman rite in the celebration of Mass and recite the Roman breviary from the time of their promotion. (P. 95.)

10. Religious upon their promotion to the cardinalitial or episcopal dignities may carry with them from their institutes all written matter of their own, all necessary personal clothing and their

breviary. For other things a legitimate permission of the religious superior is required. (Pp. 95-96.)

11. A religious by his promotion to the cardinalate or the episcopate loses any office he held in the religious institute. (P. 97.)

12. The vow of obedience virtually remains in force for dignitaries religious in regard to the religious superiors, so that upon the return of the cardinals or bishops religious to their religious institute that vow of obedience obliges them in the measure in which it obliged them before their promotion to a dignity. (Pp. 97-99.)

13. The vow of poverty in its juridic effects remains for dignitaries regular, except for the modifications in canon 628, 1°. Regulars who are abbots or prelates *nullius* acquire after their promotion the ownership of all temporal goods for their respective territories which they govern. Dignitaries regular do not have the power of making a will, except they are cardinals; but cardinals regular are limited in this matter to the provisions of canon 239, §1, 19°. Dignitaries regular cannot give donations from the temporalities accruing to them personally and of which they have the enjoyment alone, except as alms, or for other just reasons. (Pp. 102-106, 108, 109-111.)

14. The chief juridic effects of the simple vow of poverty for dignitaries religious who are professed with simple vows cease while they are outside the congregation in the exercise of the offices connected with the dignity. However, these religious remain bound subjectively by their vow of poverty, i.e., in the personal use of the temporal goods. (Pp. 113-116.)

15. Cardinals and bishops religious are under grave obligation to retain the color and material quality of their religious habit, if their Order or congregation possesses a special and distinctive habit. However, the habit is patterned in cut after the dress worn by secular prelates in the same dignities. Religious in the cardinalitial or episcopal dignity are under obligation to use the privileges of dress accorded to them as incumbents of those dignities. (Pp. 121, 122, 124-125).

16. Religious upon their abdication from the cardinalate, from the episcopal office, or from any other dignity are obliged *sub gravi* to return to their religious institute. Under the law of the

Code they are placed in the same juridic condition that obtained for them before their promotion. They must resume actively and fully the religious life along with all the obligations and duties which derive from the vows, the rule and the constitutions. However, out of deference to the dignity and high position they had attained, they may be granted by the religious superiors some liberty and freedom from the strict observance of religious discipline in minor details. (Pp. 129, 130-132, 134.)

17. Bishops and cardinals religious of exempt institutes who upon their abdication from the episcopal office or from the cardinalate have not returned to their religious institutes incur the excommunication levied against apostate religious. (Pp. 135-136.)

18. Cardinals and bishops religious upon their return to the religious life can choose for the rest of their lives any house of the institute for their residence, and, as often as they wish, can make a new choice. The lack of the right of active and passive participation in elections of the whole institute is an absolute denial, so that it effects a juridical incapacity. The deprivation of the right of active and passive participation in elections is not imposed in the nature of a penalty. (Pp. 137-139.)

19. Cardinals and bishops religious do not possess eligibility for office in their religious institutes while they are incumbents in a dignity outside the Order or congregation. Neither do they have the right to the vote in their Orders or congregations while they are outside the institute in the exercise of their dignitary offices, unless the constitutions or legitimate custom concede this right to them, or unless the dignitaries religious in extraordinary cases hold in the institute some office with which the right of voting is associated. (Pp. 139-144.)

BIBLIOGRAPHY

SOURCES

Acta Apostolicae Sedis, Commentarium Officiale, Romae, 1909–1929; Civitate Vaticana, 1929—.

Acta Sanctae Sedis, 41 vols., Romae, 1865–1908.

Benedicti XIV Bullarium, 3 vols. in 4, Prati, 1845–1847.

Bullarii Romani Continuatio Summorum Pontificum, 9 vols. in 10, Prati, 1840–1856.

Bullarum Diplomatum et Privilegiorum Sanctorum Romanorum Pontificum Taurinensis Editio, 25 vols., Augustae Taurinorum, 1857–1872.

Canones Apostolorum et Conciliorum Saec. IV–VII, 2 vols., ed. H. T. Bruns, Berolini, 1839.

Canones et Decreta Sacrosancti Oecumenici Concilii Tridentini, ed. novissima, Romae, 1882.

Codex Iuris Canonici Pii X Pontificis Maximi iussu digestus, Benedicti Papae XV auctoritate promulgatus, Praefatione, Fontium Annotatione et Indice Analytico-Alphabetico ab Emo Petro Card. Gasparri Auctus, Romae, Typis Polyglottis Vaticanis, 1917; reimpressio, 1934.

Codicis Iuris Canonici Fontes, cura Emi Petri Card. Gasparri editi, 9 vols., Romae [postea Civitate Vaticana]: Typis Polyglottis Vaticanis, 1923–1939 (Vols. VII–IX, ed. cura et studio Emi Iustiniani Serédi).

Corpus Iuris Canonici, Editio Lipsiensis II (Richter-Friedberg), 2 vols., Lipsiae, 1879–1881. Editio anastatica repetita, 1922.

Corpus Iuris Civilis, Vol. III, ed. stereotypa quinta, *Novellae Constitutiones,* quas recognovit Rudolfus Schoell, opus Schoellii morte interceptum absolvit Guilelmus Kroll, Berolini: Apud Weidmannos, 1928.

Decreta Authentica Congregationis Sacrorum Rituum ex actis eiusdem collecta eiusque auctoritate promulgata sub auspiciis SS. D. N. Leonis Papae XIII, 5 vols. et 2 Appendices, Romae: Typis Polyglottis Vaticanis, 1898–1927.

Decretales D. Gregorii Papae IX suae integritati una cum glossis restitutae, Romae, 1582.

Decretum Gratiani emendatum et notationibus illustratum una cum glossis, Romae, 1582.

Jaffé, Philippus, *Regesta Pontificum Romanorum ab condita Ecclesia ad annum post Christum natum MCXCVIII,* ed. 2. (Kaltenbrunner, Ewald, Loewenfeld), 2 vols., Lipsiae, 1885–1888.

Liber Sextus D. Bonifacii Papae VIII suae integritati una cum Clementinis et Extravagantibus, eorumque glossis restitutis, Romae, 1582.

Mansi, J. D., *Sacrorum Conciliorum Nova et Amplissima Collectio,* 53 vols. in 60, Parisiis, 1901–1927.

Monumenta Germaniae Historica:

———, *Epistolae: Gregorii I Papae Registrum Epistolarum,* Tom. I, ed. P. Ewald et L. Hartmann, Berolini, 1891; tom. II, pars I; tom. II, pars II; tom. II, pars III: Post Ewaldi obitum ed. L. Hartmann: Berolini, 1893–1899.

——— *Leges,* 5 vols.; Vols. I–IV, ed. G. Pertz; Vol. V, ed. G. Pertz-G. Waitz-H. Brunner, Hannoverae, 1835–1889.

Pallottini, Salvator, *Collectio omnium conclusionum et resolutionum quae in causis propositis apud Sacram Congregationem Cardinalium S. Concilii Tridentini Interpretum prodierunt ab eius institutione anno MDLXIV ad annum MDCCCLX, distinctis titulis alphabetico ordine per materias digesta,* 17 vols., Romae, 1868–1893.

Potthast, Augustus, *Regesta Pontificum Romanorum inde ab anno post Christum natum MCXCVIII ad annum MCCCIV,* 2 vols., Berolini, 1874–1875.

Sacrae Rotae Romanae Decisiones Recentiores, 19 partes in 25 vols., Romae, 1623–1703.

Schroeder, Henry, *Canons and Decrees of the Council of Trent, Original Text with English Translation,* St. Louis, Mo.: B. Herder Book Co., 1941.

Thesaurus Resolutionum S. C. Concilii, 167 vols., Urbini, 1718–1749; Romae, 1843–1908.

AUTHORS

Aichner, Simon, *Compendium Juris Ecclesiastici,* 6. ed., Brixinae, 1887.

Alphonsus de Ligorio, St., *Theologia Moralis,* ed. nova, cura et studio P. Leonardi Gaudé, 4 vols.; Vol. II, Romae, 1907.

Augustine, Charles, *A Commentary on the New Code of Canon Law,* 8 vols., St. Louis, Mo.: B. Herder Book Co.; Vol. III, *De Personis, or Ecclesiastical Persons, Religious and Laymen,* 2. ed., 1919.

Bachofen (Charles Augustine), *Compendium Iuris Regularis,* Neo-Eboraci: Benziger Brothers, 1903.

Bernardus Papiensis, *Summa Decretalium,* ed. E. A. Th. Laspeyres, Ratisbonae, 1860.

Berutti, Christophorus, *Institutiones Iuris Canonici,* Vol. III, *De Religiosis,* Taurini, Romae: Marietti, 1936.

Beste, Udalricus, *Introductio in Codicem,* 2. ed., Collegeville, Minn.: St. John's Abbey Press, 1944.

Biederlack, Josephus-Führich, Maximilianus, *De Religiosis Iuris Canonici,* Oeniponte: Typis Feliciani Rauch, 1919.

Blat, Albertus, *Commentarium Textus Codicis Iuris Canonici,* 7 vols., Romae: Ex Typographia Augustiniana; Vol. III, *Ius De Religiosis et Laicis iuxta Codicis Ordinem,* ed. 3., 1938.

Boich, Henricus, *In Quinque Decretalium Libros Commentarius,* Venetiis, 1576.

Bouix, Dominicus, *Tractatus de Jure Regularium,* 2 vols., Parisiis, 1857.

Bouscaren, T. Lincoln-Ellis, Adam, *Canon Law, A Text and Commentary,* Milwaukee: The Bruce Publishing Co., 1946.

Cappello, Felix, *Summa Iuris Canonici in Usum Scholarum Concinnata,* Vol. II, ed. 4., Romae: Apud Aedes Universitatis Gregorianae, 1945.

Catholic Encyclopedia, The, 15 vols. with Index and 2 Supplements, New York, 1907-1922.

Chelodi, Ioannes, *Ius Canonicum de Personis,* ed. 3. curavit Pius Ciprotti, Vicenza: Societa Anonima Tipografica, 1942.

Claeys Bouuaert, F.-Simenon, G., *Manuale Juris Canonici,* 3 vols., Vols. I, III, 3. ed., 1930; Vol. II, 1931, Gandae et Leodiensi: Prostat apud Auctores.

Cocchi Guidus, *Commentarium in Codicem Iuris Canonici ad Usum Scholarum,* 8 vols., Taurinorum Augustae: Marietti; Vol. IV, 3. ed., 1932.

Coronata, Mathaeus, Conte a, *Institutiones Iuris Canonici,* 5 vols., Taurini: Marietti; Vol. I, ed. altera, 1939.

Craisson, D., *Manuale Totius Juris Canonici,* 5. ed., 4 vols., Pictavii, 1877.

Creusen, Joseph-Ellis, Adam-Garesché, Edward, *Religious Men and Women in the Code,* 5. ed., Milwaukee: The Bruce Publishing Co., 1940.

De Meester, Alphonsus, *Juris Canonici et Juris Canonico-Civilis Compendium,* nova ed., 3 vols. in 4, Brugis: Desclee, 1921-1928.

Devoti, Ioannes, *Institutiones Canonicarum Libri IV,* 3 vols., ed. prima Romana post quintam, Romae, Vol. I, 1825.

Dictionnaire de Droit Canonique, 3. ed., M. André, P. Condis, J. Wagner, Paris: H. Walzer, 1901.

Eichmann, Eduard, *Lehrbuch des Kirchenrechts auf Grund des Codex Juris Canonici,* 2. ed., Paderborn: Ferdinand Schöningh, 1926.

Fagnanus, Prosperus, *Commentarium in Librum Decretalium,* 3 vols., Venetiis, 1709.

Fanfani, Ludovicus, *De Iure Religiosorum ad Normam Codicis Iuris Canonici,* ed. altera, Taurini-Romae: Marietti, 1925.

Ferraris, Lucius, *Prompta Bibliotheca Canonica, Juridica, Moralis, Theologica necnon Ascetica, Polemica, Rubricistica, Historica,* ed. novissima, mendis expurgata, 8 vols., Parisiis, 1852-1857.

Ferreres, Ioannes, *Institutiones Canonicae iuxta Novissimum Codicem,* ed. altera, 2 vols., Barcinone: Eugenius Subirana, 1925.

Flanagan, Bernard, *The Canonical Erection of Religious Houses,* The Catholic University of America Canon Law Studies, n. 179, Washington, D. C.: The Catholic University of America Press, 1943.

Goyeneche, S., *De Religiosis De Laicis,* Roma: Apud Herder S. A. L. E. R., Montecitorio, 1938.

Graesse, G. Th., *Orbis Latinus,* 2. ed., Berolini, 1909.

Heimbucher, Max, *Die Orden und Kongregationen der katholischen Kirche,* 3. ed., 2 vols., Paderborn: Ferdinand Schoeningh, 1933–1934.

Hostiensis, Cardinalis (Henricus de Segusio), *In Quinque Libros Decretalium Commentaria,* 5 vols. in 3, Venetiis, 1581.

———, *Summa Aurea,* Venetiis, 1570.

Hynes, Harry, *The Privileges of Cardinals,* The Catholic University of America Canon Law Studies, n. 217, Washington, D. C.: The Catholic University of America Press, 1945.

Jansen, Joseph, *Ordensrecht,* 2. ed., Paderborn: Ferdinand Schöningh, 1920.

Köstler, Rudolf, *Wörterbuch zum Codex Iuris Canonici,* München: Verlag Josef Kösel & Friedrich Pustet, 1927–1929.

Laymann, Paulus, *Quaestiones Canonicae de Praelatorum Ecclesiasticorum Electione, Institutione et Potestate ex Lib. I Decretalium,* Dilingae, 1627.

Maroto, Philippus, *Institutiones Iuris Canonici,* 2 vols.; Vol. II, Roma-Matriti, 1919.

Matulenas, Raymond, *Communication—A Source of Privileges,* The Catholic University of America Canon Law Studies, n. 183, Washington, D. C.: The Catholic University of America Press, 1943.

Meehan, Andreas, *Compendium Juris Canonici,* Roffae, 1899.

Michiels, Gommarus, *Normae Generales Juris Canonici,* 2 vols., Lublin, Poloniae: Universitas Catholica, 1929.

Migne, J. P., *Patrologiae Cursus Completus, Series Latina,* 221 vols., Parisiis, 1844–1864.

Nainfa, John, *Costume of Prelates of the Catholic Church,* new and revised edition, Baltimore: John Murphy Co., 1926.

Oesterle, Gerardus, *Praelectiones Iuris Canonici,* Tomus I, Romae: Prostat in Collegio S. Anselmi, 1931.

Ojetti, Benedictus, *Commentarium in Codicem Iuris Canonici,* Vol. III, Romae: Apud Aedes Universitatis Gregorianae, 1930.

Panormitanus, Abbas (Nicolaus de Tudeschis), *Commentaria in Quinque Decretalium Libros,* 8 vols., Venetiis, 1588.

Papi, Hector, *Religious in Church Law,* New York: P. J. Kenedy & Sons, 1924.

Parsons, Anscar, *Canonical Elections,* The Catholic University of America Canon Law Studies, n. 118, Washington, D. C.: The Catholic University of America Press, 1939.

Pejška, Josephus, *Jus Canonicum Religiosorum,* 3. ed., Friburgi Brisgoviae: Herder and Co., 1927.

Piat, F., *Praelectiones Juris Regularis,* ed. 3., 2 vols., Tornaci, 1906.

Prümmer, Dominicus, *Manuale Iuris Canonici in Usum Scholarum,* 3. ed., Friburgi Brisgoviae: Herder and Co., 1922.

Raus, J. B., *Institutiones Canonicae,* Parisiis: Typis Emmanuelis Vitte, 1923.

Regatillo, Eduardus, *Institutiones Iuris Canonici,* 2 vols., Santander: Sal Terrae, 1941–1942.

Reiffenstuel, Anacletus, *Jus Canonicum Universum,* 5 vols., Parisiis, 1864–1870.

Roelker, Edward, *Principles of Privilege According to the Code of Canon Law,* The Catholic University of America Canon Law Studies, n. 35, Washington, D. C.: The Catholic University of America, 1926.

Rufinus, *Die Summa Decretorum des Magister Rufinus,* ed. Heinrich Singer, Paderborn: Ferdinand Schoeningh, 1902.

Santi, Franciscus, *Praelectiones Juris Canonici juxta Ordinem Decretalium Gregorii IX,* 5 vols. in 2, Ratisbonae, 1886.

Schaefer, Timotheus, *De Religiosis ad Normam Codicis Iuris Canonici,* ed. 3., Roma: Typis Polyglottis Vaticanis, 1940.

Schmalzgrueber, Franciscus, *Jus Ecclesiasticum Universum,* 5 vols. in 12, Romae, 1843–1845.

Schmidt, Antonius, *Thesaurus Iuris Ecclesiastici, potissimum Germanici, sive Dissertationes Selectae in Ius Ecclesiasticum,* 7 vols., Heidelbergae, Bambergae et Wirceburgi, 1772–1779.

Schroeder, Henry, *Disciplinary Decrees of the General Councils, Text, Translation and Commentary,* St. Louis, Mo.: B. Herder Book Co., 1937.

Shuhler, Ralph, *Privileges of Regulars to Absolve and Dispense,* The Catholic University of America Canon Law Studies, n. 186, Washington, D. C.: The Catholic University of America Press, 1943.

Sipos, Stephanus, *Enchiridion Iuris Canonici,* Pécs: Ex Typographia "Haladás R. T.," 1926.

Suarez, Franciscus, *Opera Omnia,* ed. nova a Carolo Berton, Parisiis, Vol. XVI, 1860.

Thomas Aquinas, St., *S. Thomae Aquinatis Doctoris Angelici Summa Theologica diligenter emendata, de Rubeis Billuart et aliorum notis selectis ornata,* 6 vols., Augustae Taurinorum: Typographia Pontificia, Vol. IV, 1886.

Thomassinus, Ludovicus, *Vetus et Nova Ecclesiae Disciplina circa Beneficia et Beneficiarios,* 10 vols., Moguntiae, 1787.

Toso, Albertus, *Ad Codicem Juris Canonici Commentaria Minora,* Vol. V, Romae: Apud Ephemerides Jus Pontificium, 1933.

Tuschus, Cardinalis Dominicus, *Practicae Conclusiones Iuris,* 3. ed., Vols. I–VIII, Ludguni, 1634; Vol. IX: *Eminentissimi Cardinalis Tuschi Additiones ad caetera octo volumina Practicarum Conclusionum Iuris:* Opus posthumum a Carolo Tuscho et Raynaldo Cardinali Estensi, Ludguni, 1670.

Van Hove, A., *Commentarium Lovaniense,* Vol. I, *Prolegomena ad Codicem Iuris Canonici,* ed. altera, Mechliniae-Romae: H. Dessain, 1945.

Vermeersch, Arthurus-Creusen, Josephus, *Epitome Iuris Canonici,* 5. ed., 3 vols., Mechliniae-Romae: H. Dessain, 1933–1936.

Vermeersch, Arthurus, *Theologia Moralis,* 3. ed., 3 vols., Romae: Pontificia Universitas Gregoriana, Vol. I, 1933.

Vives, Cardinalis Josephus, *De Dignitate et Officiis Episcoporum et Praelatorum*, Romae, 1905.

Wernz, Franciscus, *Ius Decretalium ad usum Praelectionum in Scholis Textus Canonici, sive Iuris Decretalium,* Vol. II, 1899; Vol. III, ed. altera, 1908, Romae-Prati: Ex typographia Polyglotta.

Wernz, Franciscus-Vidal, Petrus, *Ius Canonicum ad Codicis Normam Exactum,* 7 vols. in 9, Romae: Apud Aedes Universitatis Gregorianae. Tomus II, *De Personis,* ed. 3., 1943; tomus III, *De Religiosis,* 1933.

Woywod, Stanislaus, *A Practical Commentary on the Code of Canon Law,* Revised by Callistus Smith, 8th Printing, 2 vols., New York: Joseph Wagner, Inc., 1944.

ARTICLES

A. D., "De Obligationibus et Privilegiis Religiosi ad Ecclesiasticam Dignitatem Promoti"—*CpRM,* XIX (1938), 169–192; 261–268.

Garcia, Stephanus, "Annotationes"—*CpR,* II (1921), 102–104.

Goyeneche, S., "Consultationes"—*CpR,* II (1921), 148–154.

Klewitz, Hans-Walter, "Die Entstehung des Kardinalkollegiums"—*Zeitschrift der Savigny-Stiftung für Rechtsgeschichte,* LVI, *Kanon. Abtlg.,* XXV (1936), 115–222.

Kuttner, Stephan, "Cardinalis: The History of a Canonical Concept"—*Traditio,* III (1945), 129–214.

Larraona, Arcadius, "Commentarium Codicis"—*CpR,* II (1921), 134–139.

Maroto, Philippus, "De Consultoribus Dioecesanis"—*Apollinaris,* IV (1931), 252–253.

Oesterle, G., "Annahme kirchlicher Würden durch Ordenspersonen"—*TpQ,* LXXIV (1921), 415–418.

Pauwels, Joseph, "Motu Proprio '*Episcopis*': Annotationes"—*Periodica,* X (1922), 142–143.

Voltas, Petrus, "De vi can. 515 quoad prohibitionem honorum et exemptionum"—*CpR,* I (1920), 273–275.

PERIODICALS

Apollinaris, Romae, 1928—.

Commentarium pro Religiosis (later [1935]: *Commentarium pro Religiosis et Missionariis*), Romae, 1920—.

Periodica de Religiosis et Missionariis, Brugis, 1905–1919; from 1920: *Periodica de Re Canonica et Morali utilia praesertim Religiosis et Missionariis,* Brugis, 1920–1927; from 1927: *Periodica de Re Morali, Canonica, Liturgica,* Brugis (1927–1936) et Romae (1937—).

Theologisch-praktische Quartalschrift, Linz, 1832—.

Traditio: Studies in Ancient and Medieval History, Thought and Religion, New York, 1943—.

Zeitschrift der Savigny-Stiftung für Rechtsgeschichte, Kanon. Abtlg., Weimar, 1911—.

ABBREVIATIONS

AAS—*Acta Apostolicae Sedis.*
ASS—*Acta Sanctae Sedis.*
BRT—*Bullarum Diplomatum et Privilegiorum Sanctorum Romanorum Pontificum Taurinensis Editio.*
CpR(M)—*Commentarium pro Religiosis (et Missionariis).*
Fontes—*Codicis Iuris Canonici Fontes,* cura Emi Petri Gasparri editi.
Jaffé—*Regesta Pontificum Romanorum* (edited by Ewald, Kaltenbrunner, Loewenfeld).
Mansi—*Sacrorum Conciliorum Nova et Amplissima Collectio.*
MGH—*Monumenta Germaniae Historica.*
MPL—Migne, *Patrologiae Cursus Completus, Series Latina.*
Periodica—*Periodica de Re Canonica et Morali.*
Potthast—*Regesta Pontificum Romanorum.*
S. C. C.—Sacra Congregatio Concilii.
S. C. de Prop. Fide—Sacra Congregatio de Propaganda Fide.
S. C. Ep. et Reg.—Sacra Congregatio Episcoporum et Regularium.
S. R. C.—Sacra Rituum Congregatio.
S. R. R.—Sacra Romana Rota.
TpQ—*Theologisch-praktische Quartalschrift.*
Traditio—*Traditio: Studies in Ancient and Medieval History, Thought and Religion.*

ALPHABETICAL INDEX

Canon Law Studies *

1. Freriks, Rev. Celestine A., C.PP.S., J.C.D., Religious Congregations in Their External Relations, 121 pp., 1916.
2. Galliher, Rev. Daniel M., O.P., J.C.D., Canonical Elections, 117 pp., 1917.
3. Borkowski, Rev. Aurelius L., O.F.M., J.C.D., De Confraternitatibus Ecclesiasticis, 136 pp., 1918.
4. Castillo, Rev. Cayo, J.C.D., Disertacion Historico-Canonica sobre la Potestad del Cabildo en Sede Vacante o Impedida del Vicario Capitular, 99 pp., 1919 (1918).
5. Kubelbeck, Rev. William J., S.T.B., J.C.D., The Sacred Penitentiaria and Its Relation to Faculties of Ordinaries and Priests, 129 pp., 1918.
6. Petrovits, Rev. Joseph J. C., S.T.D., J.C.D., The New Church Law on Matrimony, X-461 pp., 1919.
7. Hickey, Rev. John J., S.T.B., J.C.D., Irregularities and Simple Impediments in the New Code of Canon Law, 100 pp., 1920.
8. Klekotka, Rev. Peter J., S.T.B., J.C.D., Diocesan Consultors, 179 pp., 1920.
9. Wanenmacher, Rev. Francis, J.C.D., The Evidence in Ecclesiastical Procedure Affecting the Marriage Bond, 1920 (Printed 1935).
10. Golden, Rev. Henry Francis, J.C.D., Parochial Benefices in the New Code, IV-119 pp., 1921 (Printed 1925).
11. Koudelka, Rev. Charles J., J.C.D., Pastors, Their Rights and Duties According to the New Code of Canon Law, 211 pp., 1921.
12. Melo, Rev. Antonius, O.F.M., J.C.D., De Exemptione Regularium, X-188 pp., 1921.
13. Schaaf, Rev. Valentine Theodore, O.F.M., S.T.B., J.C.D., The Cloister, X-180 pp., 1921.
14. Burke, Rev. Thomas Joseph, S.T.D., J.C.D., Competence in Ecclesiastical Tribunals, IV-117 pp., 1922.
15. Leech, Rev. George Leo, J.C.D., A Comparative Study of the Constitution "Apostolicae Sedis" and the "Codex Juris Canonici," 179 pp., 1922.
16. Motry, Rev. Hubert Louis, S.T.D., J.C.D., Diocesan Faculties According to the Code of Canon Law, II-167 pp., 1922.
17. Murphy, Rev. George Lawrence, J.C.D., Delinquencies and Penalties in the Administration and the Reception of the Sacraments, IV-121 pp., 1923.

* From nn. 1–100 inclusive only n. 25 is still obtainable. From n. 101 onward all numbers are available except the following: 101–114, 116, 118, 120, 122, 123 and 162.

18. O'Reilly, Rev. John Anthony, S.T.B., J.C.D., Ecclesiastical Sepulture in the New Code of Canon Law, II-129 pp., 1923.
19. Michalicka, Rev. Wenceslas Cyrill, O.S.B., J.C.D., Judicial Procedure in Dismissal of Clerical Exempt Religious, 107 pp., 1923.
20. Dargin, Rev. Edward Vincent, S.T.B., J.C.D., Reserved Cases According to the Code of Canon Law, IV-103 pp., 1924.
21. Godfrey, Rev. John A., S.T.B., J.C.D., The Right of Patronage According to the Code of Canon Law, 153 pp., 1924.
22. Hagedorn, Rev. Francis Edward, J.C.D., General Legislation on Indulgences, II-154 pp., 1924.
23. King, Rev. James Ignatius, J.C.D., The Administration of the Sacraments to Dying Non-Catholics, V-141 pp., 1924.
24. Winslow, Rev. Francis Joseph, M.M., J.C.D., Vicars and Prefects Apostolic, IV-149 pp., 1924.
25. Correa, Rev. Jose Servelion, S.T.L., J.C.D., La Potestad Legislativa de la Iglesia Catolica, IV-127 pp., 1925.
26. Dugan, Rev. Henry Francis, A.M., J.C.D., The Judiciary Department of the Diocesan Curia, 87 pp., 1925.
27. Keller, Rev. Charles Frederick, S.T.B., J.C.D., Mass Stipends, 167 pp., 1925.
28. Paschang, Rev. John Linus, J.C.D., The Sacramentals According to the Code of Canon Law, 129 pp., 1925.
29. Piontek, Rev. Cyrillus, O.F.M., S.T.B., J.C.D., De Indulto Exclaustrationis necnon Saecularizationis, XIII-289 pp., 1925.
30. Kearney, Rev. Richard Joseph, S.T.B., J.C.D., Sponsors at Baptism According to the Code of Canon Law, IV-127 pp., 1925.
31. Bartlett, Rev. Chester Joseph, A.M., LL.B., J.C.D., The Tenure of Parochial Property in the United States of America, V-108 pp., 1926.
32. Kilker, Rev. Adrian Jerome, J.C.D., Extreme Unction, V-425 pp., 1926.
33. McCormick, Rev. Robert Emmett, J.C.D., Confessors of Religious, VIII-266 pp., 1926.
34. Miller, Rev. Newton Thomas, J.C.D., Founded Masses According to the Code of Canon Law, VII-93 pp., 1926.
35. Roelker, Rev. Edward G., S.T.D., J.C.D., Principles of Privilege According to the Code of Canon Law, XI-166 pp., 1926.
36. Bakalarczyk, Rev. Richardus, M.I.C., J.U.D., De Novitiatu, VIII-208 pp., 1927.
37. Pizzuti, Rev. Lawrence, O.F.M., J.U.L., De Parochis Religiosis, 1927. (Not Printed.)
38. Bliley, Rev. Nicholas Martin, O.S.B., J.C.D., Altars According to the Code of Canon Law, XIX-132 pp., 1927.
39. Brown, Mr. Brendan Francis, A.B., LL.M., J.U.D., The Canonical Juristic Personality with Special Reference to its Status in the United States of America, V-212 pp., 1927.

40. Cavanaugh, Rev. William Thomas, C.P., J.U.D., The Reservation of the Blessed Sacrament, VIII-101 pp., 1927.
41. Doheny, Rev. William J., C.S.C., A.B., J.U.D., Church Property: Modes of Acquisition, X-118 pp., 1927.
42. Feldhaus, Rev. Aloysius H., C.PP.S., J.C.D., Oratories, IX-141 pp., 1927.
43. Kelly, Rev. James Patrick, A.B., J.C.D., The Jurisdiction of the Simple Confessor, X-208 pp., 1927.
44. Neuberger, Rev. Nicholas J., J.C.D., Canon 6 or the Relation of the Codex Juris Canonici to the Preceding Legislation, V-95 pp., 1927.
45. O'Keefe, Rev. Gerald Michael, J.C.D., Matrimonial Dispensations, Powers of Bishops, Priests, and Confessors, VIII-232 pp., 1927.
46. Quigley, Rev. Joseph A. M., A.B., J.C.D., Condemned Societies, 139 pp., 1927.
47. Zaplotnik, Rev. Johannes Leo, J.C.D., De Vicariis Foraneis, X-142 pp., 1927.
48. Duskie, Rev. John Aloysius, A.B., J.C.D., The Canonical Status of the Orientals in the United States, VIII-196 pp., 1928.
49. Hyland, Rev. Francis Edward, J.C.D., Excommunication, Its Nature, Historical Development and Effects, VIII-181 pp., 1928.
50. Reinmann, Rev. Gerald Joseph, O.M.C., J.C.D., The Third Order Secular of Saint Francis, 201 pp., 1928.
51. Schenk, Rev. Francis J., J.C.D., The Matrimonial Impediments of Mixed Religion and Disparity of Cult, XVI-318 pp., 1929.
52. Coady, Rev. John Joseph, S.T.D., J.U.D., A.M., The Appointment of Pastors, VIII-150 pp., 1929.
53. Kay, Rev. Thomas Henry, J.C.D., Competence in Matrimonial Procedure, VIII-164 pp., 1929.
54. Turner, Rev. Sidney Joseph, C.P., J.U.D., The Vow of Poverty, XLIX-217 pp., 1929.
55. Kearney, Rev. Raymond A., A.B., S.T.D., J.C.D., The Principles of Delegation, VII-149 pp., 1929.
56. Conran, Rev. Edward James, A.B., J.C.D., The Interdict, V-163 pp., 1930.
57. O'Neill, Rev. William H., J.C.D., Papal Rescripts of Favor, VII-218 pp., 1930.
58. Bastnagel, Rev. Clement Vincent, J.U.D., The Appointment of Parochial Adjutants and Assistants, XV-257 pp., 1930.
59. Ferry, Rev. William A., A.B., J.C.D., Stole Fees, V-136 pp., 1930.
60. Costello, Rev. John Michael, A.B., J.C.D., Domicile and Quasi-Domicile, VII-201 pp., 1930.
61. Kremer, Rev. Michael Nicholas, A.B., S.T.B., J.C.D., Church Support in the United States, VI-136 pp., 1930.
62. Angulo, Rev. Luis, C.M., J.C.D., Legislation de la Iglesia sobre la intencion en la application de la Santa Misa, VII-104 pp., 1931.

63. Frey, Rev. Wolfgang Norbert, O.S.B., A.B., J.C.D., The Act of Religious Profession, VIII-174 pp., 1931.
64. Roberts, Rev. James Brendan, A.B., J.C.D., The Banns of Marriage, XIV-140 pp., 1931.
65. Ryder, Rev. Raymond Aloysius, A.B., J.C.D., Simony, IX-151 pp., 1931.
66. Campagna, Rev. Angelo, Ph.D., J.U.D., Il Vicario Generale del Vescovo, VII-205 pp., 1931.
67. Cox, Rev. Joseph Godfrey, A.B., J.C.D., The Administration of Seminaries, VI-124 pp., 1931.
68. Gregory, Rev. Donald J., J.U.D., The Pauline Privilege, XV-165 pp., 1931.
69. Donohue, Rev. John F., J.C.D., The Impediment of Crime, VII-110 pp., 1931.
70. Dooley, Rev. Eugene A., O.M.I., J.C.D., Church Law on Sacred Relics, IX-143 pp., 1931.
71. Orth, Rev. Clement Raymond, O.M.C., J.C.D., The Approbation of Religious Institutes, 171 pp., 1931.
72. Pernicone, Rev. Joseph M., A.B., J.C.D., The Ecclesiastical Prohibition of Books, XII-267 pp., 1932.
73. Clinton, Rev. Connell, A.B., J.C.D., The Paschal Precept, IX-108 pp., 1932.
74. Donnelly, Rev. Francis B., A.M., S.T.L., J.C.D., The Diocesan Synod, VIII-125 pp., 1932.
75. Torrente, Rev. Camilo, C.M.F., J.C.D., Las Procesiones Sagradas, V-145 pp., 1932.
76. Murphy, Rev. Edwin J., C.PP.S., J.C.D., Suspension Ex Informata Conscientia, XI-122 pp., 1932.
77. MacKenzie, Rev. Eric F., A.M., S.T.L., J.C.D., The Delict of Heresy in its Commission, Penalization, Absolution, VII-124 pp., 1932.
78. Lyons, Rev. Avitus E., S.T.B., J.C.D., The Collegiate Tribunal of First Instance, XI-147 pp., 1932.
79. Connolly, Rev. Thomas A., J.C.D., Appeals, XI-195 pp., 1932.
80. Sangmeister, Rev. Joseph V., A.B., J.C.D., Force and Fear as Precluding Matrimonial Consent, V-211 pp., 1932.
81. Jaeger, Rev. Leo A., A.B., J.C.D., The Administration of Vacant and Quasi-Vacant Episcopal Sees in the United States, IX-229 pp., 1932.
82. Rimlinger, Rev. Herbert T., J.C.D., Error Invalidating Matrimonial Consent, VII-79 pp., 1932.
83. Barrett, Rev. John D. M., S.S., J.C.D., A Comparative Study of the Third Plenary Council of Baltimore and the Code, IX-221 pp., 1932.
84. Carberry, Rev. John J., Ph.D., S.T.D., J.C.D., The Juridical Form of Marriage, X-177 pp., 1934.
85. Dolan, Rev. John L., A.B., J.C.D., The Defensor Vinculi, XII-157 pp., 1934.

86. HANNAN, REV. JEROME D., A.M., S.T.D., LL.B., J.C.D., The Canon Law of Wills, IX-517 pp., 1934.
87. LEMIEUX, REV. DELISE A., A.M., J.C.D., The Sentence in Ecclesiastical Procedure, IX-131 pp., 1934.
88. O'ROURKE, REV. JAMES J., A.B., J.C.D., Parish Registers, VII-109 pp., 1934.
89. TIMLIN, REV. BARTHOLOMEW, O.F.M., A.M., J.C.D., Conditional Matrimonial Consent, X-381 pp., 1934.
90. WAHL, REV. FRANCIS X., A.B., J.C.D., The Matrimonial Impediments of Consanguinity and Affinity, VI-125 pp., 1934.
91. WHITE, REV. ROBERT J., A.B., LL.B., S.T.B., J.C.D., Canonical Ante-Nuptial Promises and the Civil Law, VI-152 pp., 1934.
92. HERRERA, REV. ANTONIO PARRA, O.C.D., J.C.D., Legislacion Ecclesiastica sobra el Ayuno y la Abstinencia, XI-191 pp., 1935.
93. KENNEDY, REV. EDWIN J., J.C.D., The Special Matrimonial Process in Cases of Evident Nullity, X-165 pp., 1935.
94. MANNING, REV. JOHN J., A.B., J.C.D., Presumption of Law in Matrimonial Procedure, XI-111 pp., 1935.
95. MOEDER, REV. JOHN M., J.C.D., The Proper Bishop for Ordination and Dimissorial Letters, VII-135 pp., 1935.
96. O'MARA, REV. WILLIAM A., A.B., J.C.D., Canonical Causes for Matrimonial Dispensations, IX-155 pp., 1935.
97. REILLY, REV. PETER, J.C.D., Residence of Pastors, IX-81 pp., 1935.
98. SMITH, REV. MARINER T., O.P., S.T.Lr., J.C.D., The Penal Law for Religious, VII-169 pp., 1935.
99. WHALEN, REV. DONALD W., A.M., J.C.D., The Value of Testimonial Evidence in Matrimonial Procedure, XIII-297 pp., 1935.
100. CLEARY, REV. JOSEPH F., J.C.D., Canonical Limitations on the Alienation of Church Property, VIII-141 pp., 1936.
101. GLYNN, REV. JOHN C., J.C.D., The Promoter of Justice, XX-337 pp., 1936.
102. BRENNAN, REV. JAMES H., S.S., M.A., S.T.B., J.C.D., The Simple Convalidation of Marriage, VI-135 pp., 1937.
103. BRUNINI, REV. JOSEPH BERNARD, J.C.D., The Clerical Obligations of Canons 139 and 142, X-121 pp., 1937.
104. CONNOR, REV. MAURICE, A.B., J.C.D., The Administrative Removal of Pastors, VIII-159 pp., 1937.
105. GUILFOYLE, REV. MERLIN JOSEPH, J.C.D., Custom, XI-144 pp., 1937.
106. HUGHES, REV. JAMES AUSTIN, A.B., A.M., J.C.D., Witnesses in Criminal Trials of Clerics, IX-140 pp., 1937.
107. JANSEN, REV. RAYMOND J., A.B., S.T.L., J.C.D., Canonical Provisions for Catechetical Instruction, VII-153 pp., 1937.
108. KEALY, REV. JOHN JAMES, A.B., J.C.D., The Introductory Libellus in Church Court Procedure, XI-121 pp., 1937.

109. McMANUS, REV. JAMES EDWARD, C.SS.R., J.C.D., The Administration of Temporal Goods in Religious Institutes, XVI-196 pp., 1937.

110. MORIARTY, REV. EUGENE JAMES, J.C.D., Oaths in Ecclesiastical Courts, X-115 pp., 1937.

111. RAINER, REV. ELIGIUS GEORGE, C.SS.R., J.C.D., Suspension of Clerics, XVII-249 pp., 1937.

112. REILLY, REV. THOMAS F., C.SS.R., J.C.D., Visitation of Religious, VI-195 pp., 1938.

113. MORIARITY, REV. FRANCIS E., C.SS.R., J.C.D., The Extraordinary Absolution from Censures, XV-334 pp., 1938.

114. CONNOLLY, REV. NICHOLAS P., J.C.D., The Canonical Erection of Parishes, X-132 pp., 1938.

115. DONOVAN, REV. JAMES JOSEPH, J.C.D., The Pastor's Obligation in Prenuptial Investigation, XII-322 pp., 1938.

116. HARRIGAN, REV. ROBERT J., M.A., S.T.B., J.C.D., The Radical Sanation of Invalid Marriages, VIII-208 pp., 1938.

117. BOFFA, REV. CONRAD HUMBERT, J.C.D., Canonical Provisions for Catholic Schools, VII-211 pp., 1939.

118. PARSONS, REV. ANSCAR JOHN, O.M.Cap., J.C.D., Canonical Elections, XII-236 pp., 1939.

119. REILLY, REV. EDWARD MICHAEL, A.B., J.C.D., The General Norms of Dispensation, XII-156 pp., 1939.

120. RYAN, REV. GERALD ALOYSIUS, A.B., J.C.D., Principles of Episcopal Jurisdiction, XII-172 pp., 1939.

121. BURTON, REV. FRANCIS JAMES, C.S.C., A.B., J.C.D., A Commentary on Canon 1125, X-222 pp., 1940.

122. MIASKIEWICZ, REV. FRANCIS SIGISMUND, J.C.D., Supplied Jurisdiction According to Canon 209, XII-340 pp., 1940.

123. RICE, REV. PATRICK WILLIAM, A.B., J.C.D., Proof of Death in Prenuptial Investigation, VIII-156 pp., 1940.

124. ANGLIN, REV. THOMAS FRANCIS, M.S., J.C.D., The Eucharistic Fast, VIII-183 pp., 1941.

125. COLEMAN, REV. JOHN JEROME, J.C.D., The Minister of Confirmation, VI-153 pp., 1941.

126. DOWNS, REV. JOHN EMMANUEL, A.B., J.C.D., The Concept of Clerical Immunity, XI-163 pp., 1941.

127. ESSWEIN, REV. ANTHONY ALBERT, J.C.D., Extrajudicial Penal Powers of Ecclesiastical Superiors, X-144 pp., 1941.

128. FARRELL, REV. BENJAMIN FRANCIS, M.A., S.T.L., J.C.D., The Rights and Duties of the Local Ordinary Regarding Congregations of Women Religious of Pontifical Approval, V-195 pp., 1941.

129. FEENEY, REV. THOMAS JOHN, A.B., S.T.L., J.C.D., Restitutio in Integrum, VI-169 pp., 1941.

130. FINDLAY, REV. STEPHEN WILLIAM, O.S.B., A.B., J.C.D., Canonical

Norms Governing the Deposition and Degradation of Clerics, XVII-279 pp., 1941.

131. GOODWINE, REV. JOHN, A.B., S.T.L., J.C.D., The Right of the Church to Acquire Property, VIII-119 pp., 1941.

132. HESTON, REV. EDWARD LOUIS, C.S.C., Ph.D., S.T.D., J.C.D., The Alienation of Church Property in the United States, XII-222 pp., 1941.

133. HOGAN, REV. JAMES JOHN, A.B., S.T.L., J.C.D., Judicial Advocates and Procurators, XIII-200 pp., 1941.

134. KEALY, REV. THOMAS M., A.B., Litt.B., J.C.D., Dowry of Women Religious, IX-152 pp., 1941.

135. KEENE, REV. MICHAEL JAMES, O.S.B., J.C.D., Religious Ordinaries and Canon 198, V-164 pp., 1942.

136. KERIN, REV. CHARLES A., S.S., M.A., S.T.B., J.C.D., The Privation of Christian Burial, XVI-279 pp., 1941.

137. LOUIS, REV. WILLIAM FRANCIS, M.A., J.C.D., Diocesan Archives, X-101 pp., 1941.

138. MCDEVITT, REV. GILBERT JOSEPH, A.B., J.C.D., Legitimacy and Legitimation, X-247 pp., 1941.

139. MCDONOUGH, REV. THOMAS JOSEPH, A.B., J.C.D., Apostolic Administrators, X-217 pp., 1941.

140. **MEIER, REV. CARL ANTHONY, A.B., J.C.D., Penal Administrative Pro**cedure Against Negligent Pastors, XI-240 pp., 1941.

141. SCHMIDT, REV. JOHN ROGG, A.B., J.C.D., The Principles of Authentic Interpretation in Canon 17 of the Code of Canon Law, XII-331 pp., 1941.

142. SLAFKOSKY, REV. ANDREW LEONARD, A.B., J.C.D., The Canonical Episcopal Visitation of the Diocese, X-197 pp., 1941.

143. SWOBODA, REV. INNOCENT ROBERT, O.F.M., J.C.D., Ignorance in Relation to the Imputability of Delicts, IX-271 pp., 1941.

144. DUBÉ, REV. ARTHUR JOSEPH, A.B., J.C.D., The General Principles for the Reckoning of Time in Canon Law, VIII-299 pp., 1941.

145. MCBRIDE, REV. JAMES T., A.B., J.C.D., Incardination and Excardination of Seculars, XX-585 pp., 1941.

146. KRÓL, REV. JOHN T., J.C.D., The Defendant in Contentious Trials, XII-207 pp., 1942.

147. COMYNS, REV. JOSEPH J., C.SS.R., A.B., J.C.D., Papal and Episcopal Administration of Church Property, XIV-155 pp., 1942.

148. BARRY, REV. GARRETT FRANCIS, O.M.I., J.C.D., Violation of the Cloister, XII-260 pp., 1942.

149. BOLDUC, REV. GATIEN, C.S.V., A.B., S.T.L., J.C.D., Les Études dans les Religions Cléricales, VIII-155 pp., 1942.

150. BOYLE, REV. DAVID JOHN, M.A., J.C.D., The Juridic Effects of Moral Certitude on Pre-Nuptial Guarantees, XII-188 pp., 1942.

151. **CANAVAN, REV. WALTER JOSEPH, M.A., Litt.D., J.C.D., The Profes**sion of Faith, XII-143 pp., 1942.

152. DESROCHERS, REV. BRUNO, A.B., Ph.L., S.T.B., J.C.D., Le Premier Concile Plénier de Québec et le Code de Droit Canonique, XIV-186 pp., 1942.
153. DILLON, REV. ROBERT EDWARD, A.B., J.C.D., Common Law Marriage, X-148 pp., 1942.
154. DODWELL, REV. EDWARD JOHN, Ph.D., S.T.B., J.C.D., The Time and Place for the Celebration of Marriage, X-156 pp., 1942.
155. DONNELLAN, REV. THOMAS ANDREW, A.B., J.C.D., The Obligation of the Missa pro Populo, VII-131 pp., 1942.
156. ELTZ, REV. LOUIS ANTHONY, A.B., J.C.D., Cooperation in Crime, XII-208 pp., 1942.
157. GASS, REV. SYLVESTER FRANCIS, M.A., J.C.D., Ecclesiastical Pensions, XI-206 pp., 1942.
158. GUINIVEN, REV. JOHN JOSEPH, C.SS.R., J.C.D., The Precept of Hearing Mass, XIV-188 pp., 1942.
159. GULCYNSKI, REV. JOHN THEOPHILUS, J.C.D., The Desecration and Violation of Churches, X-126 pp., 1942.
160. HAMMILL, REV. JOHN LEO, M.A., J.C.D., The Obligations of the Traveler According to Canon 14, VIII-204 pp., 1942.
161. HAYDT, REV. JOHN JOSEPH, A.B., J.C.D., Reserved Benefices, XI-148 pp., 1942.
162. HUSER, REV. ROGER JOHN, O.F.M., A.B., J.C.D., The Crime of Abortion in Canon Law, XII-187 pp., 1942.
163. KEARNEY, REV. FRANCIS PATRICK, A.B., S.T.L., J.C.D., The Principles of Canon 1127, X-162 pp., 1942.
164. LINAHEN, REV. LEO JAMES, S.T.L., J.C.D., De Absolutione Complicis In Peccato Turpi, 114 pp., 1942.
165. MCCLOSKEY, REV. JOSEPH ALOYSIUS, A.B., J.C.D., The Subject of Ecclesiastical Law According to Canon 12, XVII-246 pp., 1942.
166. O'NEILL, REV. FRANCIS JOSEPH, C.SS.R., J.C.D., The Dismissal of Religious in Temporary Vows, XIII-220 pp., 1942.
167. PRINCE, REV. JOHN EDWARD, A.B., S.T.B., J.C.D., The Diocesan Chancellor, X-136 pp., 1942.
168. RIESNER, REV. ALBERT JOSEPH, C.SS.R., J.C.D., Apostates and Fugitives from Religious Institutes, IX-168 pp., 1942.
169. STENGER, REV. JOSEPH BERNARD, J.C.D., The Mortgaging of Church Property, 186 pp., 1942.
170. WALDRON, REV. JOSEPH FRANCIS, A.B., J.C.D., The Minister of Baptism, XII-197 pp., 1942.
171. WILLETT, REV. ROBERT ALBERT, J.C.D., The Probative Value of Documents in Ecclesiastical Trials, X-124 pp., 1942.
172. WOEBER, REV. EDWARD MARTIN, M.A., J.C.D., The Interpellations, XII-161 pp., 1942.
173. BENKO, REV. MATTHEW ALOYSIUS, O.S.B., M.A., J.C.D., The Abbot *Nullius*, XVI-148 pp., 1943.

174. CHRIST, REV. JOSEPH JAMES, M.A., S.T.L., J.C.D., Dispensation from Vindicative Penalties, XIV-285 pp., 1943.
175. CLANCY, REV. PATRICK M. J., O.P., A.B., S.T.Lr., J.C.D., The Local Religious Superior, X-229 pp., 1943.
176. CLARKE, REV. THOMAS JAMES, J.C.D., Parish Societies, XII-147 pp., 1943.
177. CONNOLLY, REV. JOHN PATRICK, S.T.L., J.C.D., Synodal Examiners and Parish Priest Consultors, X-223 pp., 1943.
178. DRUMM, REV. WILLIAM MARTIN, A.B., J.C.D., Hospital Chaplains, XII-175 pp., 1943.
179. FLANAGAN, REV. BERNARD JOSEPH, A.B., S.T.L., J.C.D., The Canonical Erection of Religious Houses, X-147 pp., 1943.
180. KELLEHER, REV. STEPHEN JOSEPH, A.B., S.T.B., J.C.D., Discussions with Non-Catholics: Canonical Legislation, X-93 pp., 1943.
181. LEWIS, REV. GORDIAN, C.P., J.C.D., Chapters in Religious Institutes, XII-169 pp., 1943.
182. MARX, REV. ADOLPH, J.C.D., The Declaration of Nullity of Marriages Contracted Outside the Church, X-151 pp., 1943.
183. MATULENAS, REV. RAYMOND ANTHONY, O.S.B., A.B., J.C.D., Communication, a Source of Privileges, XII-225 pp., 1943.
184. O'LEARY, REV. CHARLES GERARD, C.SS.R., J.C.D., Religious Dismissed After Perpetual Profession, X-213 pp., 1943.
185. POWER, REV. CORNELIUS MICHAEL, J.C.D., The Blessing of Cemeteries, XII-231 pp., 1943.
186. SHUHLER, REV. RALPH VINCENT, O.S.A., J.C.D., Privileges of Regulars to Absolve and Dispense, XII-195 pp., 1943.
187. ZIOLKOWSKI, REV. THADDEUS STANISLAUS, A.B., J.C.D., The Consecration and Blessing of Churches, XII-151 pp., 1943.
188. HENEGHAN, REV. JOHN JOSEPH, S.T.D., J.C.D., The Marriages of Unworthy Catholics: Canons 1065 and 1066, XVI-213 pp., 1944.
189. CARROLL, REV. COLEMAN FRANCIS, M.A., S.T.L., J.C.L., Charitable Institutions.
190. CIESLUK, REV. JOSEPH EDWARD, Ph.B., S.T.L., J.C.D., National Parishes in the United States, VI-178 pp., 1944.
191. COBURN, REV. VINCENT PAUL, A.B., J.C.D., Marriages of Conscience, XII-172 pp., 1944.
192. CONNORS, REV. CHARLES PAUL, C.S.Sp., A.B., J.C.D., Extra-Judicial Procurators in the Code of Canon Law, X-94 pp., 1944.
193. COYLE, REV. PAUL RAYMOND, A.B., J.C.D., Judicial Exceptions, X-142 pp., 1944.
194. FAIR, REV. BARTHOLOMEW FRANCIS, A.B., S.T.L., J.C.D., The Impediment of Abduction, XII-122 pp., 1944.
195. GALLAGHER, REV. THOMAS RAPHAEL, O.P., A.B., S.T.Lr., J.C.D., The Examination of the Qualities of the Ordinand, X-166 pp., 1944.
196. GANNON, REV. JOHN MARK, S.T.L., J.C.D., The Interstices Required for the Promotion to Orders, XII-100 pp., 1944.

197. **GOLDSMITH, REV. J. WILLIAM, B.C.S., S.T.L., J.C.D., The Competence of Church and State over Marriage—Disputed Points, X-128 pp., 1944.**
198. **GOODWINE, REV. JOSEPH GERARD, A.B., S.T.B., J.C.D., The Reception of Converts, XIV-326 pp., 1944.**
199. KOWALSKI, REV. ROMUALD EUGENE, O.F.M., A.B., J.C.D., Sustenance of Religious Houses of Regulars, X-174 pp., 1944.
200. MCCOY, REV. ALAN EDWARD, O.F.M., J.C.D., Force and Fear in Relation to Delictual Imputability and Penal Responsibility, XII-160 pp., 1944.
201. MCDEVITT, REV. VINCENT JOHN, Ph.B., S.T.L., J.C.L., Perjury.
202. MARTIN, REV. THOMAS OWEN, Ph.D., S.T.D., J.C.D., Adverse Possession, Prescription and Limitation of Actions: The Canonical "Praescriptio," XX-208 pp., 1944.
203. MIKLOSOVIC, REV. PAUL JOHN, A.B., J.C.L., Attempted Marriages and Their Consequent Juridic Effects.
204. **MUNDY, REV. THOMAS MAURICE, A.B., S.T.L., J.C.D., The Union of** Parishes, X—164 pp., 1944.
205. O'DEA, REV. JOHN COYLE, A.B., J.C.D., The Matrimonial Impediment of Nonage, VIII-126 pp., 1944.
206. OLALIA, REV. ALEXANDER AYSON, S.T.L., J.C.D., A Comparative Study of the Christian Constitution of States and the Constitution of the **Philippine Commonwealth, XII—136 pp., 1944.**
207. POISSON, REV. PIERRE-MARIE, C.S.C., A.B., Ph.L., Th.L., J.C.L., Droits Patrimoniaux des Maisons et des Églises Religieuses.
208. STADALNIKAS, REV. CASIMIR JOSEPH, M I.C., J.C.D., Reservation of Censures, X-141 pp., 1944.
209. **SULLIVAN, REV. EUGENE HENRY, S.T.L., J.C.D., Proof of the Reception of the Sacraments, X—165 pp., 1944.**
210. VAUGHAN, REV. WILLIAM EDWARD, J.C.D., Constitutions for Diocesan Courts, X-210 pp., 1944.
211. **PARO, REV. GINO, S.T.D., J.C.L., The Right of Apostolic Legation.**
212. BALZER, REV. RALPH FRANCIS, C.P., J.C.D., The Computation of Time in a Canonical Novitiate, X—227 pp., 1945.
213. DOUGHERTY, REV. JOHN WHELAN, A.B., S.T.L., J.C.D., De Inquisitione Speciali, XII—195 pp., 1945.
214. DZIOB, REV. MICHAEL WALTER, J.C.D., The Sacred Congregation for the Oriental Church, XII—181 pp., 1945.
215. EIDENSCHINK, REV. JOHN ALBERT, O.S.B., B.A., J.C.D, The Election of Bishops in the Letters of Pope Gregory the Great, VII—200 pp., 1945.
216. GILL, REV. NICHOLAS, C.P., J.C.D., The Spiritual Prefect in Clerical Religious Houses of Study, X—140 pp., 1945.
217. **HYNES, REV. HARRY GERARD, S.T.L., J.C.D., The Privileges of Cardinals, XII-183 pp., 1945.**
218. **MCDEVITT, REV. GERALD VINCENT, S.T.L., J.C.D., The Renunciation** of an Ecclesiastical Office, XIV—179 pp., 1945.

219. MANNING, REV. JOSEPH LEROY, J.C.D., The Free Conferral of Offices, VIII—116 pp., 1945.
220. MEYER, REV. LOUIS G., O.S.B., A.B., S.T.B., J.C.D., Alms-Gathering by Religious, XII—163 pp., 1945.
221. O'DONNELL, REV. CLETUS FRANCIS, M.A., J.C.D., The Marriage of Minors, XII—268 pp., 1945.
222. PRUNSKIS, REV. JOSEPH, J.C.D., Comparative Law, Ecclesiastical and Civil, in Lithuanian Concordat, X—161 pp., 1945.
223. SWEENEY, REV. FRANCIS PATRICK, C.SS.R., J.C.D., The Reduction of Clerics to the Lay State, X—199 pp., 1945.
224. VOGELPOHL, REV. HENRY JOHN, J.C.D., The Simple Impediments to Holy Orders, XVI—190 pp., 1945.
225. BROCKHAUS, REV. THOMAS AQUINAS, O.S.B., A.B., J.C.D., Religious who Are Known as *Conversi*, X—127 pp., 1945.
226. GRIESE, REV. N. ORVILLE, S.T.D., J.C.D., The Marriage Contract and the Procreation of Offspring, XVI-224 pp., 1946.
227. BOUDREAUX, REV. WARREN LOUIS, J.C.L., The "*ab acatholicis nati*" of Canon 1099, § 2.
228. BOWE, REV. THOMAS JOSEPH, A.B., J.C.D., Religious Superioresses, VIII-206 pp., 1946.
229. DIEDERICHS, REV. MICHAEL FERDINAND, S.C.J., J.C.D., The Jurisdiction of the Latin Ordinaries over their Oriental Subjects, XIV-153 pp., 1946.
230. DINGMAN, REV. MAURICE JOHN, A.B., S.T.L., J.C.L., The Plaintiff in Contentious Trials.
231. FRISON, REV. BASIL, C.M.F., M.MUS., J.C.D., The Retroactivity of Law, X-221 pp., 1946.
232. GALVIN, REV. WILLIAM ANTHONY, M.A., J.C.D., The Administrative Transfer of Pastors, XII-288 pp., 1946.
233. GORACY, REV. JOSEPH C., J.C.L., The Diriment Matrimonial Impediment of Major Orders.
234. HALE, REV. JOSEPH FRANCIS, M.A., S.T.L., J.C.L., The Pastor of Burial.
235. HENRY, REV. JOSEPH ARTHUR, A.B., J.C.D., The Mass and Holy Communion: Inter-Ritual Law, XII-138 pp., 1946.
236. LINENBERGER, REV. HERBERT, C.PP.S., J.C.L., The False Denunciation of an Innocent Confessor.
237. LOWRY, REV. JAMES MARTIN, A.B., J.C.D., Dispensation from Private Vows, XII-266 pp., 1946.
238. LYNCH, REV. GEORGE EDWARD, A.B., S.T.L., J.C.D., Coadjutors and Auxiliaries of Bishops, X-107 pp., 1947.
239. LYNCH, REV. TIMOTHY, M.S.SS.T., J.C.D., Contracts between Bishops and Religious Congregations, XIV-232 pp., 1946.
240. McCLUNN, REV. JUSTIN DAVID, A.B., S.T.L., J.C.D., Administrative Recourse, VII-142 pp., 1946.

241. Lohmuller, Rev. Martin Nicholas, A.B., J.C.D., The Promulgation of Law, XII-140 pp., 1947.
242. McGrath, Rev. James, A.B., J.C.D., The Privilege of the Canon, XII-156 pp., 1946.
243. Marbach, Rev. Joseph Francis, A.B., J.C.D., Marriage Legislation for the Catholics of the Oriental Rites in the United States and Canada, XIV-314 pp., 1946.
244. Shimkus, Rev. Bernard Aloyius, A.B., J.C.L., The Determination and Transfer of Rite.
245. Smith, Rev. Vincent Michael, A.B., S.T.L., J.C.L., Ignorance Affecting Matrimonial Consent.
246. Wachtrle, Rev. Paul Anthony, A.B., J.C.L., The Baptism of the Children of Non-Catholics.
247. Crotty, Rev. Matthew Michael, J.C.L., The Recipient of First Holy Communion.
248. Eagleton, Rev. George, J.C.L., The Quinquennial Faculties, Formula IV.
249. Gibbons, Rev. Marion Leo, C.M., J.C.L., Domicile of the Wife Unlawfully Separated from Her Husband.
250. Kelly, Rev. Bernard Matthew, S.T.L., J.C.D., The Functions Reserved to Pastors, IX-141 pp., 1947.
251. Kilcullen, Rev. Thomas John, LL.M., J.C.D., The Collegiate Moral Person as Party Litigant, X-150 pp., 1947.
252. Lafontaine, Rev. Germain Joseph, W.F., J.C.L., Relations Canoniques entre le Missionaire et Ses Superieurs.
253. Lane, Rev. Loras Thomas, J.C.L., Matrimonial Procedure in Ordinary Court of Second Instance.
254. Lover, Rev. James Francis, C.Ss.R., J.C.L., The Master of Novices.
255. McNicholas, Rev. Timothy Joseph, J.C.L., The *Septimae Manus* Witness.
256. Marositz, Rev. Joseph John, M.S.C., J.C.L., Obligations and Privileges of Religious Promoted to the Episcopal or Cardinalitial Dignities.
257. Murphy, Rev. Francis Joseph, J.C.L., Legislative Powers of the Provincial Council.
258. O'Brien, Rev. Romaeus William, O.Carm., J.C.L., The Provincial Superior in Religious Orders of Men.
259. Pfaller, Rev. Benedict Anthony, O.S.B., J.C.L., *The ipso facto* Effected Dismissal of Religious.
260. Popek, Rev. Alphonse Sylvester, J.C.L., The Rights and Obligations of Metropolitans.
261. Ristuccia, Rev. Bernard Joseph, C.M., J.C.L., Quasi-Religious.
262. Sonntag, Rev. Nathaniel Louis, O.F.M.Cap., J.C.L, Censorship of Special Classes of Books.
263. Stadler, Rev. Joseph Nicholas, J.C.L., Frequent Holy Communion.

264. SZAL, REV. IGNATIUS JOSEPH, J.C.L., The Communication of Catholics with Schismatics.
265. WAGNER, REV. URBAN STANLEY, O.F.M.Conv., J.C.D., Parochial Substitute Vicars and Supplying Priests, IX-126 pp., 1947.

BIOGRAPHICAL NOTE

JOSEPH JOHN MAROSITZ was born on September 13, 1917, in Nazareth, Pennsylvania. After completing his elementary education in the Holy Family Parochial School, Nazareth, Pennsylvania, he enrolled for one year at the Public High School of the same town. He entered the Sacred Heart Mission Seminary, Geneva, Illinois, the minor Seminary of the Missionaries of the Sacred Heart, in September, 1932. On August 12, 1936, he became a Postulant at the Sacred Heart Seminary, Shelby, Ohio, and a month later entered the Clerical Novitiate of the Congregation of the Missionaries of the Sacred Heart. After the completion of the Novitiate he made his religious profession on September 13 of the following year. His seminary course was made at the major Seminary of the Missionaries of the Sacred Heart in Shelby, Ohio. Having completed his course of Philosophy, he was transferred to the minor Seminary of the Society, where he taught for one year. Thence he returned to the major Seminary for his course of Theology. He was ordained to the priesthood on June 19, 1943, at the Queen of the Most Holy Rosary Cathedral, Toledo, Ohio, by the Bishop of the diocese, Karl J. Alter. In October of 1944 he entered the Catholic University of America to pursue graduate studies in the School of Canon Law. He received the degree of the Baccalaureate in Canon Law in May, 1945, and the degree of the Licentiate in Canon Law in June, 1946.

www.ingramcontent.com/pod-product-compliance
Lightning Source LLC
LaVergne TN
LVHW050234080826
844660LV00012B/528

* 9 7 8 0 8 1 3 2 2 4 3 4 3 *